Growing into G

Exploring our call to grow
into God's image and likeness

CHURCHES TOGETHER
IN BRITAIN AND IRELAND

Growing into God

A collection of papers resulting from a study process conducted by Churches Together in Britain and Ireland, which included three special consultations

Edited by Jean Mayland

This collection of papers is offered to readers as of value in itself but also as challenging background material to be read alongside the Ecumenical Lent Course for 2004 entitled *Face to Face*.

Churches Together in Britain and Ireland
Inter-Church House,
35-41 Lower Marsh,
London SE1 7SA

Tel: +44 (0) 20 7523 2121
Fax: +44 (0) 20 7928 0010
info@ctbi.org.uk
www.ctbi.org.uk

ISBN 085169 282 6

Published 2003 by Churches Together in Britain and Ireland

Produced by Church House Publishing

Further copies available from CTBI Publications
31 Great Smith Street, London SW1P 3BN
Tel: +44 (0) 20 7898 1300; Fax: +44 (0) 20 7898 1305
orders@ctbi.org.uk
www.chbookshop.co.uk

Unless otherwise stated, the Scripture quotations contained herein are from the
New Revised Standard Version Bible, copyright © 1989, by the Division of Christian
Education of the National Council of the Churches of Christ in the United States of
America, and are used by permission. All rights reserved.

Scripture quotations marked 'RSV' are from the Holy Bible, Revised Standard
Version © 1952 and 1946, by the Division of Christian Education of the National
Council of the Churches of Christ in the United States of America. Scripture quotations
marked 'NEB' are from The New English Bible, © 1961 and 1970, by The Delegates
of the Oxford University Press and the Syndics of the Cambridge University Press.

Cover designed by Church House Publishing
Printed by The Cromwell Press Ltd, Trowbridge, Wiltshire

Contents

Contents

Contributors

Revd Archimandrite Ephrem Lash is a monk of the Greek Orthodox Church. He has responsibility for a parish in Manchester and travels around the country to celebrate the Liturgy for groups of Orthodox who have no resident priest. He has provided many interpretations in English of liturgical texts.

Ms Zoë Bennett Moore is Director of Postgraduate Studies in Pastoral Theology with Anglia Polytechnic University and the Cambridge Theological Federation. She is a lay member of the Church of England and author of *Introducing Feminist Perspectives on Pastoral Theology.*[1]

Mr David Carter is a Methodist Local Preacher and Associate Lecturer in Religious Studies with the Open University. He is involved in ecumenical work and research.

Revd Colin Coward is an Anglican priest who is Director of 'Changing Attitude', an organization working for gay and lesbian affirmation within the Anglican Church.

Ms Elisabeth Davies-John is a Methodist laywoman. She is deeply involved in CHAD (Church Action on Disability).

Revd Lorraine Dixon is a priest and Church Army Sister of the Anglican Church. She is currently Chaplain at Chester College of Higher Education in the city of Chester. Ms Dixon is also a part-time PhD candidate of the Theology Department at the University of Birmingham. Her area of research concerns black religious history in late eighteenth-century England.

Professor Mary Grey is D. J. James Professor of Pastoral Theology at the University of Wales, Lampeter.

Revd Dr David Hilborn is a priest of the Church of England who is currently Theological Adviser to the Evangelical Alliance.

Mr Martin Hogg is a lawyer and a lecturer in law at Edinburgh University. He is a member of the Scottish Episcopal Church. He is a Director of the Lesbian and Gay Christian Movement.

Revd Dr Alastair Hunter is a minister of the Church of Scotland who is currently a senior lecturer in the Department of Theology and Religious Studies of the University of Glasgow.

Dr Donald Macaskill, formerly Vice-Principal of the Scottish Churches Open College, is currently Head of Training and Leadership at Scottish Human Services Trust, a values led organization working to promote inclusion and participation for excluded individuals in the fields of health, education and criminal justice in Scotland. He is the co-author of *Rediscovering Faith: explorations in Christian belief.*[2]

Mr David Melling is an Orthodox layman. He has retired from his post as Lecturer in Philosophy but is still actively involved in teaching and writing. He is a gifted musician and a choir leader.

Dr Anne Primavesi is a former Research Fellow in Environmental Theology at Bristol University. She is now at the Centre for the Interdisciplinary Study of Religion, Birkbeck, University of London. Her latest book is *Gaia's Gift: Earth, Ourselves and God after Copernicus.*[3]

Revd Canon Dr John W. Rogerson is Emeritus Professor of Biblical Studies at the University of Sheffield, where for many years he taught in the Biblical Studies Department. He is the author of numerous books and commentaries on the Old Testament.

Revd Dr Professor Mary Seller is Professor of Development Genetics, Division of Medical and Molecular Genetics at Guy's Hospital. She is also Head of Developmental Biology Research Group. In addition she is a non-stipendiary priest in the Anglican Diocese of Southwark.

Revd Dr Chris Sunderland was originally a research biochemist, studying the biochemistry of graft rejection at Oxford followed by postdoctoral research in feto-maternal immunology. He was ordained as an Anglican priest and served as vicar of a tower block estate in inner-city Bristol. He later studied to develop a new practical approach to theology that would allow the Church to engage more clearly with issues of public life. This has recently led to the founding of a company known as AGORA, dedicated to rebuilding trust and providing opportunity for discussion of public issues.

Revd Arlington Trotman is a minister in the Wesleyan Holiness Church. He is currently Secretary of the Churches' Commission for Racial Justice (CCRJ) of CTBI.

Revd Henry Wansbrough is a Roman Catholic priest, monk and scholar who teaches at St Benet's Hall, Oxford.

Revd Canon Michael Williams is the Vicar of Bolton and a former Principal of the Northern Ordination Course. Before that he was lecturer and tutor in ethics at St John's College, Durham.

Revd Dr Stephen Wright is an Anglican priest who is Director of the College of Preachers, an ecumenical in-service resource centre for preachers, based at Spurgeon's College.

The Editor: Revd Jean Mayland is an Anglican priest who is currently Coordinating Secretary for Church Life at CTBI.

Secretarial Assistance: Ms Katrina Bradley, Administrative Secretary for Church Life and Publications.

Acknowledgements

Our warmest thanks go to the writers of the papers who, while retaining the copyright of the individual papers for themselves, have allowed us to publish them in this collection.

We are grateful to the following for permission to use material for which they hold the copyright. Every effort has been made to trace and contact copyright holders. If there are any inadvertent omissions we apologize to those concerned and will ensure that a suitable acknowledgement is made at the next reprint.

We thank:

Abingdon Press, Nashville, extracts from *Becoming A Self Before God: Critical Transformations*, Romney M. Moseley, 1991;

The American Academy of Religion, Atlanta, *White Women's Christ and Black Women's Jesus*, Jacquelyn Grant, 1989;

The Archbishops' Council, Collect for the First Sunday of Christmas, *Common Worship*: *Services and Prayers for the Church of England*, Church House Publishing, 2000;

Archimandrite Ephrem Lash for permission to use his interpretative translations from the writings of the Fathers and the Liturgy;

Blackwell, Oxford, extract from *On Christian Theology*, Rowan Williams, 2000;

Cambridge University Press, extract from *Individuals, Relationships and Culture-Links between Ethology and Social Sciences*, R. A. Hinde, 1987;

Cambridge University Press, extracts from *The Call to Personhood: A Christian Theory of the Individual in Social Relationships*, Alistair McFadyen, 1990;

Continuum International Publishing Group Ltd, extract from
*Interpreting God and the Postmodern Self: On Meaning,
Manipulation and Promise*, Anthony Thiselton, 1996;

Crossroad, New York, extract from 'Hildegarde of Bingen Scivias'
cited in *She Who Is*, Elizabeth Johnson, 2002;

Wm B. Eerdmans Publishing Co., Michigan, extract from *Freedom
for Ministry*, Richard John Neuhaus, 1992;

Extracts from 'Vocation and the People of God' in Scottish
Journal of Theology 33, Iain G. Nichol, 1980;

Harper, San Francisco, extract from *A Testament of Hope –
The Essential Writings and Speeches of Martin Luther King
Junior*, James Washington (ed.), 1991, reprinted by arrangement
with the Estate of Martin Luther King Jr, c/o Writers House as agent
for the proprietor, New York, NY;

HarperCollins Publishers USA, extract from *Christ and Culture*,
H.R. Niebuhr, 1975;

Harvard University Center for the Study of World Religions,
Cambridge Mass., extract from 'The Wounded Spirit as the
Basis for Hope in an Age of Radical Ecology', Mark Wallace
in *Christianity and Ecology: Seeking the Well-Being of Earth
and Humans*, Dieter T. Hessel and Rosemary Radford Ruether
(eds), 2000;

Harvard University Press, Cambridge Mass., *Good Natured:
The Origins of Right and Wrong in Humans and Other Animals*,
Frans de Waal, 1996;

Harvard University Press, Cambridge Mass., extract from
Is There a Text in This Class?, Stanley Fish, 1980;

Orbis Books, New York, extract from *The Black Christ*, Kelly
Brown Douglas, 1994;

Palgrave Macmillan, extract from *Evil and the Love of God*,
John Hick, 1966;

SCM Press, London, extract from *The Hope of Happiness: A Sketch for a Christian Humanism*, Helen Oppenheimer, 1983;

St Vladimir's Seminary Press, New York, extract concerning St Ephraim from *The Orthodox Way*, Kallistos Ware;

Thomson Publishing Services, Andover, extract from *Negative Dialectics* (Negative Dialektik), Theodor Adorno, 1973;

The Women's Press, London, extract from *In Search of Our Mothers' Gardens*, Alice Walker, 1984;

University of America Press, Washington, extract from *The Redemption of God*, Carter Heyward, 1982;

Yorkshire Art Circus, Castleford, 'When Our Ship Comes in; Black Women Talk', extract from article by Katie Stewart, 1992.

We thank the following for permission to use their illustrations:

Photo SCALA, Florence, 'Il Volto Santo', Lucca Cathedral;

Rijksmuseum, Amsterdam, 'The Threatened Swan', Jan Asselijn;

St Paul's Multimedia Press for the two reproductions of icons from the Tretyakov Gallery, Moscow.

Introduction

Jean Mayland

In 1996 the Churches set out to explore some of the most fundamental questions of our human existence. Who are we? Why are we here? What is our destiny? What is the point of life? The process they followed, undertaken through Churches Together in Britain and Ireland (CTBI), led them in different ways to reaffirm a common answer. We are beings made in the image of God with the potential to grow more fully into God's likeness so that we can find the point, purpose and fulfilment of life here in this universe in eternal life with God. While we are on this earth, we should care for it well and treat our fellow human beings with love and respect.

The papers that together form the content of this book arose from this process. CTBI is publishing them in the belief that they have a useful part to play in wider discussions today about the relevance of the Bible and the meaning and purpose of life. They are published in association with a study course, to be used, initially, in Lent 2004, but available for use at other times and in other years by local groups. This course (entitled *Face to Face*) has been produced in cooperation with Bible Society. It also considers our call to 'grow into the image and likeness of God', but deals with the issues by means of special studies of parts of the opening chapters of the Gospel according to Luke. These two publications are the visible results of the process, but they are not the whole story; on the way many people have been touched, encouraged or stimulated by the consultations and the wider discussions and activities that it has inspired.

The beginning of this process

The seeds of the process begun in 1996 were planted eight years earlier, when the World Council of Churches (WCC) inaugurated a special decade to affirm women's contribution in church and community, and empower and support their struggle against discrimination on grounds of gender. Visiting teams to each country challenged the Churches on their response. It was when the report of the team that visited these islands was being discussed by Church leaders at the Church Representatives'

Meeting (which is the biennial decision-making gathering of CTBI) that it was recognized that more work on 'being made in the image of God' was required. In responding to that need, it quickly became apparent that the concept of the 'image of God' was being found highly relevant to discussions about human rights and to many groups in society who felt marginalized, whether through ethnicity, disability or sexual orientation.

A small consultation was held at Whirlow Grange Conference Centre in Sheffield in December 1998, and a second, much larger, consultation was held in November 2001. A special consultation on some issues of sexuality was held in November 2002. The papers in this collection result from these consultations and the interplay and exchange of views between those who originally gave the papers. Some of this led to modification of the papers given, although in a number of places they continue to reflect varying points of view.

During this process there was a shift from merely considering the issues raised by those made to feel that they are not made fully in God's image to considering a whole range of issues arising from the concept of our being made and remade in the image of God. Part of this consideration led to the claim that we are not made and remade but that at the heart of the matter is the concept of our *growing* into our potential to be like God or, as the Orthodox would put it, our 'divinization'.

The biblical and theological background

There are some key biblical passages and theological debates that form a common background for those who wrote papers for this volume. When they refer to them, there is an assumption that the reader will recognize and understand the references and the way most scholars have handled the issues. The next few pages seek to provide readers less familiar with this background with a map to help them find their way through it.

Starting from Genesis

In Chapter 1 of the first book of the Bible, namely Genesis, we read one of the stories of how God created the world. A second version follows in Chapter 2. Scholars on the whole agree that the second story is the earlier one and the account in Genesis 1 probably was not completed until after the time of the exile of

Jews into Babylon, the first wave of which took place in 597 BCE and the second in 587 BCE. These stories are what can be described as 'myths'. Many people today think that a myth is a kind of fairy story, something that has no basis in fact, is therefore not ' true' and has no meaning for intelligent people today. There are, however, more kinds of truth than strictly historical factual truth. (There is, actually, little of that as most history is written from a particular angle.) Myths are stories, often arising from particular cultures, that contain deep and eternal truths that go on being true, however much life and culture change.

For Christians (and for Jews) the creation myths of Genesis contain the truths that God created the whole world (indeed the whole universe) and that, in the scheme of life, human beings occupy a distinct and privileged position in relation to the Being of God. In Genesis 1, human beings are described as being made 'in the image of God', and in Genesis 2, God breathes 'the breath of life' into the nostrils of 'man' – in this case, male human being. Human beings are also given a special position to care for and control nature. Some would also say that both stories describe man and woman as equal (Genesis 1: man and woman are both created in God's image; Genesis 2: woman is created from man's side but he is not fully 'whole' until she is created). Others would say that the story in Genesis 2 speaks of the subservience of woman to man while yet others would say that is only part of the 'fallen' world and not part of God's original concept.

The concept of the 'Fall' is one that belongs to the Creation Story of Genesis 2 and is set out in Chapter 3 of Genesis. According to this story, the man and the woman were told that they could eat from any tree in the Garden of Eden except the tree in the middle (the tree of the knowledge of good and evil). The woman, Eve, was tempted by the serpent to eat of the fruit. She did so and offered some to her husband, who also ate. As a result they became aware that they were naked and so 'fell' from their original innocence. They were turned out of the garden, the man had to toil hard, the woman to bear children in pain and be ruled over by her husband.

This story is still one of the best known in these islands and there are frequent references to it in literature. Most people know about Eve and the apple – even though the fruit is not actually named in Genesis and, in some cultures, the tree is considered to have been a fig tree! One of the many problems about this story is that it often polarizes the position of believers and unbelievers. Unbelievers may know it as a story but reject it as a myth in the fairy story sense and believe that its only relevance to life today is that it has been, and still is, used to oppress women. Some believers think that it must be taken literally or we are failing to show proper respect to the authority of the Scriptures. Some people think that there was a time when human beings were perfect, bearing the image of God and alive with his breath. Then there came the cataclysmic 'Fall' and human beings lost the image of God. Since then, human beings have been stained by original sin and can only become fit to live with God because Jesus, his Son, who was the perfect image of God, died on the cross and gave his life as 'a ransom for many' (Matthew 20.28b).

The Influence of St Augustine

This concept of the 'Fall' and that of original sin were given a huge boost by the teaching of St Augustine. According to St Augustine, God created a universe out of nothing. The universe contained all kinds of creatures, each good but spanning many grades of goodness with angels as the highest in the scale. By a wilful misuse of their freedom some of the angels rebelled and were expelled from heaven into misery. This story was then repeated with human beings. Adam and Eve in the Garden of Eden were immortal. They did not grow old, they had complete control over their bodily passions and they lived in joy. Once they ate from the forbidden fruit, they fell and so lost their freedom for ever. Their descendants had lost the image of God, were tainted by original sin and, as a result, they were punished by suffering. Human beings are born as sinners and endowed with a nature that is bound to lead them daily into further sin. According to Augustine, not only do human beings inherit sinfulness or tendency to sin but they also inherit guilt. The stain of sin and guilt can only be washed away by baptism and so unbaptized babies go to hell. Only by God's free and incomprehensible grace will some human beings (but not all) eventually be saved. It is not only unbelievers who have problems with all this!

Problems with science

In addition to the troubling concepts about the nature of God, which this theory entails, there are troubling facts about evolution and scientific knowledge of the universe. Evolution gives the lie to any idea of perfect human beings who then fell. It rather demonstrates a process by which human beings evolved from lower forms of life. At the time when Darwin published his *Origin of the Species*,[1] it appeared that one had to choose between believing what he claimed or accepting the literal truth of Genesis. For a time it seemed that the Church might drive itself down this cul-de-sac. Fortunately, common sense prevailed. Christians came to see that the revelations of science were compatible with the vital truths contained in the myths of Genesis. God could indeed still have created the whole universe but through the marvellous processes being revealed by science rather than in a literal six days of the first Genesis story. There are still Christians in these islands who take Genesis literally, as well as in the United States, but, thankfully, in these islands they are a small minority. We do no service to Christianity by trying to insist on the literal truth of the Genesis myths.

Professor John Hick expressed this forcibly in 1966 when he wrote as follows in his book *Evil and the God of Love*:

> Only a drastic compartmentalization of the mind could enable one to believe today in a literal historical fall of man from paradisal perfection taking place in the year X B.C. It is not necessary to go back over the biological, anthropological, geological, and palaeontological work of the past century and a half to relive the battles between advancing science and retreating theological dogmatism. Let us simply say without equivocation that the fall is a mythic conception, which does not describe an actual event in man's history or prehistory . . . Man [sic] has never lived in a pre- or un-fallen state, in however remote an epoch. He has never existed in an ideal relationship with God, and he did not begin his career in paradisal blessedness and then fall into sin and guilt. From his first emergence from the lower forms of life he has been in other than perfect fellowship with his Maker. We cannot speak of a radically better state that **was**; we must speak instead in hope of a radically better state which **will be**.[2]

The teaching of Irenaeus

Centuries before Hick, Irenaeus (*c*.130–*c*.200 CE), Bishop of Lyons and author, in response to Gnosticism, of the Church's first systematic theology, had spoken of human beings as originally immature beings on whom God could not bestow his highest gifts. He pictured our present life as a scene of gradual spiritual growth. He saw that the problems and suffering of beings could develop towards the perfection that is God's will and purpose for them. In other words, he thought of this world as a 'vale of soul making'³ rather than as a place of punishment. Irenaeus was also one of the first to give expression to the view, taken up by later Greek Fathers, of the distinction between the image (*eikōn*) of God and the likeness (*homoiōsis*) of God. The *imago* represents human nature as intelligent beings endowed with moral freedom and responsibility. Humans are, however, only at the beginning of a process of growth and development which, with the help of the Holy Spirit, will culminate in being in the likeness of God. Human beings, he believed, are made in the image of God but, during their lifetime, they should take all their opportunities to grow into the likeness of God.

This basic Irenaean concept of human beings made initially in the image of God and gradually being brought through their own will into the divine 'likeness', this creative process being interrupted by the Fall (or failure to climb aright) and set right again by the incarnation, has continued to operate in the minds of theologians of the Orthodox Church down to this day. In their view the 'Fall' marred the image of God in human beings but did not destroy it nor did it destroy human potential to grow into the likeness of God.

Many Western Christians accept the idea of individuals and communities growing to be more like God but they still talk of growing into the 'image of God'.

The teaching of Teilhard de Chardin

Pierre Teilhard de Chardin (1881–1955) was a Roman Catholic priest who was also a distinguished palaeontologist, professionally respected as such. He wrote fascinating books dealing with the borderland between science and theology. His activities in this field were restricted in various ways by the Jesuit Order of which he remained a loyal member. He was unable to obtain an official *imprimatur* for the publication of many of his philosophical writings, which appeared after his death as a result of the activity of an international committee composed of scholars and scientists. In his book *The Phenomenon of Man*,[4] de Chardin presents Christ as the peak of evolution. Christ is completely in the image and likeness of God – the only one ever to reach such perfection and the goal of human beings is to grow to be like him. In his writings he also, as a Western Christian, was influenced by the writings of Irenaeus and Orthodox theologians.

Section One – Reflections on the Biblical Background

Made in the image and likeness of God – John W. Rogerson

At the first consultation a paper on the Old Testament view of our being 'made and remade in the image of God' was given by the Revd Canon Dr John Rogerson, Emeritus Professor of Biblical Studies at the University of Sheffield. As already indicated, he did not enter into the issues set out above. Taking them as understood, he went on to challenge the whole concept of our being made and remade in God's image and put forward the basic thesis that the idea of our being made in God's 'image' must be thought of as a process. He claimed that the Old Testament narrative is the story of the 'Divine Project' to produce humankind in community, including in community with the natural order. It describes how God chose a people and through them attempted to create structures of grace. It is the story of leading people on to grow into God's image, not only as individuals but also as a community. Professor Rogerson regards this project as an ongoing one in which the more human people become as individuals and in community, the more they reflect the divine image. This concept of 'growing into the image of God' as individuals and communities is an exciting one, which we do need to share with the people in our churches, as is the concept that the more we become truly human the more we become divine. The implications for discussion with people of other faiths are also considerable.

The phrase 'image of God' in the New Testament – Stephen I. Wright

The Revd Dr Stephen Wright sets out his purpose as a limited one, namely to attempt to summarize the meaning and implications of the phrase 'image of God' as it occurs in the New Testament. He summarizes the New Testament usage of this phrase in two assertions. 'First the New Testament writings bear witness to Jesus Christ as the one who bears God's image in perfect form. Second, they also speak of those "in Christ" as being in a process of renewal in God's image. Thus through being joined to Christ, God's perfect image, human beings may embark on a new course whereby their true character as humans is restored.'

In Dr Wright's view, the implications of this for Christians today are enormous. Firstly, he would say that, in the teaching of the New Testament, although all people are made in God's image, it is only through Christ that we are enabled to fulfil our destiny and that the broken image of God is restored. Secondly, this process of renewal demands a comprehensive moral commitment to put to death the habits and practices of the old humanity and put on those of the new. We need to pattern ourselves on Jesus. Thirdly, being renewed in God's image is something that happens to people *together.*

Once more we have the same concepts of *growing into God's image, patterning ourselves on Jesus in whom the fullness of God's image dwells and doing this as members of a community.*

Made and remade in the image of God – The New Testament evidence – Henry Wansbrough OSB

Father Wansbrough suggested that a more fitting title might have been 'Made in the image of God and remade in the image of Christ'. In referring to the Pauline evidence in the New Testament he points out that Paul considered the Christian rather than human beings in general and is interested only in salvation through Christ. The hymn in Philippians 2 contrasts the obedience of Christ with the disobedience of Adam. God humbled Adam but raised Christ high. For Paul, Adam is the 'archetype and myth of unredeemed humanity'. He is the image of man as sinful and ready to be remade. This 'remaking' is begun by a Christian's being baptized *into* Christ. We were *buried* with him so that we too should begin living a new life. The completion of this new life is found in our resurrection. 'Just as all die in Adam, so in Christ will all be brought to life.' Christ is the first fruits of the resurrection of all who believe in him. Father Wansbrough goes on to say that the advance in Christology made in the Deutero-Pauline epistles 'does, however, raise the Christian remade in the image of Christ into being remade in the image of God'. The implications of this remaking in the image of God are far reaching but, for Father Wansbrough as for St Matthew, the most important one is to show 'perfect love for all'.

Father Wansbrough ended his paper with a comment on those who had often been made to feel that they were not fully made in the image of God, namely black people and women. He says 'it should be a significant support for two groups who often feel themselves underprivileged in Christianity that the first Christian outside the Holy Land was black and the first Christian of Europe was a woman.'

Section Two – Insights from Orthodox Christians

Two presentations of insights from the Orthodox Church were given by **Archimandrite Ephrem** and **David Melling**. Father Ephrem did not present a paper as such but a series of short readings from his own translations of the Fathers and the Liturgy illustrated by slides of icons. Icons are for the Orthodox 'windows into heaven', in other words, not mere images but symbolic representations that allow us a glimpse into the divine. The papers by the two Orthodox representatives resonate with a positive hope. Human beings had lost the likeness of God through sin but are still in God's image, even 'though that image is tarnished'. The purpose of the incarnation is stressed as one of salvation 'so that what we had lost in Adam – namely to be according to the image and likeness of God – we might recover in Jesus Christ' (St Irenaeus). This concept is also expressed vividly in texts such as the following:

> For you fashioned a man by taking dust from the earth, and honoured him, O God, with your own image. You placed him in the Paradise of pleasure and promised him immortal life and the enjoyment of eternal good things if he kept your commandments. But when he disobeyed you, the true God, who had created him . . . you banished him by your just judgement, O God, from Paradise into this world, and returned him to the earth, from which he had been taken; while, in your Christ, you established for him the salvation which comes through rebirth.
>
> *(Anaphora of St Basil, Post-Sanctus)*

> Give rest with your chosen ones, O Lover of
> humankind, to your faithful servants who have
> departed to you, their only Benefactor, in places of
> refreshment, amid the splendours of your Saints. For
> you are the one who wishes to show mercy and as
> God you save those whom you fashioned according
> to your image, for you alone are full of mercy.
>
> *(Prosomion for the Dead, Tone 6)*

The texts quoted also make it quite clear that all this applies to
women as much as men. For example:

> She is a woman who, while others have been
> honoured and extolled for natural and artificial
> beauty, has acknowledged but one kind of beauty,
> that of the soul, and the preservation, or restoration
> as far as possible, of the divine image.
>
> *(St Gregory the Theologian on his mother Nonna)*

There are also important parallels with Professor Rogerson's
concept of the 'process' of growing into the image of God. Christ
became human so that humans might grow to be like God. This
process of 'divinization' is a process of growing into the likeness
of God as we are led by the Spirit 'from glory to glory'.

In his paper **In the image and likeness of God** Mr David Melling
speaks of the distinction between 'image' and 'likeness'. The
image is 'obscured, damaged, almost lost as the result of sin. The
likeness is attained by virtuous conduct responsive to grace.' He
points out that 'the salvation of humanity is very frequently seen
in terms of the restoration of the damaged image by the descent
of the True Image into our humanity, to share our humanity so
that we may be deified in him.' In fact, at the heart of the joyous
message of hope of Orthodoxy lies the belief that Jesus assumed
the poverty of our flesh so that we may assume the richness of his
Godhead. Our destiny is to become like God – so to grow into
God that we share the life of his Godhead.

The image of God in humankind – A bridge between the Eastern and Wesleyan theological traditions – David Carter

The joy and hope of the Eastern teaching about our growing into
God – sanctification or 'theosis' – was for many centuries lost in

the Western tradition, which laid a much greater stress on sin and the loss of God's image in humankind. As David Carter pointed out, however, in an original and stimulating paper, 'one major Western theological tradition, the Wesleyan, has emphasized the concept rather more than most, and behind much of the attitude to worship and holiness within the Wesleyan tradition lies a strong awareness of the vocation to share in the divine energies.' For both the Orthodox and the Wesleyan traditions, 'worship is primarily celebratory of the great mystery of divine love and grace in creation and redemption'.

Section Three – But what if your experience makes you feel that you are not fully made in God's image?

One of the starting points of this study process was an observation, worldwide, that many women are oppressed and marginalized in our churches because of an underlying belief (usually unspoken but occasionally voiced openly) that women are secondary and subservient to men and as such are not as completely in the image of God. In this section there are papers by a black man, a white woman, a black woman, a disabled woman and two gay men – one lay and one ordained. All of them reflect on their experience while at the same time rejecting the concept that a white, heterosexual, able-bodied male is in any way automatically more fully made in God's image than they are.

Black people made in the image of God – Arlington Trotman

The Revd Arlington Trotman started his original presentation by explaining that he had been brought up by his father to be proud of being black and to be self confident about his person and nature. As a result, although throughout his life others had tried to make him feel inferior and 'less than fully in God's image', he had always brushed it off. His paper, therefore, has a positive purpose to present his 'understanding of what it means that a black person is made in the image and likeness of God'. This leads him to the conclusion that 'we must come to appreciate that, having been made in the image of God, all people must continue the fight against racism and xenophobia in British society, and make obsolete the question about what this means for a black person.'

'One ladies'; one normal': Made in the image of God – issues for women – Zoë Bennett Moore

Ms Bennett Moore's wryly amusing title, drawn from the experience of buying a rucksack for her daughter, leads into the central question of her paper – are women regarded as 'subnormal' human beings? For her this is a vital question as in many parts of the world 'the undervaluing of women literally kills them'. This takes us back to one of the themes arising from the original WCC team visits in the second half of the 1990s. Ms Bennett Moore speaks strongly of 'the connection between gendered violence and the image of God. Value is intimately linked to godlikeness.' She claims that 'It would appear that in different ways in many of our Churches worldwide women are less highly valued than men.' Ms Bennett Moore's paper takes us into very practical areas of concern in Church and society – but she does more. She carries the challenge to the concept of God itself: 'Who has decided what this God is like: in whose image is this God made?'. She also claims that 'Jesus Christ as the image of God holds up an ambiguous picture to women.' There is strong stuff for the Churches to face here but it is a vital challenge.

Made in the image of God: A womanist perspective – Lorraine Dixon

'Feminist to womanist is as lavender to purple' says Ms Dixon in her paper, quoting the African American author Alice Walker. She writes from the point of view of a person who has received a 'double whammy' – marginalized as a woman and as a black person but expressing through her womanist theology that she believes herself to be made as fully in God's image as anyone else, however much others may try to deny it. Her paper reflects both black liberationist struggles against white supremacy and women's struggle against men. Unlike white feminists, black womanists do not have a problem with the maleness of Jesus because 'gender issues have been only one aspect of the struggle for liberation and personhood for the black woman. Jesus as God with us in the struggle for personhood has been a key issue.' She agrees that the Bible has been used as an instrument of oppression but calls on Christians to follow the example of black women and 'read' the Bible in creative ways that are liberative. One of the purposes of publishing these papers is to help Christians to do just that.

Disabled and made in the image of God –
Elisabeth Davies-John

'Freak, devil, saint, the possessor of special wisdom, subhuman, supra-human . . . sometimes the overt statement that the person is not created by God. All these attitudes have been attached to people with disabilities in what little history has been discovered. If feminist theologians think that the history of women has been one of hardship then that of the disabled has been much worse.' This statement is at the centre of the paper by Ms Elisabeth Davies-John. She herself is proud of what she is and has no doubt that she is made in God's image, but she is suspicious of what the Church really thinks. She objects particularly to the view, prevalent in many churches, that disabled people want to be healed. After the discussion following the presentation of her paper at the first consultation, Professor Rogerson said that he must go home and reread and rethink the healing stories in the Gospels. Perhaps we all need to do the same!

Gay and lesbian and in God's image – Martin Hogg

Mr Hogg suggested 'that we should begin our thinking by remembering that it is not really an "issue" at all. It is about the Church's theological pronouncements on the lives of *real people* – people, moreover, for whom sexuality is *only one part of their lives*, but who are forced to think of themselves *only* as sexual beings because of their rejection by the Church on the grounds of their sexuality.' He called on the people present at the consultation (and through them the Churches) to be prepared to listen to gay and lesbian people. 'Only if we listen to gay and lesbian people, can we then begin to work out how to tie in this listening to our view of God and humanity, to our understanding of what the "image of God" means.' Martin Hogg was himself confident that he was both gay and made in God's image and the members of the consultation agreed with him. Where the disagreement came was when he claimed the right to exercise his sexuality within a committed and faithful relationship. At that point half the people present said that he and other gay and lesbian people must be celibate. At this Martin Hogg reiterated the question in his paper. 'What kind of God gives human beings an overwhelming desire to share their lives in a loving way, including a physical, sexual way, but then simply says "But you cannot do it"? He does not even justify his decision, he just says "thou shalt not". Such a God would be a tyrant and not worthy of our love and obedience.'

What do I want to say to the Churches about my God-given sexuality? – Colin Coward

The Revd Colin Coward began his paper by saying that he was a gay man, a Christian, an ordained priest and he wanted to share his story. His story was that of a young man who had many problems at home but who was inspired by his parish priest to become a committed Christian. Having become aware of his sexuality at an early age, a painful experience of sexual abuse in his teenage years reinforced his sense of vulnerability, loneliness and isolation. He was later inspired by the work of gay clergy to seek ordination himself. To him his sexuality is normal and ordinary and was with him at birth although its particular version was 'formed by my childhood and parenting and the traumas of life'. He begins from story and not from Scripture but his life and faith bring him close to God 'who created a world in which he delighted'. He ends with a list of things he wishes to say to the Churches which includes:

- Grow up in your attitude towards human sexuality.

- Recognize the integrity of lesbian and gay identity.

- Respect God's creative activity and intention even if at first it seems at odds with what you have been taught.

Section Four – Back to the Bible

At the first consultation on these issues a division arose between those who did their theological reflection beginning from the tradition – the biblical text or the writings of the Fathers – and those who began their reflection from their experience. Those who began from the tradition were not convinced that the experience of women, black people or gay and lesbian people had anything to do with what the Bible said about being made in the image of God. They denied that people were marginalized in the Church because of perversions of what the Bible said about 'being in God's image', to which those who had been marginalized for one reason or another replied 'Well that has been our experience and we know it whatever you say.' This led on to further discussions about the authority of the Bible and how far it was legitimate for individuals or church communities to read the Bible with new eyes and interpret it in new ways. In order to take this matter forward at the second consultation, **Alastair Hunter** of the University of Glasgow was asked to give a paper on the

methodology of reading the Bible. He duly gave a paper entitled
**Gone fishing *or* Saussure *or* not so sure: Why we need a
methodology to read the Bible.** He gave his paper this punning
title 'in order to alert the hearer/reader to what some perceive to
be the fundamental instability of the process of interpretation, and
others see as a glorious opportunity'. He accepts the importance of
the place of communities of the Church in the reinterpretation of
the text but warns that we cannot, therefore, expect a consensual
outcome. 'What we must concede is the right of each community
interpretation to coexist with others and to make its own way in a
sort of free market of opinion. Even the CTBI – even Rome – has to
accept this reality.'

At the special consultation on issues of sexuality there was a
very deep division between those who began their theological
reflection from the tradition and those who began from experience
as did Colin Coward. For those who began from the tradition,
often with a very high view of the authority of the Bible, the
importance of what certain verses of Leviticus or the Pauline
Epistles said about homosexual practices was very great. Such
practices are sinful actions of fallen human nature. Those coming
from the experience of being faithful Church members who
gradually came to realize that they were gay or lesbian reflected
on the Scriptures in rather different ways. They were more
influenced by the Gospel picture of a Jesus who mingled with
those on the margins and condemned the legalism of the religious
authorities of his day. They would welcome the comment of Dr
Hunter that ethics 'represents a *process* from which none of us
can resile; and in so far as the Bible has a role, it is surely in the
processual exchange of views between reader-in-community and
text, and not in any "reading off" of rigid rules.'

Within the members of the consultation who were not gay or
lesbian, there were very different ways of reading the Scriptures,
which were influenced by the particular communities from which
they came. Sadly there seemed little willingness to 'concede the
right of each community interpretation to coexist with others'.
Instead there was deep division and painful polarization. For many
of us the most bitter lesson of this special consultation was the
need for Christians to live together with deep difference of belief,
interpretation and practice in a much more loving, understanding
and caring way.

At this consultation there were two papers presented about homosexuality and the Bible. **David Hilborn** presented a paper entitled **Homosexuality and Scripture**. His paper paid careful attention to specific texts in Genesis, Leviticus and the Pauline Epistles but he was anxious to stress that 'these more explicit texts belong to a much broader biblical discourse on creation, love, holiness and human relationships – a discourse which goes to the heart of God's purpose for humankind . . .' He firmly believes that 'biblical models of sex, marriage and reproduction must be related in turn to the essential quality of love.' On the basis of Old Testament texts Dr Hilborn has no problem with gay or lesbian people expressing friendship with one another or committing themselves to chastity but he believes that the texts in Leviticus clearly show that homosexual intercourse is wrong and sinful. He argues strongly that the Epistle to the Romans also makes it clear that homosexual activity is prohibited for those who would claim to be followers of Christ. Similarly he asserts that in both 1 Timothy and 1 Corinthians Paul teaches that homosexual practices are sinful and are 'incompatible with authentic participation in the community of God's people'.

Dr Hilborn is, however, anxious to avoid any special scapegoating of homosexual people. He comments 'Importantly for current debate, the context of Paul's remarks in both 1 Timothy 1 and 1 Corinthians 6 is eligibility for God's kingdom in general, and for church membership in particular. As in Romans 1, homoerotic sexual practice here belongs to a catalogue of sins: it is apparently no better, and no worse, than fornication, adultery, theft, greed, drunkenness, slander and robbery. This surely confirms that the Church is a community of sinners, and disallows the singling out of homosexual sin for special condemnation.'

Michael Williams gave a paper entitled **Interpreting the biblical texts on homosexuality**. He confessed that he approached the issues from his stance as an open evangelical. He rejected the stance of liberalism which 'sees only a symbolic role for the Bible in current day ethics at best or, it regards the book simply as an antique to be left behind in favour of a "common sense" or "spirit ethics".' For him, as for Dr Hilborn, 'Christian ethics must be ethics guided by the Bible and the New Testament in particular.'

Nevertheless, he comes to rather different conclusions. He prefaced his exploration with the comment 'Let me say, therefore, at the outset, that the texts which we will consider do seem to give us a clear prohibition of homosexual sex, I do not wish to deny that, but my argument will be that this is not the deeper meaning of the texts, nor is it the teaching of the Bible as a whole.' This is the thesis that he works through in the various texts he considers.

Commenting on the Leviticus texts he says that they are part of a section of 'cleanliness texts'. He adds that 'the reason that we do not apply these texts today is that in Christian theology they have been transformed by the life and teaching of Jesus. To put it very simply Jesus and the New Testament *keep* the theme of cleanliness but transpose it to a matter of the heart.' He concludes 'looking at these texts in this way could lead us to say that gay and lesbian sex is no longer a physical taboo but has now become a matter of the sincerity of the heart.' When considering the Pauline texts Canon Williams advised 'Follow the deeper logic not just the surface of the text. Look below the surface to find the centre of the argument.' Following his own advice Canon Williams observed that Paul's 'deeper argument is that disordered sexuality is the result of idolizing human desire instead of worshipping God'. His own conclusion is that 'loving homosexual relationships and loving heterosexual relationships can both be places where sexual desire finds proper expression instead of rampant self-indulgence.'

We did not have a paper looking at the biblical texts on these issues from a convinced liberal point of view but if we had done so it may have contained comments such as that expressed at the earlier consultation by Dr Hunter, namely that 'there are good grounds for the claim that the Bible has more in common with contemporary Afghanistan than with Britain or North America. We ought to reflect on that uncomfortable probability: the Bible's assumptions about women, gay men, ethnic minorities, blasphemy, slavery, war and capital punishment are decidedly pre-modern, and must be offensive to every liberal, democratic, inclusive-minded Christian.'

Section Five – Pushing Out the Boundaries

The four papers in this section press the implication of the claim that human beings are made in God's image rather further than we have gone so far. In her paper **Made and remade in the image of God**, **Anne Primavesi** asks 'why the dignity of every living being created, we would say, by God, is comprehensively denied once they are classed as "non-human"'. She objects strongly to the way in which the teaching of Genesis has been used by human beings to justify their exploitation of the earth, which has resulted in 'the monumental chemical, physical and biological changes in the earth's surface and biosphere brought about by Western industrialized nations belonging to and/emerging from Christian traditions . . .' She asks 'so what image of God are we talking about when we equate it with a human rationality which is commonly seen to exclude any kind of emotion or empathy with our non-human fellow creatures?'

Chris Sunderland takes these issues further in his paper **Human nature and image of God – Social and biological factors**. Dr Sunderland begins by saying that 'the narrative of creation in Genesis 1 would suggest that humanity was both created as an integral part of the whole creation and is therefore creature, yet at the same time it speaks of us as made in the image of God, as if special.' We define such abilities as reason, conscience, moral capacity 'over against a "lower" animal nature, which is to be repressed or overcome'. The advent of socio-biology raised further spectres such as 'selfish genes' and raised fears of 'extraordinary reductionism' and dangerous individualism. By contrast, sociology 'failed to give adequate consideration to the freedom and creativity of the individual'.

For Dr Sunderland 'the good news is that postmodern criticism has enabled many to expose the ideological undercurrents in our previous approaches to the subject of human nature and allowed us to work with a new humility that genuinely crosses disciplines, and builds a more complex and subtle view of our humanity.' This Dr Sunderland sets out to do in the rest of his paper. In this process he gives an important place to biblical narratives. Narratives in general, he believes, are important in explaining social structures but also in changing them. This creative tension he finds to be at work in a vital way in the biblical narratives. Belief in God 'means that the social order can be upheld in a creative way that allows challenge and change'. Human beings bear the image of God in relational terms and the stories of the Scriptures reflect the struggles of the community of faith to understand and discern the divine nature.

Mary Seller gave a paper entitled **Theological reflections on aspects of modern medical science – A point of view in favour**. A non-stipendiary Anglican priest, she is also Head of Development Genetics, Division of Medical and Molecular Genetics at Guy's Hospital in London. She describes very complex processes to treat infertility in terms of crystal clear simplicity and also meets head on questions such as 'Are we interfering with nature?' She concludes that helping childless couples 'is not interfering in nature, it is simply doing what people have always done in their Godlike image, being inventive and creative, and also doing what is already going on in nature: instituting change.' Faced with the question 'Are we playing God?' she replies 'we are the ones to carry out God's purposes, and we believe that we are called to cooperate with him in bringing both individuals and the world to good. So, in many respects, we should be acting as God – "playing God".' She also regards the new techniques she develops as 'an aspect of the healing ministry we are all called upon to exercise at this juncture in our history and evolution. God's creativity through scientists is unbounded.'

She is not in favour of cloning, which she regards as morally wrong for a variety of reasons. She does, however, point out that the idea that cloning will produce an identical person to the donor of the nucleus is basically flawed, as we are more than the sum of our genes. Christianity she regards as basically non-reductionist in regarding the mystery of human identity as relational, intellectual, cultural and spiritual. By being made 'in the image of God', a uniqueness is conferred upon us through our personal relationship with God which is continuous throughout our lives.

In his paper **Human individuality and inclusive community: Concepts of self, vocation and *imago Dei*, Donald Macaskill** agrees that 'to be created in the image of God is somehow to be made a unique individual, specially and specifically created.' He goes on to say 'and yet, according to traditional theology, to be created for community and for relationship to others'. The question he poses is 'How is this tension held in place? Indeed, is there a tension?' In his paper Dr Macaskill argues that 'it is intrinsic to the human self made in God's image that we are related to those who are different from us and that inclusive community, far from being an optional extra, is an imperative for humanness. Such community is within our vocation to be human, made in God's image.'

Human relations at a personal level, he believes, 'take their form from the relations in the Trinity'. Humanity is formed by the nature of its response to God's call. In this his view is very close to that of Dr Seller even though he approaches the issues from a different discipline. He goes on further to claim that human vocation is rooted in the call of God and the individual's response to the vocation of God is unique and irreplaceable. This vocation, he believes, is 'intrinsic to *imago Dei*', yet it is always a call to action in community. He concludes by stressing 'the need to rediscover a truly inclusive human community as the basis for Christian witness to *imago Dei*'.

Section Six – The Church 'Between Suffering and Hope'

There is only one paper in this section – a paper by **Mary Grey** entitled **Created in the image – The suffering, broken Body of Christ, the Church**. For Professor Grey *Between suffering and hope* sums up one of the ways the Church's life is lived out as the suffering, broken Body of Christ, the social and corporeal expression of *imago Dei*.

As she develops her narrative she holds in tension the Western theology that 'we lose the image through sin and the Fall' and the Orthodox belief that we 'retain the image with the invitation to become the *likeness* of God through virtue, through Christian sacramental life and practice'. The creating, relational God is the 'Trinitarian God of faith, a God of communion, movement, dynamism'. She continues 'thus, created as *imago Dei,* the anthropology of the human person is based on this iconicity of the divine, and increasingly we begin to see the person in relationship as being an ecological self, in relationship with the environment and with the earth as filled with divine presence . . . this passionate God-in-movement and relationship became flesh in Jesus of Nazareth', the 'embodiment of a relational God'. Moreover 'the pattern and practices of his relating are significant for messianic community . . . Christ as *imago Dei* is also *living dynamic presence'* in marginal communities today. In this situation the Church is called to be 'the drawing together of each of us, in all our diversity, created in the image, within a social vision of *imago Dei'*. It is the Spirit who 'keeps open the questioning and searching, pushing towards a new social shape and inviting Christian discipleship to embody an authentic Christic patterning in society'. This social body of the Church needs also to be *imago Trinitatis.*

Professor Grey concludes that 'becoming *imago Trinitatis* as the social body of the Church is a call to begin to nurture and empower the rejected and neglected parts of the suffering Body; to build communion on authentic mutuality; to enable processes of encountering otherness with a spirit of conversion and to follow the energizing spirit across boundaries into as yet uncharted territories.' This is the challenge to the Church with which Professor Grey and this collection of papers concludes.

Postscript

Those who read all these papers will travel a long way. We begin with a discussion of two stories in Genesis, go on to consider the meaning of being created in God's image, are challenged by the views of those made to feel that they are not fully in that image, read the varying ways of studying Scripture, pay attention to the other parts of God's created world, face up to issues of *in vitro* fertilization and cloning, are drawn into new concepts of personhood and finally are challenged as members of the Church to become *imago Trinitatis*, empowering the rejected and following the Spirit into the future as we go on 'growing into God' as individuals and as a community. What greater calling can there be for all whom God has created and will create?

> Almighty God,
> who wonderfully created us in your own image
> and yet more wonderfully restored us
> through your Son Jesus Christ:
> grant that, as he came to share in our humanity,
> so we may share the life of his divinity;
> who is alive and reigns with you and the Holy Spirit
> one God, now and for ever. Amen.[5]

From glory to glory advancing we praise you O Lord.[6]

Section One –
Reflections on the
Biblical Background

Made in the image and likeness of God

John W. Rogerson

Theo Kobusch in *Die Entdeckung der Person: Metaphysik der Freiheit und modernes Menschenbild* draws attention to the United Nations 'Universal Declaration of Human Rights' of 10 December 1948 and its belief in 'the value and worth of the person', and asks where this conception of a person with rights comes from.

> Notoriously, it belongs to the terminological reservoir of western, logical thought; but Plato and Aristotle, all the Greeks, the Romans and the ancient world and also Christian antiquity did not know this notion of a person equipped with rights . . . The discovery of the person began at a particular time, but it is not yet complete. In reality it is a process which extends over centuries. (translation mine)[1]

The purpose of this quotation is not to equate modern notions of personhood and rights with humankind being made in the image and likeness of God. It is, rather, to alert us to the fact that we cannot assume that what we understand today by terms such as 'person' is what everyone has always taken the term to mean. Further, if Kobusch's claim is true, that 'the discovery of the person . . . is not yet complete', this has implications for any theological claim that people (persons) are made in the divine image and likeness. One of the most important parts of the December 1998 consultation was the section devoted to the speakers from black, gay and lesbian, feminist, womanist and disabled points of view. What they said challenged conventional ideas of what it means to be human and indicated that their contribution to the 'discovery of the person' must be taken very seriously.

Some language about being made in the divine image and likeness implies that, on the basis of Scripture and tradition, a kind of ontological definition of the *imago Dei* can be given that will then serve to guide Christian ethical teaching on social and other matters. The December consultation indicated that this implication is both true and false. The contributors in the section representing black, gay, etc. Christians used the notion of the *imago Dei* to argue that their humanity and their standing as Christians needed to be recognized and accepted in a new way. Their implicit definition was a relational one: if God accepted them as they were, how could it be maintained that their humanity was in some way defective? (Some might reply that God's acceptance of sinners does not justify evil; but it is doubtful whether this line of argument is relevant to the powerful cases made by those speaking from black, gay, etc. standpoints.) What no one was willing or able to do was to present a definition of the *imago Dei* that contested the claim of the black, gay, etc. contributors to be made in the divine image. It was argued by some, at least, that the 'image of God' was an empty concept even though it could be effectively used in support of black, gay, etc. Christians.

That this should be so should come as no surprise in view of the history of the *imago Dei*, the understanding of which has been affected by the history of the concept of the 'person' as well as the history of the interpretation of the Bible. Key texts have been Genesis 1.26, 1 Corinthians 15.49 and Colossians 1.15.

Irenaeus (*c*.130–*c*.200 CE) deduced from the Old Testament and New Testament texts that Adam was a copy of the divine image whereas Christ was the original. The 'image' was not complete in Adam. Other lines of thought (found also in Wisdom 8.13) associated the image (or the likeness) with the soul (disagreeing about whether the soul was immortal), or the intellect. These lines of thought tended to hold that the 'image' was complete in Adam.

There was also a conflict in interpretation between seeing the 'image' in terms of fellowship with God, and the 'image' as human stewardship of the world, although the two trends are not necessarily contradictory.

There was some understandable disappointment at the consultation that an 'answer' had not been found to the question 'what does it mean to be made in God's image and likeness?'; but it was unlikely that an answer would be forthcoming in a way that would be generally agreeable, given the divergences in the history of theology. Good accounts of this history are given, for example, in Volume 2 of Pannenberg's *Systematic Theology*,[2] and of particular value is G. A. Jónsson, *The Image of God: Genesis 1.26-28.*[3]

If modern thinking about personhood, which has stressed its corporate dimension and that personhood is a complex of roles and relationships, is taken seriously, this will have implications for thinking about the *imago Dei.* A strand in theology from at least the eighteenth century has understood the 'image' in terms of a process, and in what follows here, this line of thought will be developed.

In the narrative structure of Genesis 1–11, the vegetarian world of Genesis 1.30 is deliberately the description of a world that is not the world of our experience. The world of our experience does not appear until Genesis 9 when a compromise – and no longer a vegetarian world – is sanctioned after the flood. The implication of this is that whatever is meant by humankind being made in the divine image in Genesis 1.26-8, this was meant for a world that (for the biblical author(s)/editor(s) of Genesis) no longer exists. It can be argued that Genesis 1–11 prefaces and introduces a divine project whose aim is to produce a humankind in community, including in community with the natural order, that will more and more adequately reflect the divine nature. That this is something that cannot be done without God, and indeed something that is difficult even with God (!), is abundantly illustrated in the Old Testament. Israel, as the people of God chosen by God to be a light to the nations, finds it difficult to accept this divine vocation; and visions of a recreated world (in which the vegetarian world reappears – cf. Isaiah 65.17ff) make it clear that this is God's new creation and not a human achievement.

In spite of these realistic assessments of the unlikelihood that humanity could ever adequately reflect the divine image, there are driving forces in the Old and New Testaments that indicate how efforts in that direction could be made. The laws of the Old Testament – which are only a selection of those that would have been needed to regulate Israel's life – lay particular stress on compassion. Slavery is limited to six years, the charging of interest on loans is prohibited, there are periodic arrangements to cancel debts and to tithe the people so that what is collected from the tithe can be allocated to the aliens (Israelites forced to live apart from their supporting kin), orphans and widows (Exodus 21.1-6, 22.25-7, Deuteronomy 14.28-9). A version of the Sabbath commandment (Exodus 23.12) makes the chief beneficiaries of the Sabbath rest the domesticated ox and ass, with the aim of preventing these animals from exploitation. These and other provisions can be called 'structures of grace' – proposed administrative arrangements designed to enable social interaction and the distribution of resources to manifest graciousness. The 'structures of grace' are enjoined as human responses to 'imperatives of redemption', that is, courses of action motivated by and in imitation of God's redemptive actions towards his people.

A good example of this can be found in Deuteronomy 15.12-18. This limitation of slavery, which grants to women the same conditions of release as men, contains an imperative of redemption in v. 15:

> Remember that you were a slave in the land of Egypt, and the Lord your God redeemed you; for this reason I lay this command upon you today.

Further, in enjoining the 'structure of grace' an appeal is made to the creative generosity of Israelite masters whose slaves are being freed:

> And when you send a male slave out from you a free person, you shall not send him out empty-handed. Provide liberally out of your flock, your threshing floor, and your wine press, thus giving to him some of the bounty with which the Lord your God has blessed you. (15.13-14)

On the basis of the presence in the Old Testament of 'structures of grace' enjoined in response to 'imperatives of redemption', it can be said that being made in the divine image is a matter of responding creatively and sensitively to experiences of divine graciousness. It is an ongoing project in which the more human people become as individuals and in community, including in community with the created order, the more they reflect the divine image. In the New Testament, the revelation in Jesus Christ of new facets of what it means to be human in terms of being for others, and of divine forgiveness and hope as aids in this process, adds a new dimension to the project of being in the divine image. The Early Church sought to create a new kind of humanity in the way it shared resources, cared for widows and orphans, and welcomed slaves into its fellowship, in some cases allowing them to have leading positions in local congregations.

The biblical examples of attempts to devise 'structures of grace' are examples. They cannot be transferred to a modern world that has abolished slavery and in which urban Christians, at any rate, do not own domesticated beasts of burden. They are, however, pointers to a theological task in theory and practice. We have to discover what, for our day, the relevant 'imperatives of redemption' are, and we have to embody them in 'structures of grace' that meet the needs of today's world. In so doing, we 'answer' the question of what it means to be made in the divine image. The advantage of having an understanding of being made in the divine image that works in terms of an ongoing project is that it enables contributions to be made by people who have often been marginalized – as the December consultation showed.

It also enables theological reflection on the matter to be undertaken in conjunction with what can be learnt from secular thinkers who are reflecting on what it means to be human in today's world. It is notable how many recent writers have addressed this theme, including Charles Taylor,[4] Seyla Benhabib[5] and Anthony Giddens.[6]

There are two possible directions in which things could be worked out. The first would be T. W. Adorno's insistence on the importance and uniqueness of individuals. Without being individualistic, Adorno's approach stresses the primacy of the individual over the general, and develops a view of society that is sharply critical of all social and economic processes that rob individuals of their uniqueness. 'Genocide', says Adorno, 'is the ultimate form of integration' (i.e. the elimination of an ethnic group implies that all its members are 'the same'), and he proposes a 'categorical imperative' in terms of the prevention of a recurrence of Auschwitz.[7] At the December consultation, the contributions from the black, gay and lesbian, etc. representatives were a series of calls for their uniqueness to be taken seriously as instances of the divine image.

The other direction in which things could be worked would be in terms of communicative ethics, the attempt to achieve a coercionless harmony of individuals.[8]

The 'image and likeness of God' is an empty concept that works negatively. It dares us to affirm that people of a certain colour, class, gender, sexual orientation, physical or mental handicap, religion or lack of it are not made in the divine image. When we decide (wisely) not to take up the challenge of denying the divine image to such people, we are left with the need for an open-ended concept that grows in accordance with our understanding of God and of what it means to be human. In practical and theological terms for believers, an *imitatio Dei* leads to a more profound realization of the *imago Dei*.

The phrase 'image of God' in the New Testament

Stephen I. Wright [1]

1 Introduction

The purpose of this chapter is to attempt to summarize the meaning and implications of the phrase 'image of God' as it occurs in the New Testament.[2] Another chapter in this book, by Henry Wansbrough, takes the discussion further by exploring the concept as it appears in some important passages (e.g. Philippians 2.5-11, Romans 5.12-21) where the phrase itself is not used.[3]

The phrase and concept have given rise to a rich history of theological reflection, which is beyond the scope of this chapter. My purpose here is to try to get the actual usage of the phrase in the New Testament into focus, so that others may take that theological reflection forward, perhaps in fresh ways, or rediscover the strengths of older perspectives in Christian tradition. At the same time, I am fully aware that one cannot come to a subject like this innocent of all theological presuppositions. Any description of the usage of a phrase like this is bound also to be an interpretation; all interpreters have aims, and bring something of themselves to the task of interpretation. My aim is the rather old-fashioned, but I think still interesting one, of trying to discover what the New Testament authors were thinking of when they used this particular phrase. I bring to the task a belief in the inherent importance and coherence of the concept, faith in the Christ who is at the centre of it, and a desire not only to analyse it but also to live inside its reality. Brevity and clarity require that interaction with the rich variety of views on particular passages is excluded; those who want to investigate the issue further can turn to the relevant commentaries and scholarly studies.

The New Testament usage of the phrase 'image of God' may be summarized quite briefly, in two assertions. First, the New Testament writings bear witness to Jesus Christ as the one who bears God's image in perfect form. Second, they also speak of those 'in Christ' as being in a process of renewal in God's image. Thus, through being joined to Christ, God's perfect image, human beings may embark on a new course whereby their true character as humans is restored.

Below I shall explore these twin truths more closely, with reference to key texts (section 3). I will go on to draw out some implications of them, arising directly from the New Testament (section 4). But first we need to set the scene by outlining the scriptural background for the term 'image of God'.

2   The Old Testament background

It is interesting to note that the idea of humanity being 'in the image of God' comes early in the story told by the Old Testament, but late in the historical development of Israel. On the one hand, Genesis 1.26f. is the climax of the first chapter of our Bibles, and of the first of the creation stories. Thus those who ordered the Hebrew Scriptures gave the nature of men and women as God's image an important place at the outset of the great narrative. This has enabled readers to interpret all that would be said about Israel, and the world, and individual human beings, in that overarching light. On the other hand, Genesis 1 was almost certainly composed quite late, during the Babylonian exile. So the span separating it from the New Testament literature is comparatively small – perhaps five or six hundred years. Genesis 1 can be seen, therefore, as the crystallization of a faith that was undoubtedly present before (evidenced for example in the worship of Israel – see Psalm 8), but which found new clarity in the wake of that world-shattering event for God's people. Not only was Yahweh, Israel's God, the creator of the whole world, including humanity; he created humanity *as his image*.

This would have been a particularly powerful assertion for the Israelites in exile. In the ancient Near East, 'images' were statues that 'expressed the "presence" of an absent lord in the sphere of his own dominion'.[4] The thirteenth-century BCE Pharaoh Rameses II had his image hewn out of rock on the Mediterranean coast north of Beirut: a very visible sign that this was his territory, even though he might not have lived there.[5] (We may think also of the Roman coinage in the time of Jesus, bearing the Emperor's image – Matthew 22.20; even of our own coins today, with the Queen's head.) But the idea of image was taken a stage further. Images were made of *gods* who were believed to rule over some or all of the earth. Moreover, believing that a 'god' was in ultimate authority over a particular territory, people regarded *kings or rulers* as being the 'image of god'. In their magnificence, the elites of empires such as Babylon were held to reflect the gods of those empires and mediate their power. This was a successful way of legitimating the status quo and keeping the majority of human beings in a state of subservience. So, for the people of Israel in exile, the confident credo of Genesis 1.26, 27, that human beings *as human beings* were created in the image of God, was both a subversive and a potentially liberating and exhilarating thought. They did not have to accede to the depressing choice between aspiring to unattainable power and splendour, like that of the Babylonian royalty, and accepting a status as essentially subhuman slaves of the gods.[6]

For this is the simple yet hugely significant centre of the account of God's creation of humanity in Genesis 1. Humankind, men and women as such (quite explicitly, male and female are both included in the collective term *adam*, 'humankind') were created *as* God's image (a more precise rendering than 'in').[7] It is in humanity *as such* that God is reflected and revealed in the world he has made. Not, in other words, in some humans only, like royalty – as many ancients thought; nor in some *aspect* of humanity only, such as rationality, morality, spirituality and so on – as many in the classical Christian tradition have thought. Quite straightforwardly, human beings themselves, in their collective identity, are the mirrors of God.

As a consequence of this identity, there is a commission, described in Genesis as dominion over the earth. Like the statue of the Egyptian ruler in Lebanon, human beings are the physical embodiments – across the whole world – of the rule of an invisible lord. 'Dominion' is a strong word, too strong perhaps for many of our sensibilities. Hans Walter Wolff clarifies it helpfully for us. Although in some places in the Old Testament the word denotes violent actions, in others it denotes a refashioning activity, such as treading the winepress and turning grapes into wine. Wolff says that the giving of dominion to humanity empowers us 'to make comparable useful alterations' to the earth itself. He also points out that there is no decree that men and women should have *dominion over other men and women*; and that 'dominion over the earth' should be distinguished from 'subjection to technology', which is its characteristic modern perversion.[8]

The key feature, then, of the Old Testament picture of the creation of humanity in God's image is the pivotal place it gives to humanity, in relation to both God and the world. Being in the image of God gives to humanity an extraordinary dignity and power in relation to the rest of the world. The implication of this, not fully drawn out in the Old Testament but necessary to make proper sense of the New Testament, is that precisely because humans are made as the image of *God*, God ceases to be reflected through them and exercise his rule through them in so far as they cease to acknowledge him as the one who possesses the greater and ultimate authority. In biblical terms, the disorder and imbalance in the world and in humanity itself can be traced to humanity's repudiation of this pivotal role. Human beings have swapped their created dignity for various kinds of slavery; instead of being rulers of the world under God they have effectively let the world rule *them*, and trampled on God. Shared dominion over the earth has become oppression of, and subservience to, one another. A constructive relationship with the created order, allowing us to make 'useful alterations' without violating its essential nature, has been replaced by one in which it is seen not as a partner, but as an enemy to be tamed.

3   The New Testament viewpoint

It is important first to reiterate the familiar point that the New Testament does not give us 'doctrine' in the abstract. Statements of faith are forged in the fires of experience; injunctions and exhortations arise in pastoral contexts. With regard to our theme, we find exalted affirmations about the nature of Jesus Christ being made because there was no lesser way to do justice to the impact he had made and the light that had dawned. And we find assertions about the renewal of humanity being made, not in a detached way, as if they were simply the logical consequences of what was believed about Jesus, but because in the young churches the signs of the renewal happening were excitingly visible.

The New Testament assumes the viewpoint of Genesis 1.27: that humankind is created in God's image. This is seen in an almost incidental way in James 3.9. Drawing attention to the perverse manner in which human beings use their tongues, James points out that although we 'bless the Lord and Father' with them, we also 'curse those who are made in the likeness of God'. We have forgotten the noble status of our fellow-humans, thinking blithely that we can go on 'blessing God' while denying the worth of those made to reflect him. In a much more obscure and contentious passage, Paul writes that a man (unlike a woman) ought not to have his head veiled in the Christian gathering, 'since he is the image and glory (*doxa*) of God; but woman is the glory of man' (1 Corinthians 11.7). The whole passage is deeply rooted in contemporary mores of honour and shame, as well as notions of what is 'natural'; we cannot get mired in it here. Suffice it to say that, like the verse from James, it assumes (following Genesis) that humanity *as created* – and even in its present very imperfect state – reflects God. It introduces an ordering into the male-female relationship not seen in Genesis 1 (though it may be discerned in the narrative of Genesis 2, to which Paul alludes in vv. 8, 9). This is not, however, a distinction of status or dignity. If man is the 'glory' of God, and woman the 'glory' of man, both are bearers of the 'image' in equal measure; Paul's point, following the detailed creation account of Genesis 2, is that, as it were, the image of God reached woman via man.[9] He drew implications from this for the practices of the Corinthian Church, whose logic is difficult for us to follow, but we should not lose sight of the underlying point: Paul assumes that humanity reflects God's image.

These two almost incidental references reveal the basic acceptance by James and Paul of the viewpoint of Genesis 1. It is not doubted that humanity as such is created in God's image. However, and without repudiating this belief, the main thrust of the New Testament on this theme is the twofold one we noted in the introduction. New Testament writers see the image of God as uniquely apparent in Jesus. And, although they do not use specific language concerning the 'spoiling' or 'tarnishing' of God's image to describe the state of humankind, they clearly assume the *need* for the restoration of the image of God in people, and see Christ as the clue to it.

Christ the image of God

The passages to which we draw attention here have been the subject of vast, profound and intricate reflections and dissections over the centuries. We can do no more than outline the contributions they make to the overall picture.

2 Corinthians 4.4

In this passage Paul is defending his ministry of the gospel against the charge (implicit in his answers to it) that it is somehow ineffective or inauthentic because of all the suffering it seems to bring him. His response to this accusation is rich and many-sided. The point here is that, if the good news appears at all 'veiled', it is not because of the manifest frailty of the human messenger, but because 'the god of this world' has blinded people's minds. This prevents them 'from seeing the light of the gospel of the glory of Christ, who is the image of God' – which otherwise, by implication, they *would* see. By contrast Paul, and his fellow-Christians in Corinth and elsewhere, have come to know the glory of God in the face of Jesus Christ, by God's own creative act of illumination (v. 6).

The suffering and ignominy of Christ's messengers, then, is in itself no barrier to the revelation of God through Christ. On the contrary, the Christ who died (v. 10) is specifically revealed in the suffering of his people, and revealed there *as* the image of God. Here, then, is no Babylonian-style 'image of god' reeking of extravagant wealth and oppressive exercise of power, but one who reflects God precisely in vulnerability. The image of God in humanity was spoiled as humanity became possessive about its prerogatives – and it is exactly so that the greatness of *God's* power may be seen again in human beings that, according to Paul, he is such a weak 'earthen vessel' (v. 7). But it takes a new divine *fiat lux* for God to be seen in so strange and humble a guise.

Colossians 1.15-20

Here is the most explicit extended exposition of Christ as the image of God in the New Testament. We note several features.

a)   Christ is the image of the *invisible* God (v. 15): this links back to the fundamental emphasis of Genesis on *humanity* as the visible representation of the 'absentee' owner. Christ is now seen as the true fulfilment of humanity's purpose. As Jesus of Nazareth, he had made the invisible God visible, and exercised true and wise dominion.

b) He is the *firstborn of all creation* (v. 15): a contentious statement in Patristic times because of its apparently less than unambiguous affirmation of Christ's divinity, this simply continues the theme of Christ as the true representative of humanity. Like humanity in Genesis 1, he is at the pinnacle of the created order.

c) The writer of Colossians goes beyond the affirmations of Genesis about humanity in what he says about Christ: not only was everything created *for* him, everything was created *in* or *by* and *through* him (v. 16). Here there are echoes of the language used about 'Wisdom' in the Old Testament (Proverbs 8.22-31; and see Wansbrough's chapter). Especially we note the reference to 'thrones or dominions or rulers or powers'. All forms of authority, whether human or angelic, are ultimately subservient to him. The writer has confidence that, unlike the first humanity, Christ will exercise his vocation as God's image successfully; he will not be defeated, deflected or thrown off course. All other 'powers', benevolent or malign, will ultimately find themselves caught up in his wise rule. The Gospel stories of Jesus' encounters with various 'powers', human and spiritual, provide telling demonstrations of this truth, and profound material for reflection on this theme, which we cannot engage with further here.

d) Christ's being the image of God is linked to his being the head 'of the body, the church'. Not only is he 'the firstborn of all creation', he is also 'the firstborn from the dead' (v. 18). His pre-eminence arises not only from his place in the order of creation but also from the fact that he has been through, and gone beyond, death. It is death that marks out most starkly the painfully split identity of humanity as we know it: created as the image of God, yet mortal, and often tasting death even in life. Through his death and resurrection Christ is able to gather up lost humanity so that together, as his body the Church, they may be God's image in the world.

e) 'In him all the fullness of God was pleased to dwell' (v. 19). Here is an eloquent expansion of the idea of 'image'. God in all his Godliness thought it fitting to live in Christ.[10]

f) The concrete outworking of the appearance of God on earth, in Christ his image, and his self-giving to death, is the reconciliation to himself of 'all things' (v. 20). Human beings' estrangement from God and, therefore, from each other, and the travails of the creation of which they were meant to be the wise guardians, are overcome through Christ.

Hebrews 1.1-4

The writer to the Hebrews closely echoes the thought of Colossians 1, though the words used are rather different. Introducing his appeal to his readers to remain faithful to Christ as the fulfilment of the old covenant, and not regress in nostalgia for the old system of sacrifices, he describes the status of Christ in a way that makes it clear that God could have sent no higher messenger into the world: 'He is the reflection of God's glory and the exact imprint of God's very being' (v. 3). 'Imprint' is the Greek word from which we get *character*, and suggests the impress of an image on a coin. This in itself might sound rather mechanical but, as in Colossians, the picture is filled out considerably. Christ is not only image: he is Son, heir, agent as well as pinnacle of creation, sustainer of all things, purifier, and now agent of God's rule over all. Hebrews' emphasis on the superiority of Christ to angels parallels that of Colossians on his ascendancy over all earthly and heavenly powers. Further, as in Colossians, the fact that this is *the human Jesus* is never lost sight of. It was only after 'he had made purification for sins' that he 'sat down at the right hand of the Majesty on high'. Again we find the striking picture: God is supremely reflected, and exercises his rule, in a human who suffered and died.

In all these three passages, then, it is precisely the *man Christ Jesus* who is seen as bearing the image of God. What Genesis saw as true of all humanity is seen by the New Testament as supremely true of Jesus of Nazareth. For the time, and still today, this is a startling claim: that the ultimate representative 'image' of God is not some wealthy, successful potentate able to sweep away all opposition to God's lordship, but a person who yielded to violence, shame and death.

We have already seen, especially in 2 Corinthians 4 and Colossians 1, that the identity of Christ as the image of God is inseparable from what he has achieved for humanity. His suffering has opened the way for the restoration of the human race to its true destiny as bearer of the image of God; the glory of God is now revealed not only in the face of Christ, but in the wounds of his people. We turn now to consider four passages where the emphasis is on this restoration of human beings.

Humanity being renewed in God's image

Two key things stand out about the renewal of humanity in God's image in the New Testament picture. First, it is still in process. Secondly, it happens in and through Christ alone. This means that, in at least two of the passages below (Romans 8.29 and 1 Corinthians 15.49), the transformation is explicitly stated in terms of conformity to the *image of Christ.*

Colossians 3.1-17

This is one of the great 'therefore' passages in the epistles. Having recalled his readers to the wondrous nature of what Christ has done for them, and their status in him, the writer points to the way this must be worked out in their lives. But this, like similar passages, is far from being a mere list of instructions. The logic and basis of this new way of life are repeatedly returned to, from one angle or another.

For our purposes the key verses are 9-11. Paul tells the Colossian Christians not to lie to one another, because they have 'stripped off the old self with its practices' and clothed themselves 'with the new self, which is being renewed in knowledge according to the image of its creator' (vv. 9, 10). In the act of baptism (something imbued with far greater life-changing significance in that context than, normally, in ours) they had died and risen with Christ; they had cast off an old identity and put on a new. It was because they were new people that they could, and should, live in new ways.

Interestingly, the writer describes this new self as being renewed in *knowledge.* 'Knowledge' in the biblical sense is much more than the intellectual grasping of facts. It involves relationship, commitment, involvement. So humans, unlike mute statues, are made to be living, knowing, relating beings, like their creator. In Christ they are being renewed in this true knowledge. This is necessary because in our natural state our 'knowledge' is tainted and perverted. The characteristic sin of humanity is expressed in the Adam and Eve story as grasping at the 'knowledge of good and evil', i.e. seeking first-hand experience of what it is like to do wrong as well as to obey God (Genesis 3.1-7). This first-hand

experience of evil as well as good has turned sour; while
appearing to promote human freedom it has led to human slavery,
and though promising joy it has only brought misery. Christ
restores a true relationship to God in which we know him as the
one whose image we bear, and know ourselves as humans who do
not have complete and ultimate autonomy, and know one another
as fellow-humans not as slaves or demigods, and know the world
as the sphere in which we exercise a *delegated* rule on God's
behalf. Again, the Gospel stories of Jesus' liberation of human
beings from the powers to which they have become enslaved
provide an eloquent commentary on the theme.

But the writer's sentence has not finished: he continues with
verse 11, 'where there is no longer Greek and Jew . . .'. The
difficulty of translating this 'where', and seeing just what it refers to,
is overcome in the NRSV by the paraphrase 'in that renewal . . .'.
The point surely is that the new 'self' that the Colossians have put
on is not a merely individual identity. It is, rather, that they have
clothed themselves in a new corporate humanity – like the
humanity God originally created. The key feature of this new
humanity is precisely this: that it is being *human* that matters.
Differences of race, religious tradition, social status (and we might
add gender – Paul does not specifically mention that here, though
he does in the similar verse, Galatians 3.29) still of course exist,
but they are seen at last as irrelevant beside the truth of one
humanity, gathered around one 'icon' of God: 'Christ is all,
and in all.'[11]

2 Corinthians 3.18

This verse gives a vivid picture of how the process of renewal
takes place. The passage contains notorious difficulties. In brief,
Paul writes that the 'veil' of the law, which had previously kept
people from seeing the full glory of God, is now removed 'when
one turns to the Lord' (v. 16). Thus, through Christ, we are enabled
to see 'the glory of the Lord as though reflected in a mirror' (v. 18).
This translation partly combines the two options given in the RSV,
which offers both 'beholding the glory of the Lord' and, in a
footnote, 'reflecting the glory of the Lord'. But however the
participle here should be translated, the general sense is clear.
Seeing the glory of God, we become reflectors of it (like Moses
when he met with God, v. 13). But unlike the case of Moses and
the Israelites, there is no interruption to our meeting with God.
There is no end to the glory. So we are 'transformed into the same

image (*eikōn*) from one degree of glory to another'. 'Same' perhaps implies 'same as each other': not that we are becoming identical, but that we share a common humanity bearing God's image. In any case, the corporate dimension is strong here too. It is not just a matter of an individual's face getting brighter 'the nearer they get to God'. It is much more a matter of Christian people, as the first fruits of a new humanity, reflecting to each other, and seeing in each other, the human race as God's image on earth, being renewed through Christ. Note the 'we *all*' at the beginning of the verse!

Romans 8.29

This verse, in which Paul writes that those whom God foreknew 'he also predestined to be conformed to the image of his Son', makes quite explicit that the image of the creator is restored in us through our increasing conformity to Christ. This is in order 'that he might be the firstborn within a large family'. The personal, familial dimension is prominent here. Humankind is not destined to be a frozen, static mirror, but a living, dynamic family, and as such to reflect God. The first member of this new family is Christ, and he is the model for the rest.

1 Corinthians 15.49

We cannot go into Paul's discussion about resurrection, which forms the context of this verse; we simply note his confidence that 'just as we have borne the image of the man of dust, we will also bear the image of the man of heaven' (throughout this passage gender-neutral terms are used). The hope is that we shall be transformed into the image of Christ, the one who is 'from heaven'. The contrast between what the original image of God has become and the new image of God being forged through Christ lies precisely in death, whose sting is sin (v. 56). We inherit a mortal nature from the 'first Adam', but it will be swallowed up in the immortal nature that we inherit from the 'last Adam', who went through death with us and for us.

Let us summarize. The New Testament testifies that, in the man Christ Jesus, God is seen in pristine clarity; and that, through being joined to Christ, humanity is being renewed in God's image. That means, as it meant in Genesis, humanity *as humanity* – not as a mere collection of individuals or aspects of individuals, but the human race as a body and a family, of which the Church is the first sign and foretaste. For it is precisely as a *human being*, and

41

one, moreover, who suffered, died and was raised, that Christ is recognized as the image of God, and it is through conformity to that perfect human image that together, ultimately, we will reflect God perfectly again. Meanwhile, through Christ and his people joined to him, the true function of those 'in the image of God' is beginning to be exercised again, in wise dominion over the earth, and in anticipation of the renewal of all creation.

4 Some concluding implications

For those who take seriously this New Testament picture of a Christ who fulfils human destiny as God's image and gathers up human beings with him in it, what are the consequences? I will briefly outline three, under the headings of Christ-centred thinking, behaviour and society.

Christ-centred thinking

It is manifestly clear from the New Testament that though (as in the Old Testament) *all* humanity is made in the image of God, and no characteristic of any individual human excludes him or her from this, it is only through Christ that we are enabled to fulfil our destiny, and that the broken image is restored. Any doctrinal thinking, church programmes or social action, which ignore this centrality of Christ in the purposes of God may still (because we *are* made in God's image!) contain elements of truth and usefulness, but it will not be in accordance with New Testament Christianity.

Christ-centred behaviour

The most central passages concerning our renewal in God's image, Colossians 3.9-11 and Ephesians 4.22-4, make it unequivocally clear that the process of renewal that is actually happening enables, inspires and demands a comprehensive moral commitment to put to death the habits and practices of the old humanity and put on those of the new. In the first category are sexual impurity, evil desires, greed, hatred, abusive words and lies. In the second are compassion, kindness, humility, meekness and patience. This challenge is not imposed upon us as a set of legal requirements alien to our nature. It is set before us as a vision of the beauty of holiness, which is *true* to the *new* nature we have put on. This is what it means, in practice, to reflect the image of God more and more.

If it is to Jesus that we are to be conformed, studying and imitating the pattern of his life is central to our part in the renewal process. Reading the Gospels is, of course, deeply instructive in this respect. For though Jesus is not described there as 'the image of God', and nor is that phrase used of the calling of human beings, we may recognize in the words and actions of Jesus the true fulfilling of humanity's destiny as described in Genesis 1. Jesus is the one who exercises wise and powerful dominion over the natural world, but who demonstrates that true dominion does not mean dominating over other people. He exercises true freedom in submission to his Father, not being subject to the slaveries that others have taken upon themselves. He subdues the sins, diseases and mortality that mar humanity's reflection of God, by taking the taint and the pain and the death on himself. And he does all this precisely as the truly human being: the one who goes ahead of us as the restorer of our true dignity, but also the one who continually stands before us and beside us as the model for our living.

Christ-centred society

As we have seen, the Bible's teaching about the image of God concerns a *corporate* reality. Being renewed in God's image is something that is happening to people *together*. If, in practice, human beings are not demonstrating the entirely secondary nature of such distinctions as 'Greek and Jew, circumcised and uncircumcised, barbarian, Scythian, slave and free', the image of God is not being disclosed in them – which means that God himself is not being disclosed in them. In New Testament terms, the Church is (in theory) the arena where this common humanity is discovered and celebrated most fully. But verses such as Colossians 3.11 suggest that Paul would be unwilling to tie the sphere of God's renewing work too tightly to a particular body of people. Through Christ we enter into something much bigger than an organization or a club: we enter into God's new humanity – that 'where' that translators find difficult! And while the shared knowledge of Christ experienced in Christian fellowship is celebrated in the New Testament, the one who has seen God in Christ 'with unveiled face' also sees, inevitably and gloriously, *every* human being with new eyes. Even before they discover through Christ something of what it is to be 'renewed in *knowledge*' according to the creator's image, people can be

known, by those with opened eyes, as those who were originally
made in that image – even sometimes as those in whom the
renewal process is at work without their realizing it! A vision of
Christ and what he has done leads to a new glimpse of God in
everyone. And when we 'know' another person as being in God's
image, it may be a vital link in the chain, which, under God, can
lead to their own 'renewal in knowledge': and thus to a new
society, and a new creation.

Made and remade in the image of God – The New Testament evidence

Henry Wansbrough OSB

For this second consultation of Churches Together in Britain and Ireland I have been given a double remit. I am to complete with the New Testament evidence the survey given by Professor John Rogerson, which was centred on the Old Testament evidence; this I shall attempt to do. It was also felt important to include the Roman Catholic point of view. Here I feel less secure, since I cannot in any way claim to be a spokesperson for the Roman Catholic Church. I can only say that I hope to be a faithful member of that Church and to be formed in that tradition. When I received the papers of the first consultation it became clear that the genesis of this series was the position of women in the Church, as a follow-up to the World Council of Churches (WCC) decade of 'Churches in Solidarity with Women'. Furthermore, at the first consultation, the position of other apparently neglected groups, such as black Christians, featured largely in the discussion. I shall turn to these questions in a second part of the paper.

1 The Pauline evidence

Paul would, I think, like my title to be adjusted in two ways. First, he considers the Christian rather than human beings in general; he is interested only in salvation through Christ. Secondly, he would prefer the title, 'Made in the image of God and remade in the image of Christ'.

At the root of Paul's thinking about salvation is the figure of Adam. Whether this comes from his own reflection or whether it was given to him is not clear. One very strong expression of it comes in the so-called Hymn to Christ in Philippians 2. There are good reasons for thinking that this hymn was not composed by him, but was taken over by Paul from some earlier Christian source. It may well have been one of those hymns that Pliny, half a century later, describes the Christians as singing *christo ut deo*. The balance, symmetry and rhythm evident in this hymn are not features of Paul's writing elsewhere and are indeed somewhat broken by features that could well be characteristic Pauline additions (e.g. 'death on a cross', typical of Paul's emphasis on the cross). Its positioning also suggests to me that it has been adopted from elsewhere, for it is rather a sledgehammer to crack a nut: Paul is making the simple point, 'Let this mind be in you which was in Christ Jesus',[1] and gets carried away by this full hymn, simply because of its beauty and of his own devotion to Christ. If this is so, then it attests to the comparison and contrast of Adam to Christ from the very earliest Christian generation. (It is difficult to date Philippians but, if Paul is quoting, it is in any case impossible to know when this hymn came into his ken.)

The central point of this hymn is that Christ's obedience corresponds in detail with Adam's disobedience. Both were made in the image of God but, while Adam tried to make himself like God, Christ did not count equality with God a thing to be grasped (or perhaps 'exploited'). Adam tried to exalt himself, but Christ humbled himself. Adam tried to evade death, but Christ accepted death (Paul adds 'death on a cross'). God humbled Adam, but raised Christ high by giving him the name of *Kurios*, which is above all other names, the Greek form of the sacred Tetragrammaton. The dignity of this elevation is then further expanded by the unimaginably bold *bravura* of attributing to Christ a homage that Isaiah 45 allows only of God himself, that 'all beings should bend the knee and that every tongue should acknowledge' Jesus Christ as Lord. To complete the picture, the hymn concludes that this attribution of divine status to Christ, far from instituting a rivalry to God, is 'to the glory of God the Father'.

This comparison of Christ to Adam is carried further in a key passage of Romans. Here we see more fully what Adam means to Paul. Adam is the archetype and myth of unredeemed humanity. It is common to congratulate ourselves in this generation on seeing at last the true meaning of the creation stories of Genesis: our generation has been clever enough to penetrate to the fact that they are not historical stories of what happened in the remote past, but a theological analysis of the present and permanent relationship of the world to God, and of the moral relationship of human beings to God, aware that even in sin we are cradled in the love of God, conscious of moral standards but prone to failure and sustained only by hope in the divine promise that God's power will finally prevail over evil. Paul would not yet, I think, deny that these stories are historical stories, but he certainly treats Adam as a myth as well as a historical figure, in the sense that

Adam stands for humanity as a whole, in its nobility and its failure. In the famous passage (*in quo omnes peccaverunt*) on whose misunderstanding the strange doctrine of original sin was founded, Paul teaches that in so far as we sin (*eph'hō*) we are united to Adam in sin. Other explanations of the origin of evil were current in contemporary Judaism, for example, the presence of two conflicting tendencies in the human heart, the good tendency and the evil tendency, warring against each other, or other stories of Genesis 1-11 (Cain and Abel, focusing on jealousy as the root of all evil, or the Tower of Babel, focusing on pride). Paul's reason for dwelling primarily on Adam as the initiator of evil may well be that Adam forms such a strong antitype to Christ. For Paul, then, Adam is primarily not so much man made in the image of God as man sinful and ready to be remade. The dark side is only the preface and counterweight to the bright side seen in the work of Christ, 'As through one man sin entered the world and through sin death, and thus sin spread to all men in so far as all have sinned . . .' (Romans 5.12).

That Adam is the myth of human failure is seen again in that tortured passage where Paul cries out in agony at his inability to keep to his own moral standards: 'the good thing I want to do I never do, the evil thing which I do not want – that is what I do' (7.19). In the same passage he actually says 'Sin beguiled *me*' (7.11), with clear allusion to the passage in the Garden of Eden where the serpent beguiles not Adam but the woman. It is, of course, heavily disputed whether the 'I' in this dramatic passage is Paul himself, or (rhetorically) Israel or humanity in general. I would prefer to adopt the widest interpretation: Paul is describing his own struggle as typical not only of Israel (a chief concern of his in Romans) but of every human being, every child of Adam, or rather of Adam and Eve.

The point being made in the earlier passage of Romans, and indeed throughout the letter, is the contrast between Adam and Christ: 'Just as by one man's disobedience many were made sinners, so by one man's obedience are many to be made upright' (5.18). By 'upright', *dikaios*, Paul means 'at peace with God' or perhaps one might understand it more widely, 'in a state of perfection'. This uprightness comes by being plunged into Christ, for this is the basic meaning of 'baptize'. The Christian is baptized not *in* Christ but *into* Christ, and the image of being plunged into water (as into the River Jordan) is filled out almost spatially: 'by our baptism into his death we were *buried* with him, so that as Christ was *raised* from the dead by the Father's glorious power, we too should begin living a new life' (6.4). This new life is Christ's risen life, as Paul so often says, 'It is no longer I who live but Christ lives in me' (Galatians 2.20; Philippians 1.21). The modality of this new life was aptly expressed by John A. T. Robinson 'the new tissues take on the rhythms and metabolism of the body into which they have been grafted.'[2] To express this union with Christ, Paul coins a whole series of barbarous neologisms, which occur seldom, if ever, elsewhere. They are all formed with the Greek prefix *sun-* (compare 'synchronize', 'synthetic', etc.): *sunmorphoi* (Romans 8.29; Philippians 3.21), 'sharing the form, shape or mould'; *sunphutoi* (Romans 6.5), 'con-grown with' – the word is used of a wound healing or a broken bone fusing together again; *suntaphentes* (Romans 6.4; Colossians 2.12), 'con-buried with'.

In his use of these words Paul is careful to distinguish what has already happened from what is still to come. By baptism the Christian has already joined Christ in his death, but – as he stresses in 1 Corinthians 15 – has not yet gone forward to resurrection. The remaking in Christ is not yet complete. Our former self was crucified with him (Romans 6.6) in the past, but dying with Christ in baptism is not the end of the matter; it is a process that leaves no room for premature triumph. Some of Paul's expressions accordingly suggest an ongoing relationship in a process that is still in progress: *sunestaurōmai Christō* (Galatians 2.19) could well be translated 'I *have been and am now* fixed to the Cross with Christ.' This compares with the process signalled as taking place in 2 Corinthians 3.18: 'we *are being* transformed into the image that we reflect in brighter and brighter glory.'

We have already received a spirit of adoption that enables the Christian to cry out, in the person of Christ, '*Abba*, Father' (cf. p. 20). The Aramaic word *abba* is retained as a sort of talisman, harking back to Jesus' own use of the term, and denoting an awareness of sharing in the intimacy of this sonship of Jesus. In accordance with this, *sunklēronomoi* (Romans 8.17), 'co-heirs' with Christ, in itself suggests a shared inheritance. But in itself the fact of being an heir is still looking to an inheritance in the future. Still another expression, *sundoxastheis* (Romans 8.17), 'con-glorified', again refers to the future, and is dependent on sharing Christ's sufferings (yet another of these formations: *sumpaskomen*). The remaking in the image of Christ is real but not yet complete,

and this explains why Paul can still agonize over his inability to
accomplish what he wills.

Immediate moral perfection is not yet part of the remaking.
However, the completion of the theology of the Second Adam
occurs in 1 Corinthians: 'Just as all die in Adam, so in Christ will
all be brought to life, but all of them in their proper order: Christ
the first fruits, and next, at his coming, all those who belong to
him' (1 Corinthians 15.22-3). Christ, the first fruits, is the exemplar
of the resurrection of all those with him. What this eschatological
completion will be is described in Paul's attempted answer to
what he considers a silly question: 'Someone may ask, how are
dead people raised and what sort of body do they have when they
come?' To answer this he can only use imagery, and his answer is
given in three contrasts, summed up in a fourth. Each of these
describes a transfer into the sphere of the divine, or perhaps,
more properly, a transformation into divine qualities.

1   'What is sown is perishable, but what is raised is
     imperishable.' Imperishability or eternity is a properly
     divine quality, for we are changing, subject to decay and
     dissolution, while only God is eternal and unchanged.

2   'What is sown is contemptible, but what is raised is glorious.'
     It is human to err and to earn contempt, so that each of us
     has something of which to be ashamed. All this will be
     washed or purged away by transformation into that awesome
     concept of divine glory, the glory that Moses was privileged
     only to glimpse, which set Isaiah cowering in the Temple at
     his vocation-vision, the glory the disciples saw in Christ.

3   'What is sown is weak, what is raised is powerful.'
     Frightening and absolute power, expressed in the terrifying
     natural phenomena of thunder, lightning and earthquake,
     is a feature of God. The weakness to which flesh is heir will
     be taken up into that divine power.

4   'What is sown is a natural body, what is raised is a spiritual
     body.' This I take to mean that the animating principle will
     no longer be the human soul, the life-principle of the body,
     what makes the difference between a hunk of flesh and a
     living human being (the word *psuchē* is here translated by
     'natural body'). In the resurrection, the animating principle

will be the *pneuma* of God. 'Spiritual' is a dangerous word, which might suggest that the risen body is a spirit, in the sense of a ghost, but the S/spirit here meant is surely the Spirit of God. I say that this fourth contrast sums up the others because it is surely the cause of all the other transformations, properly divinizing the Christian remade in Christ.

2   The Deutero-Paulines

We characterized the remaking of the image of God that exists in Adam as remaking in the image of Christ. The advance in Christology made in the Deutero-Paulines does, however, raise the Christian, remade in the image of Christ, into being remade in the image of God.

The scintillating and rich hymn in Colossians 1.15-20 (again, often thought not to originate with but to have been incorporated by the author of the letter) presents Christ in two parallel stanzas as the firstborn of all creation and the firstborn of the resurrection. In the first stanza Christ is presented as the Wisdom of God. To him are applied the images applied in the Wisdom Literature to the Wisdom of God: 'he is the image of the unseen God' (Wisdom 7.26), 'he exists before all things' (Proverbs 8.22-31). The divine wisdom is the means by which the problem is solved that, on the one hand, God is so exalted and 'other' that he cannot mix with the world and, on the other hand, that he is the sovereign creator. God's Wisdom is the agent and template by which God creates. In the Colossians hymn Christ now plays the part in creation played in the earlier writings by God's Wisdom in creating all things in the image of God. In the second stanza Christ is, in an echo of 1 Corinthians 15, seen as 'the firstborn from the dead'. There follows one of the great pleonastic phrases so typical of these letters, 'so that he should be supreme in every way, because God wanted all fullness to be found in him'. The fullness or *plērōma* is a term much used in these letters, signifying in an awesome and perhaps undefined sort of way the all-encompassing divine power, as in Ephesians 1.23, 'He is above all things, the head of the Church, which is his Body, the fullness of him who is filled, all in all' or 'the fullness of him who fills all things in all'. This obscure but magnificent expression is surely intended, without excessively close definition (scholars fight endlessly over whether *plēroumenou* is meant to be middle or passive – but did the author intend this to be clear?), to convey the limitless grandeur with which God pervades the universe. The Christian, taken up into Christ in the resurrection, is, therefore, somehow taken up into the firstborn from the dead who is this fullness, filled all in all, or filling all in all. We are trying to express what Paul himself calls *arrēta*, which cannot be expressed in words and can only be roughly evoked in this imagery. The Book of Revelation, using typically apocalyptic imagery, expresses the same idea in the picture of the followers of the Lamb sharing his throne.

3 Matthew

The implications of this remaking in the image of God are too far-reaching to be fully catalogued or examined. I would just like to touch on one. Typically Jewish, Matthew expresses his teaching in terms of orthopraxy as much as orthodoxy. He gives us six 'antitheses' by which the Jesus of the Sermon on the Mount conveys the new attitude to the Law, and the way in which Christian *dikaiosunē* must transcend that of the scribes and Pharisees. The last of these, on perfect love for all, sums them all up, and concludes 'Be perfect as your heavenly Father is perfect' (5.48; the word *teleios* occurs elsewhere in Matthew only at 19.21 – 'if you would be perfect . . .').

'Love' is often used in a vague and undefined sense. It is useful, therefore, to see the modality in which the human image of God is expressed in the imitation of God's love. First, the love that Matthew has in mind is *eleos*, the love that is mentioned in his three quotations of Hosea, 'What I want is love not sacrifice' (9.13; 12.7; 23.23). In Hosea 6.6 the word used is *hesed*. This is the word for the revelation of God's endlessly forgiving love in the great revelation of the divine nature in Exodus 34.6, a passage that is central for the whole of Israel's understanding of God, 'Yahweh, Yahweh, God of tenderness and compassion, slow to anger, rich in faithful love (*hesed*) and constancy, maintaining his faithful love to thousands'. Matthew shows that for him this quality is the keynote of Jesus' interpretation of the Law, using it as a principle of application of the Law in the two legal controversies, and attributing the failure of the scribes and Pharisees to their lack of this quality. It is not surprising that half of Matthew's chapter (18) on relations within the Christian community is taken up with forgiveness, and that the chapter concludes with the stark warning of the Parable of the Unforgiving Servant.

4 Women in the New Testament Church

The second part of this paper must be devoted to a brief examination of the position of women implied by the New Testament. Does the New Testament suggest that they share in, or are excluded from, the remaking in the image of God? It is not my business to paint a picture of women in pre-Christian Judaism or in the Bible. I would simply insist that, in the Old Testament, the image of God as Father is fully balanced by the image of God's love as a maternal love.

As regards the New Testament, I would stress that there is important development within the New Testament itself. On this issue the major development seems to me to occur when the gospel moves into the Hellenistic sphere, where women held a different status from that of the Semitic world. One only needs to look at the statues of female civic dignitaries, which line the road, for example, at the Greek city of Palmyra, to see that these women are not to be trifled with. There is a commanding presence about these statuesque figures, with their carefully coiffed hair and elaborate jewellery, which can cow lesser mortals even today. Even within Judaism this is the case, for there is a host of Jewish inscriptions that show that women could hold the position (at least honorarily, but there is no evidence that it is merely honorary) of *prutanis* or *archisunagōga*. Archaeologists are beginning to doubt whether any of the first-century synagogues really provide evidence of the notorious gallery for women, which later turns them into second-class citizens.

Luke wrote his Gospel for Hellenistic Christians, and it is characterized to a striking degree by the care that he takes always to introduce women alongside men. In Luke's eyes women are not an underprivileged class. The pairs proliferate: Zechariah and Mary, Simeon and Anna, the widow's son and Jairus' daughter, the shepherd who loses a sheep paired by the woman who loses a drachma, two men in bed and two women grinding corn (17.34), Ananias and Sapphira – and so on and on. By contrast with Mark and Matthew, Luke alters the scene of the rejection of Jesus by his family to paint Mary, once more, as at the Annunciation, as the ideal disciple who 'hears the word of God and keeps it'. This is no doubt why – possibly in defiance of convention – he is careful to show her as present also at Pentecost. Similarly, the first European Christian is a woman, Lydia of Philippi (Acts 16.14).

Nor is Luke the only witness. A number of women play important parts in Paul's missionary effort. In the greetings at the end of Romans, four of the first seven persons to be mentioned are women. The letter seems to be carried by Phoebe, a deacon of the church at Cenchreae. Prisca and Aquila appear frequently, the married couple whom Paul describes as 'my fellow-workers in Christ Jesus' (Romans 16.3), with the woman Prisca often being named before her husband. Then there is Junia, who is 'well-known among the apostles' (16.7), whether this means 'a well-known member of the apostolic group' or (which seems philologically more likely) 'well known to the apostles'. Another personage important enough in the world and in the Church to have a household, which she can send to Paul at Ephesus, is Chloe of Corinth (1 Corinthians 1.11). It may not be without significance that the only Gentile with whom Jesus has dealings in the Gospel of Mark is a woman too, the Syro-Phoenician, again no tender flower.

There are, of course, the notorious passages that deny women permission to speak in the assembly and consign them to a subordinate part (1 Corinthians 14.34-5; 1 Timothy 2.9-15). It does not seem to me plausible to explain the passage in the Corinthian letter as one of the Corinthian slogans quoted by Paul. It is far longer than any of the other neat little slogans ('For me everything is permissible') and far too long to be any use as a slogan. To make matters worse, it cannot be regarded as a merely local rule, for Paul maintains that this is the situation 'in all the churches of God's holy people' (14.34). It is hard to see how this regulation is compatible with the missionary activities listed above. Even elsewhere in the same letter it is clear that women do pray and prophesy in the assembly – presumably aloud; there Paul prescribes only a dress code, not complete silence (11.5). Could it be explained simply as the evidence of a clash of cultures, Near Eastern reticence and mistrust of women colliding with the more confident attitude of the Hellenistic world?

An interesting and important parallel is provided by the biblical attitude to black people. There is what might be at least a shade of colour prejudice in the early story of the death of Absalom, before Israel has begun to move among the nations. The unpopular task of announcing the death of his much-loved son to the aged King David, who had been forbidden to take part in the actual battle, is allotted to 'the Cushite', therefore an Ethiopian (2 Samuel 18.21).

This may be colour prejudice, or it may be that his colour makes him a suitable messenger, or simply that any foreigner will do for this dismal task. However, if there is prejudice here, it soon disappears. Once Israel has been scattered among the nations, all the nations are considered equal, and all alike will come to Jerusalem to pay homage: 'I number Rahab (Egypt) and Babylon among those that acknowledge me, Tyre, Philistia, Ethiopia' (Psalm 87.4). When we come to the New Testament, it is an Ethiopian, the queen's official, who is the first foreigner to be baptized and numbered among the disciples of Christ (Acts 8.26-40). Is colour prejudice more a matter of colonialism than anything else? It is hard to think that any sort of colour bar could exist in the varied racial and cultural hotchpotch of the Roman world.

It should be a significant support for two groups who often feel themselves underprivileged in Christianity that the first Christian outside the Holy Land was black and the first Christian of Europe was a woman.

Section Two –
Insights from
Orthodox Christians

Reflections from texts and icons

Ephrem Lash

(Archimandrite Ephrem did not present a paper on the issue of
being made and remade in the image of God. Instead he reflected
on short passages from the Fathers and from the Orthodox Liturgy
together with slides of icons. Sadly all we can do in this book is
record the quotations. In so doing it is important to reflect that
there are a variety of ways of doing theology. For the Orthodox,
the writings of the Fathers are of vital importance and capable of
reinterpretation in our modern life. Icons are more than pictures.
They are 'windows into heaven' through which the saints are also
alive with us still today. The Liturgy is where we meet with God
and are strengthened.)

> None other could create anew the likeness of God's
> image for humankind, save the image of the Father.
>
> *(St Athanasios of Alexandria)*

> In what then does the greatness of humanity consist,
> according to the doctrine of the Church? Not in its
> likeness to the created world, but in its being in the
> image of the nature of the creator.
>
> *(St Gregory of Nyssa)*

> At that time God said, Let us make man after
> our image and after our likeness. And the image
> he received, but the likeness through his disobedience
> he obscured.
>
> *(St Cyril of Jerusalem)*

> The Son of God when he was incarnate, and had
> become a human being, he began afresh the long
> line of human beings, and furnished us, in a brief,
> comprehensive manner, with salvation; so that what
> we had lost in Adam – namely, to be according to the
> image and likeness of God – we might recover in
> Christ Jesus.
>
> *(St Irenaeus of Lyons)*

Blessed are you, O Lord, teach me your statutes.
The choir of Saints has found the source of life and
the door of Paradise; may I too find the way through
repentance; I am the lost sheep, call me back, O
Saviour, and save me.

(*Evlogitaria for the Dead*)

It was necessary, therefore, that the Lord, coming to
the lost sheep, recapitulating such a comprehensive
dispensation, and seeking after his own handiwork,
should save that very man who had been created after
his image and likeness, that is, Adam, filling up the
times of his condemnation, which had been incurred
through disobedience, – [times] 'which the Father had
placed in his own power'.

(*St Irenaeus*)

The Shepherd of the whole rational creation,
left in the heights of heaven his unsinning and
supramundane flock, and, moved by love, went after
the sheep which had gone astray, even our human
nature. For human nature, which alone, according to
the comparison in the parable, through vice wandered
away from the hundred rational beings, is, if it be
compared with the whole, but an insignificant and
infinitesimal part.

(*St Gregory of Nyssa*)

He who lays down his life for his sheep, came to seek
for the one which had strayed upon the mountains
and the hills, on which you were then sacrificing, and
found the wanderer; and having found it, took it
upon his shoulders – on which he also took the wood
of the Cross; and having taken it, brought it back to
the higher life; and having carried it back, numbered
it amongst those who had never strayed.

(*St Gregory the Theologian*)

For he, the God who was well pleased without father
to become man from you, declared you to be mother,
source of life, that he might refashion his own image,
corrupted by passions, and, having found the lost
sheep wandering on the mountain and laid it on his

shoulders, he might bring it to his Father; and by his
own will unite it to the heavenly powers and save the
world, O Mother of God, he the Christ who has great
and rich mercy.

(Tone 4, Saturday Vespers, First Theotokion)

He lighted a candle – his own Flesh – and swept the
house, cleansing the world from sin; and sought the
piece of money, the royal image that was covered up
by passions.

(St Gregory the Theologian)

The parable therefore suggests that a candle should
first be lit, signifying doubtless our reason which
throws light on hidden principles; then that in one's
own house, that is, within oneself, we should search
for that lost coin; and by that coin the parable
doubtless hints at the image of our King, not yet
hopelessly lost, but hidden beneath the dirt, and
by this last we must understand the impurities of
the flesh, which, being swept and purged away by
carefulness of life, leave clear to the view the object
of our search.

(St Gregory of Nyssa)

Mary once, with aged Joseph, went to be enrolled in
Bethlehem, for they were of David's line; and she bore
in her womb the fruit unsown. The time of the birth
was at hand and there was no room at the inn; but the
cave proved a fair palace for the Queen. Christ is
born, that he may raise up again his image that of
old had fallen.

(Apolytikion, Christmas Eve)

You set alight, like a lamp, your sacred flesh in the
midst of Jordan and sought out the image which had
been befouled by sin and the passions; and when you
had found it you made it fair by your baptism, loving
Lord, therefore we sing your praise.

(Theophany)

Manifest yourself, Lord, in this water, and grant that
the one being baptized in it may be transformed for

the putting off of the old self that is corrupted after
the desires of deception, and may put on the new that
is renewed after the image of the One who created
him/her.

(Baptism, Blessing of the Water)

Her nobility consisted in the preservation of the
image, and the perfect likeness to the Archetype,
which is produced by reason and virtue and pure
desire, ever more and more conforming, in things
pertaining to God, to those truly initiated into the
heavenly mysteries; and in knowing whence, and of
what character, and for what end we came into being.

(St Gregory the Theologian)

She is a woman who, while others have been
honoured and extolled for natural and artificial
beauty, has acknowledged but one kind of beauty,
that of the soul, and the preservation, or the
restoration as far as possible, of the divine image.

(St Gregory the Theologian)

In you, Mother, was preserved unimpaired that
which is according to God's image; for you took up
the Cross and followed Christ, and by your deeds you
have taught us to despise the flesh, for it passes away,
but to care for the soul, you might renew the image
smothered by the passions; and having overthrown
hell you raised up the dead with yourself.

(2nd Sunday after Pascha, Of the Myrrhbearers, Canon, Ode 7)

Bearing the image of a servant in your surpassing
compassion, O Word, you passed by on your way and
restored health to the man who had lain sick for many
years, and ordered him to take up his bed.

*(3rd Sunday after Pascha, Of the
Paralysed Man, Matins, Canon, Ode 4)*

Let us listen to John teaching us of the holy mysteries
which happened in Samaria; how the Lord spoke with
a woman, asking her for water, he who gathers the
waters to their gatherings, equal in majesty with the

Father and the Spirit; for he came seeking out his image, as eternally glorious.

(4th Sunday after Pascha, Of the Samaritan Woman, Ikos)

The man born blind reasoned with himself: 'Was it through my parents' sin that I was born blind? Or was I born because of the unbelief of the nations as an accusation? I am not competent to ask when it is day, when night. My feet cannot detect the stumbling blocks of the stones. I have not seen the sun shining, nor him who fashioned me in his image. But I beg you, Christ God: Look on me and have mercy on me.'

(5th Sunday after Pascha, Of the Blind Man, Vespers, Idiomel)

Alas, wretch that I am, through my incontinence of old I was thrust by God's action from the greater image in which I shared. But you, O Christ, in your compassion, ineffably became my fellow and shared that which was worse, renewing me, O Saviour, from virgin blood.

(6 September, Matins, Exapostilaron, Theotokion)

Having penetrated the impenetrable darkness and become familiar with the Sun of justice, having touched divinely the image that appeared spiritually from high through an animal, you became a living image, Efstathios. Therefore, having acquired the force from Spirit the water and washed yourself with the blood of martyrdom, you were found worthy to dance with the heavenly companies of the angels. Meanwhile bring us near to Christ our Saviour and God.

(20 September, St Efstathios, Lauds, Idiomel)

When he had thus reached maturity he was well loved by the great Theodosios; and so he was worthy of the Holy Spirit, and having kept intact that which is according to the image [*to kat eikōna*], he made wild beasts subject to him; for once finding a she bear in the garden eating the lettuces, he took it by the ear and, kept safe by the prayer of the great saint, led it outside. On another occasion he was going up the

mountain with the donkey to collect wood, as he
used to do the collecting, when a she bear appeared
and struck the beast in the thigh. Copris seized the
bear and loaded the wood onto it with the words:
'I'm not letting you go; for you'll do the donkey's
service until it gets well.' And by the prayer of the
great saint the bear was subject to him, and carried
the wood. Once, when he was on duty in the kitchen,
the brass cauldron was boiling over and the lentils
were spilling out. Unable easily to find the usual stick
of wood, he plunged in his bare hand and stopped
the boiling, and remained unharmed.

(24 September, St Copris, Synaxarion)

By his mercy the creator is willingly created as an
infant from your pure blood, guarding you wholly
purified after childbirth, O Pure one, and purifying
his polluted image; therefore he is depicted with
you, having become mortal by nature, who is God
by nature.

(Sunday of the Holy Fathers of the Seventh
Ecumenical Council, Matins, Ode 8)

When the ewe-lamb saw the Lamb and Shepherd
hanging on the Cross, her inward parts were in agony
and she lamented as a mother: Alas! Light of the
world, my God and Lord, for what reason do you
now willingly endure all this? Because you wish to
save entirely those born of earth and for your
corrupted image to change its dwelling to divine life.
I magnify your sufferings; you endured them through
the compassion of your pity, completely curing the
pains of all by your own.

(Matins Kathisma, Theotokion, Tone 8)

O Christ, you have established singers of your
greatness, spiritual in their nature, imperishable by
your grace; you have created your angels in your
image, O Incomprehensible.

(8 November, The Archangels, Matins, 1st Canon, Ode 5)

The Word, consubstantial with the Father and the
Spirit, willingly appeared from the Virgin with the
same form as us, not mingling the elements of the
dread union; for he is shown to be one in both, in
the two natures and one person; the image of whose
likeness we now worship.

(8 November, The Archangels, Matins,
2nd Canon, Ode 8, Theotokion)

Having, like Moses of old, made use of divine ascents,
you longed to gaze on God; and you clearly saw his
image, having received it in accordance with the
likeness; for the Son is concise knowledge and
demonstration of the Father; while the one Essence
of Son and Begetter is made known, and its identity
through all times is reverently revealed, and its
kingship and power, glory and worship.

(14 November, Holy Apostle Philip,
Vespers, Prosomion of the Apostle)

By the Father's good pleasure the Son became
incarnate through the Spirit of God in your womb,
pure Mother of God, and saved the former image.

(30 November, Holy Apostle Andrew,
2nd Canon, Ode 6, Theotokion)

Man of God and faithful servant and steward of his
mysteries, and man of the desires of the Spirit, living
monument and breathing image, with wondering
admiration the Church of Myra has received you as
a divine treasure and intercessor for our souls.

(6 December, St Nicolas of Myra, Liti)

Bethlehem prepare; Eden is opened for all. Make
ready Ephratha, because the tree of life has flowered
in the cave from the Virgin. For her womb has been
revealed as the spiritual Paradise in which is the plant
of life; eating from it we shall live; we shall not die as
Adam. Christ is born to raise up his image which
had fallen.

(Nativity of Our Lord, Apolytikion of the Forefeast)

Raising mortals up from earth, the creator has come,
renewing once again the royal image; powers of
things above, rejoice together, sing your hymn; the
middle wall of enmity is abolished; he has come for
whom it was laid up; for God becomes a mortal;
Christ, the King of Israel, is at hand.

(20 December, Pre-Christmas, Lauds)

Living monument and breathing image, your yearly
festival is here, God-bearer Ignatios, and proclaims
your priestly service and your deeds of valour; your
resistance to shedding of blood on behalf of the faith;
that blest and revered voice which said: I am God's
wheat, and am being ground by the teeth of wild
beasts; and so, as you became an imitator of Christ,
intercede that our souls may be saved.

(20 December, St Ignatios of Antioch, Lauds, Aposticha)

That you may cleanse the poison of corruption and
refashion for me the original image, you become
incarnate and take suck, and you, who at your behest
cause the universe to revolve, are wrapped around
in swaddling clothes; O Word, who work wonders,
I hymn you, Angel of the Father's counsel, through
which I am made immortal.

(21 December, Pre-Christmas, Lauds)

O mysteries beyond mind and speech! God in his
compassion is born on earth, putting on the image of
a servant that he may snatch from the servitude of the
enemy those who cry with fervent longing: Blessed
are you, O Saviour, only lover of humankind!

(24 December, Lauds, Prosomion)

Ruined through transgression, the one made in
God's image became wholly subject to corruption,
fell stumbling from a better and divine life. Him the
wise creator now refashions, for he has been glorified.

*(25 December, Nativity of Our
Lord, 1st Canon, Ode 1, Troparion)*

As many of you as are friends of Christ, but a little distressed for him who has been formed and appeared like us, and who hastens to receive baptism for the purifying of his image.

(*3 January, Before Theophany, Compline, Canon, Ode 7*)

Having preserved that which is according to God's image [*to kat eikōna*] unblemished, by ascetic endeavour determining the mind as leader against destructive passions, you ascended as far as possible to that which is according to God's likeness. For bravely overmastering nature, you hastened to submit the worse to the better and to make the flesh the slave of the spirit. Therefore you were named 'summit of monastics', 'founder of the desert', 'trainer of those who run well', 'most accurate rule of virtue', and now in heaven, Antony, where mirrors are abolished, you look directly on the holy Trinity, appealing with no intermediary on behalf of those who honour you with faith and love.

(*17 January, St Antony the Great, Vespers, Doxastikon*)

Holy Virgin, Bride of God, we sing your praise as the one who gave birth to God and as protector of the faithful; for you raised up the fallen nature of Adam and made new the image by alone giving birth to the pre-existent God.

(*1 August, The Holy Maccabees,*
Matins, 2nd Canon, Ode 4, Theotokion)

For you fashioned a man by taking dust from the earth, and honoured him, O God, with your own image. You placed him in the Paradise of pleasure and promised him immortal life and the enjoyment of eternal good things if he kept your commandments. But when he disobeyed you, the true God, who had created him, and when he had been led astray by the deception of the serpent and been slain by his own transgressions, you banished him by your just judgement, O God, from Paradise into this world, and returned him to the earth, from which he had

been taken; while, in your Christ, you established
for him the salvation which comes through rebirth.

(Anaphora of St Basil, Post-Sanctus)

Master and Lord, the One who Is, who made man
according to your image and likeness and gave him
the power of eternal life; then, when he fell through
sin, did not disdain him, but provided for the
salvation of the world through the incarnation of
your Christ, do you yourself receive also this creature
of yours, whom you have redeemed from the slavery
of the foe, into the heavenly kingdom.

(Baptism, 3rd Exorcism)

Master, Lord our God, who honoured mortals with
your image, furnishing them with a rational soul
and a comely body, so that the body might serve the
rational soul, you placed the head at the very top and
in it you planted the majority of the senses, which do
not interfere with one another, while you covered the
head with hair so as not to be harmed by the changes
of the weather, and you fitted all the limbs most
suitably to each one, so that through them all they
might give thanks to you, the master craftsman.

(Baptism, Prayer at the Tonsure)

Acknowledging you, O Christ, as Lord of the living
and Master of the dead by your divine authority, we
entreat you: give rest with your chosen ones, O Lover
of humankind, to your faithful servants who have
departed to you, their only Benefactor, in places of
refreshment, amid the splendours of your saints. For
you are one who wishes to show mercy and as God
you save those whom you fashioned according to
your image, for you alone are full of mercy.

(Prosomion for the Dead, Tone 6)

Let us reverence the calling, let us honour the
dignity, and in fear let us also preserve the original
of the image.

(Office of the Great Schema, Canon, Ode 3)

You made humankind from earth, according to
your image and likeness, granting it the enjoyment
of Paradise.

(Anaphora of St James, Post-Sanctus)

Finally you sent your only-begotten Son, our Lord
Jesus Christ, forth into the world, to come and renew
and raise up your image.

(Anaphora of St James, Post-Sanctus)

And so I too, though I am unworthy of heaven
and earth and of this transient life – for I have made
myself wholly subject to sin, have become enslaved
to pleasures and defiled your image – but am
nevertheless your creature and your handiwork,
and do not despair of my salvation, wretch though
I am, but made bold by your measureless compassion,
I draw near.

(Preparation for Communion, Prayer of St Basil)

Now restrain your hand. I have found your faith
pure, as I wish, therefore I foreshadow in you what
is mine.
Yes, just man, for you are clearly an image of me.
Do you wish to know the things that after you will
come from yours? It was for this that I brought up
here, to show them to you.
So, just as for my sake you did not spare your son,
I too for the sake of all will not spare my Son.
I give him to be slain on behalf of the world,
for I alone am the Giver of good things and the
Saviour of your souls.

(St Romanos the Melodist, Kontakion on Abraham and Isaac)

If inanimate and irrational creatures are made radiant
and lovely by the resplendent Resurrection, how
much more ought we, who have been honoured with
reason and the image of God, make ourselves bright
by our life and give off sweet fragrance by the spirit.

(St Theodore the Studite, Catechesis 6, Mid-Pentecost)

I saw him and I cannot rest content to overlook his
nakedness; I cannot endure to see my divine image
like this.
For the disgrace of my child is my shame;
I will consider the glory of my child my own glory.
Hurry then, my servants and ministers
to make all his limbs beautiful once again, for they are
objects of my love. For I judge it improper to see
unprovided for or unadorned
the one who has run to me in repentance
and been found worthy of forgiveness.
Clothe him with the robe of grace, as I have
commanded, I the Master and Lord of the ages.

(*St Romanos the Melodist, Kontakion on the Prodigal Son*)

Lord our God, in your ineffable wisdom you created
humankind from the dust, transforming it into shape
and beauty and made it fair as a precious and
heavenly possession for the glorification and majesty
of your glory and kingdom by producing it in
accordance with your image and likeness. But when
it transgressed the order of your commandment, both
sharing in the image and not preserving it, for this
reason, in your love for humankind, lest the evil
become immortal, as God of our Fathers by your
divine will you ordered that this mixture and
combination and this unbreakable bond of yours
should be severed and dissolved, so that the soul until
the general resurrection goes to where it also received
its existence, while the body is resolved into the
elements from which it was put together. Therefore
we pray you, immortal Father without beginning,
and your only-begotten Son and your all-holy,
consubstantial and life-giving Spirit, to effect the
separation of the soul of your servant N. from the
body in repose.

(*Prayer for the Dying*)

In truth, to be wealthy does make people senseless
and mad. Did their power reach to such an excess,
they would have the earth too of gold, and walls of
gold, perchance the heaven too, and the air of gold.
What a madness is this, what an iniquity, what a

burning fever! Another, made after the image of God,
is perishing of cold; and do you furnish yourself with
such things as these? What senseless pride! What
more would a madman have done? Do you pay
such honour to your excrements, as to receive them
in silver?

(St John Chrysostom)

Someone that was made in the image of God stands
in unseemly plight, through your inhumanity; but the
faces of the mules that draw your wife glisten with
gold in abundance, as do the skins and woods which
compose the canopy. And if it is a seat that is to be
made, or a footstool, they are all made of gold and
silver. But the member of Christ, for whom also he
came here from heaven, and shed his precious blood,
does not even enjoy the food that is necessary for him,
owing to thy rapaciousness. But the couches are
mantled with silver on every side, while the bodies of
the saints are deprived even of necessary clothing.
And Christ is less precious to you than anything else,
servants, or mules, or couch, or chair, or footstool; for
I pass over furniture of still meaner use than these,
leaving it to you to know of it.

(St John Chrysostom)

In the image and likeness of God

David Melling

1 The biblical text

When commenting on the Old Testament, the Fathers of the
Eastern Church are almost always reading and commenting on
the Septuagint text (the LXX) which Eastern Orthodox have always
accepted as the Christian Church's Old Testament. The LXX text
of Genesis 1.26 translates the *adam* of the Hebrew not as a
proper name but by the word *anthropos*, 'man', 'human being'.
St Gregory of Nyssa comments on this:

> What is it then which we understand concerning these
> matters? In saying that 'God created man' the text
> indicates, by the indefinite character of the term, all
> mankind; for was not Adam here named together
> with the creation, as the history tells us in what
> follows? Yet the name given to the man created is not
> the particular, but the general name: thus we are led
> by the employment of the general name of our nature
> to some such view as this – that in the Divine
> foreknowledge and power all humanity is included in
> the first creation; for it is fitting for God not to regard
> any of the things made by Him as indeterminate, but
> that each existing thing should have some limit and
> measure prescribed by the wisdom of its Maker.
>
> Now just as any particular man is limited by his
> bodily dimensions, and the peculiar size which is
> conjoined with the superficies of his body is the
> measure of his separate existence, so I think that the
> entire plenitude of humanity was included by the
> God of all, by His power of foreknowledge, as it were
> in one body, and that this is what the text teaches us
> which says, 'God created man, in the image of God
> created He him.' For the image is not in part of our
> nature, nor is the grace in any one of the things found
> in that nature, but this power extends equally to all
> the race: and a sign of this is that mind is implanted
> alike in all: for all have the power of understanding

and deliberating, and all else whereby the Divine
nature finds its image in that which was made
according to it: the man that was manifested at the
first creation of the world, and he that shall be after
the consummation of all, are alike: they equally bear
in themselves the Divine image.

For this reason the whole race was spoken of as
one man . . .[1]

Gregory sees all humanity as created according to the image of
God, and every individual human being as created according to
the image of God. (The distinction between male and female he
sees as something secondary, something God introduces to ensure
humanity has a suitable means of reproduction in the fallen state.)

A parallel text to Genesis 1.26 is to be found in Wisdom 2.23:

That God founded the human being on incorruption,
and made him the image of His own individual
nature.

Who addresses whom when God says 'Let us make . . .'? The
consensus of the Fathers is that it is the Father who is addressing
the Logos, who is his perfect image.

2 The dimensions of the image

The early theologians of the East sought the image of God in many
aspects of human nature. St Gregory of Nyssa, for example, sees in
the human being the image of God's kingship:

For as in our own life artificers shape a fool in the
way appropriate to its use, so the best Artificer made
our nature, as it were, a formation fit for the exercise
of kingship, preparing it both by superior advantages
of soul, and by the very form of the body, to be
suitable for kingship: for the soul immediately shows
its royal and exalted character, being far removed
from the lowliness of private station, in that it has no
lord and is self-governed, swayed autocratically by its
own will; for to whom else does this belong other
than to a king? And besides this, its being the image

of that Nature which rules over all means that our nature was created to be royal from the first. For just as in normal human practice, those who make images of princes both mould the figure of their form and also represent the royal rank by means of purple robes – and even the likeness is commonly spoken of as 'king', so too, human nature, since it was made to rule the rest, was made, as it were, a living image by means of its likeness to the King of all, partaking with the archetype both in rank and in name, not robed in purple, nor giving indication of its rank by sceptre and diadem (for the Archetype itself is not arrayed with these), but instead of the purple robe, clothed in virtue, which is in truth the most royal of all raiment, and in place of the sceptre, leaning on the bliss of immortality, and instead of the royal diadem, decked with the crown of righteousness; so that it is shown to be perfectly like to the beauty of its archetype in all that belongs to the dignity of royalty.[2]

In the next chapter of the same text he sees the image of God in the human mind, 'word', understanding and love:

And if you were to examine the other points also by which the Divine beauty is expressed, you will find that to them too the likeness in the image which we present is perfectly preserved. The Godhead is mind and word: for 'in the beginning was the Word' and the followers of Paul 'have the mind of Christ' which 'speaks' in them: humanity too is not far removed from these: you see in yourself word and understanding, an imitation of the very Mind and Word. Again, God is love, and the fount of love: for this the great John declares, that 'love is of God', and 'God is love': the Fashioner of our nature has made this to be our feature too: for 'hereby,' He says, 'shall all men know that ye are my disciples, if ye love one another': thus, if this be absent, the whole stamp of the likeness is transformed. The Deity beholds and hears all things, and searches all things out: you too have the power of apprehension of things by means of sight and hearing, and the understanding that inquires into things and searches them out.

With various differences of emphasis and detail, the Eastern
Fathers are in general agreement with Gregory's analysis. Most
emphasize that the intellect (*nous*) is the main aspect of human
nature that is according to the image of God; human freedom is
probably the next most emphasized aspect. There is, however, a
wide range of other issues raised by various writers many of which
are recorded by the Catholicos of the Church of the East, Isho bar
Nun (823–828) in his discussion of the text of Genesis:

QUESTION: What then are the obvious reasons
because of which man is called an 'image' and
'likeness' of God.

ANSWER: One [reason], and the foremost, is because
only in man is there a complete *theoria*, which
concerns the qualities of the Persons of the Godhead.
For, as the Father is not begotten, Adam (possessing
the quality of an 'image') is not begotten. And as the
Son is begotten, Seth (possessing the quality of an
'image') is begotten. And as Eve who proceeded from
Adam, the Holy Spirit (possessing the quality of an
'image') is proceeding. Joined to the possessing of the
quality of an 'image' of the three of them is the
possessing of the quality of a 'likeness [and this too]
in a threefold sense. Furthermore, there is seen in the
soul, in its essence, an 'image' and 'likeness' of the
Father. In the word which is being born from it [the
soul] without pain; being not later in time than it, we
see, properly a prefiguration of the begotten quality of
the Son who is from the Father, [born] without pain,
who is not [later] than Him in time. And in its [the
soul's] own spiritual quality, which it possesses by
nature (possessing the quality of 'image') the Holy
Spirit is prefigured. In addition, man (possessing the
quality of an 'image') is called, in a proper way,
'image' and 'likeness' of God because he is the
summing up of creation: and especially (that is to say,
in a special way) because the man Jesus Christ would
be assumed from this lineage and race, [Jesus Christ]
who would be the image of God who is not seen in
His nature, as He really is, by the creatures.[3]

The first of Isho Nun's reasons is fascinating: he sees the image of God in Trinity in the nature and attributes of Adam, Eve and Seth – as a triad they are the image of the Trinity as well as being each and collectively in their shared humanity images of God. The presentation of Eve as in the image of the Holy Spirit is particularly fascinating. Equally interesting is Isho Nun's seeing the human soul as itself an image of the Trinity, something also canvassed by St Augustine of Hippo among others.

Isho Nun's relating the status of the human being as in the image of God to the status of Christ as the express image of the Father marks a point of great theological importance for the East, where the salvation of humanity is very frequently seen in terms of the restoration of the damaged image by the descent of the True Image into our humanity, to share our humanity so that we may be deified in him, and to pour out his Spirit on us to transform us into his living likeness.

> He who gives riches becomes poor, for he assumes the poverty of my flesh, that I may assume the richness of his Godhead. He that is full empties himself, for he empties himself of his glory for a short while, that I may have a share in his fullness. What is the riches of his goodness? What is this mystery that is around me? I had a share in the image; I did not keep it; he partakes of my flesh that he may both save the image and make the flesh immortal. He communicates a second Communion far more marvellous than the first, inasmuch as then he imparted the better nature, whereas now himself partakes of the worse. This is more godlike than the former action, this is loftier in the eyes of all men of understanding.[4]

Clarke records yet other issues as raised by Ishodad of Merv (consecrated Bishop of Hadita, 837) in his biblical commentaries:

- The human soul with its powers of speech and spirituality represents the Father who contains within himself the Son and Spirit.

- The human being symbolically represents the Trinity of Divine Persons and the Unity of the Divine Nature.

- The human being is like visible things through the body, like spiritual things through the soul, and like God through the power to hold dominion.

- The whole world is united in the human being (an important theme in John of Damascus), just as a king sets his image on his city.

- Like God the human being can create, though unlike God the human being cannot create out of nothing.

- The human being is like God in his Kingship and Judgeship.[5]

3 The image and the likeness

An image as such need not be a likeness. Even faced with a portrait we often say 'It's a good likeness' or 'It hasn't captured her likeness at all'. The Quinisext Council (691), recognized by Eastern Orthodox as of ecumenical authority, in its 72nd canon, forbids the symbolic depiction of Christ as a lamb. The lamb was clearly an icon of Christ, the Lamb of God, but was not, in the normal sense of the words, a likeness.

Eastern theologians see human nature as created according to the image of God, and see that image obscured, damaged, almost lost as the result of sin. The likeness is attained by virtuous conduct responsive to grace: it is the work of the Spirit. In the state of original innocence the likeness is there. In the state of sin it is lost. Its restoration is not a matter of all or nothing; if we respond to its promptings, we are led by the Spirit from glory to glory.

St Diadochos (*c.* 400–486), Bishop of Photild, makes the difference clear:

> All we human beings are in God's image: to be in his likeness belongs only to those who through much love have subjected their freedom to God.[6]

> Holy grace bestows two good things on us through the baptism of regeneration, one of which infinitely exceeds the other. The one is granted directly; for it renews us in the actual water and brightens all the outlines of the

soul, i.e. that which is according to the image, washing away every stain of our sin. The other – that which actually is according to the likeness – needs our cooperation. When indeed the intellect begins to taste the goodness of the All-Holy Spirit with great awareness, then we ought to know that grace is beginning to paint, as it were, the likeness over the image – just as portrait painters mark out the outlines of the person in monochrome then little by little adorning colour with colour, until they capture the appearance of the subject down to each hair. In the same way God's holy grace shapes through baptism the image the human being possessed at his coming into existence, but when it sees us filled with longing and yearning for the beauty of the likeness and standing naked and undaunted in its workshop, it adorns virtue with virtue and leads the soul's form up from glory to glory, preserving for her the impression of the likeness.[7]

The image of God in humankind – A bridge between the Eastern and Wesleyan theological traditions

David Carter

The biblical motif of the creation of humankind in the image of God has, in general, received much more extensive reflection within the Eastern theological tradition than in the West. There are many reasons for this, perhaps the most important one being the Western sense of the immense gap between a holy God and a sinful humanity. The East, of course, does not lack a profound sense of sin, which is amply reflected in the Liturgy and such works as the Canon of St Andrew of Crete. However, for the East, the 'very great promises' of God, referred to in 2 Peter 1.4, whereby we may be made 'participants of the divine nature' have always remained central and have controlled the development of the Eastern understanding of sanctification or 'theosis'.

Some Western theologians, most especially in the reformed tradition, have tried to maintain that the concept is marginal to the biblical tradition. While explicit references to it are limited to Genesis 1.26, James 3.9 and 2 Peter 1.4 just cited, the concept is widely implicit elsewhere in Scripture. One can hardly make sense of our Lord's injunction to 'be perfect, therefore, as your heavenly Father is perfect' (Matthew 5.48), unless there is that in our nature that, renewed and empowered by the Holy Spirit, can respond fully to such an invitation. Nor can we make sense of the Pauline injunction to have 'the mind that was in Christ Jesus'. However, one major Western theological tradition, the Wesleyan, has emphasized the concept rather more than most, and behind much of the attitude to worship and holiness within the Wesleyan tradition lies a strong awareness of the vocation to share in the divine energies.[1]

In many respects, and not only in this one, the Wesleyan tradition straddles the emphases of East and West. Within the overall Western tradition, the divine image has been seen primarily in terms of certain human attributes, such as reason and conscience. These are, so to speak, 'bolted on' to humanity's more purely animal characteristics as shared with the rest of the animal kingdom.[2] Wesley, in common with the Eastern tradition, saw the 'image' more relationally. Ted Runyon, an American Methodist dogmatic theologian, who, with others, has particularly emphasized Wesley's debt to the Eastern Fathers such as Ephraim Syrus and Gregory of Nyssa, argues that, for the Eastern Fathers and for Wesley, the image was not so much a matter of a series of human capacities as a 'living relationship called forth by divine grace'.[3] The modern French Orthodox theologian, Olivier Clément, also emphasizes this relationality. Human beings are created in the image of the supremely relational Trinity. They are invited to enter into that relationality to find themselves fully in that giving and receiving that constitute true human and divine communion.[4] Clément emphasizes that, just as the three persons of the Trinity are ever at one in mind and purpose, so human beings are called to become a 'sole person in a multitude of persons'.[5] In Charles Wesley's ecclesiological hymns we find a similar emphasis. Thus, in a hymn still perennially popular within Methodism, we sing:

> The gift which He on one bestows
> we all delight to prove;
> the grace through every vessel flows,
> in purest streams of love
> We all partake the joy of one
> the common peace we feel,
> a peace to sensual minds unknown,
> a joy unspeakable.[6]

One of Wesley's great hymns on the Holy Spirit sings lyrically of the lavish gift of the Spirit and the exultant and unending response of praise on the part of the Church. It is 'the Spirit of Thy Son' that makes 'the depths of godhead known', to which the Church responds:

> So shall we pray and never cease,
> so shall we thankfully confess
> thy wisdom, truth and power and love;
> with joy unspeakable adore,
> and bless and praise Thee evermore,
> and serve Thee as Thy hosts above.[7]

The great nineteenth-century Wesleyan ecclesiologist, Benjamin
Gregory, opens his work *The Holy Catholic Church* with a
contemplation of the Church's unceasing life of praise across
every generation, citing Paul's great introductory paean of praise
from Ephesians. He talks of Paul's vision of the 'unintermitted
anthem of praise' to be offered in every generation. Significantly
he begins his reflection thus, 'The Apostle, gazing entranced at the
boundlessness of God's love to man, yearns for an ascription of
praise which may, at least in infinity of duration, correspond to
that illimitable love.'[8]

The consequences of this common relational emphasis in their
understanding of the divine image in humanity can be seen in
the similarity of approach to worship of Methodists and Orthodox.
For both traditions, worship is primarily celebratory of the great
mystery of divine love and grace in creation and in redemption.
As Olivier Clément puts it, 'grace resides in the very act of
creation' and the vocation of humankind is to become 'the
celebrant of this great mystery'.[9] The overriding spirit both of the
Orthodox liturgies and of Wesleyan hymnody is one of wonder at
the sheer lavishness of God's love, in creation, in the Incarnation,
in the outpouring of the Holy Spirit, in the miracles of grace daily
worked in the Church of God, in the vision vouchsafed to the
people of God, who even now, and especially in the Eucharist,
taste the reality of the age to come.[10] To take just one or two
examples, in St Ephraim the Syrian, we read these words:

> Whom have we, Lord, like you
> the Great One who became small,
>   the Wakeful who slept,
> the Pure One who was baptized,
> the Living One who died,
> the King who abased Himself to ensure
>   honour for all.[11]

and an echo from Charles Wesley:

> Stand amazed ye heavens at this,
> see the Lord of earth and skies,
> humbled to the dust he is
> and in a manger lies.[12]

A valuable study by Professors Ford and Hardy, *Jubilate*, has illuminated the nature of worship as the most utilitarian and sublimely joyful of all human activities.[13] It is the most natural and necessary, yet, paradoxically, also freest, of all human activities, the response of those who know themselves to be created in the image of God and eternally held in his loving relationship. It is, in a very real sense, a counterpart of God's own joy and delight in that creation that he beholds as 'very good'.[14] It is a human expression of delight in his activity; as the psalmist puts it, 'Thou hast made me glad through thy works and I will rejoice in giving praise for the operations of thy hands' (Psalm 92.4).[15] It is in worship that human beings are taken outside of themselves, and are, literally, in an 'ecstasy', the word meaning precisely 'standing outside of oneself'. In response to the God who goes outside of himself in creation, we respond in going beyond ourselves into his eternal self-giving joy. Human beings were made for this. In the nineteenth century, Metropolitan Filaret of Moscow, echoing St Paul, said 'we are not the masters of your faith but the servants of your joy'. The early Wesleyan preachers sang,

> Tis worth living this
> to administer bliss and salvation in Jesus' name

and

> My remnant of days, I spend in His praise.[16]

Though one does not doubt that, in the present imperfect state both of the world and of the Christian community, acts of penitence and intercession are necessary components of worship, its central aim is the celebration of God's sheer goodness and of our immense privilege in being invited to share in his loving work and creation.

That, I hope, sets the overall scene. I now want to explore further the emphases within the Wesleyan tradition, making links and comparisons with the Eastern tradition. We shall look first at the work of John Wesley, then at the motif in the hymnody of his brother Charles, and, lastly, at the greatest Wesleyan systematic theologian of the nineteenth century, W. B. Pope.[17] Finally, I shall make a few concluding points about the centrality of the doctrine for our contemporary Christian mission and the search for unity.

John Wesley regarded human beings as imaging God in three
ways, which he described as the 'natural', 'political' and 'moral'
images. By the 'natural' image, he meant, 'a spirit like his Creator;
a being endued not only with sense and understanding, but also
with a will exerting itself in various affections. To crown all the
rest; he was endued with liberty, a power of directing his own
affections and actions, a capacity of determining himself, of
choosing good or evil.' We should note, at this point, that Wesley
was very Western in one aspect of his belief about the 'image'.
He believed that it had been totally destroyed by the Fall;
however, he also believed that, by 'prevenient grace', God had
restored a measure of both conscience and freedom to human
beings that predisposed them to receive the gospel and the Holy
Spirit, who could then restore the image of God in them and bring
it to the fullness of its potential.[18]

By the 'political' image, Wesley meant God's endowment of
humankind with the capacity for managing the world, for being
'vicegerent upon earth; the prince and the governor of this lower
world'.[19] Significantly, in view of current ecological concerns,
Wesley saw this political image as involving not the right to be
exploitative of the rest of the creation, but rather the duty to tend
it. As Runyon puts it, 'to humanity as the political image was given
the special responsibility of being the "channel of conveyance"
between the creator and the rest of creation, so that "all the
blessings of God flowed through him" to the other creatures. Thus
humanity is in the image of God insofar as the benevolence of
God is reflected in human actions towards the rest of creation.'[20]
Wesley had a great love of animals and a concern that they,
especially those that laboured for the benefit of humankind
domestically, should be well treated. For Wesley, human power
over any creature should be responsible, stewarding, tending
power, reflecting, as it were, ironically, the benevolent care of
God for his creation. His attitude can be summed up in a couplet
by his brother, Charles:

> The bountiful donor of all we enjoy,
> our tongues to Thine honour and lives we employ.[21]

Finally, there is the 'moral' image. Ted Runyon sums it up as
'a relationship in which the Creature receives constantly from
the Creator and mediates further what is received'. Christian
obedience is essentially, 'the continuing openness to welcome

life from the creative source, to receive love, justice, mercy and truth from God, and, as the image of God, to exercise and communicate further what we have received', a relationship that Wesley terms 'spiritual respiration'.

> God's breathing into the soul, and the soul's breathing back what it first receives from God; a continual action of God upon the soul, the reaction of the soul upon God . . . the offering up all the thoughts of our hearts, all the words of our tongues, all the works of our hands, all our body, soul and spirit, to be an holy sacrifice, acceptable unto God in Christ Jesus.[22]

We have already stressed the consummation of this exchange in worship within both traditions. Eastern Christian thought emphasizes the divinely initiated exchange, which reaches its logical conclusion in the Incarnation in which 'God becomes man in order that we might become like God'. Wesleyan theology, in line with the words spoken by the Father at the baptism of Christ, emphasizes God's good pleasure in this. Methodists recall this aspect of their tradition whenever they sing the words:

> And if thou art well pleased to hear,
> come down and meet us now. [23]

The Eastern emphasis upon the natural vocation of humanity to act as the priest of creation, so strongly stressed in the work of the late Alexander Schmemann, complements the insights of the Wesleyan tradition into the 'political' and 'moral' images of God in humanity.[24]

There is, as far as I am aware, no specific exploration in Wesley of the distinction, in Genesis 1.26, between 'image' and 'likeness'. Modern biblical scholarship has tended to see no deep significance in the use of the two terms; rather just one of the conventions of Hebrew poetry. However, it is interesting to note that another French Orthodox, Paul Evdokimov, does argue that the Hebrew term *tsemach* implies growth and development.[25] Implicitly, the Wesleyan tradition agrees with its emphasis upon journeying ever deeper into God as in one of Wesley's most famous hymns, 'Love divine, all loves excelling', especially in the last verse, which begins 'Finish then thy new creation' and leads to:

Till we cast our crowns before Thee,
lost in wonder, love and praise.[26]

Turning to the hymns of Charles Wesley, far more important for
popular Methodist consciousness than the sermons or occasional
writings of his brother, we find an emphasis upon 'love' as the
essential and prime characteristic of the image of God. Thus in
the hymn 'Let us join, 'tis God commands' we read these four
encapsulating lines:

Love thine image, love impart,
stamp it on our face and heart.
Only love to us be given Lord,
we ask no other heaven.[27]

These four lines alone sum up so much in Wesleyan theology
and experience. For the Methodist Christian, the reception,
communication and radiation of God's love sum up the whole
content of Christian faith and practice. It is, even in this life, 'life
everlasting and heaven below'.[28] James Rigg, the great nineteenth-
century Wesleyan theologian and ecclesiologist, emphasized the
distinctiveness of the Wesleyan typos of Christianity with its
emphasis upon a 'full, present and free salvation'.[29] John Wesley
emphasized this in a famous passage:

The ground of a thousand mistakes in religion is the
not considering deeply, that love is the highest gift
of God, humble, gentle, patient love. The heaven of
heavens is love. There is nothing higher in religion:
there is in effect, nothing else.[30]

The Wesleyan emphasis coheres with what Paul Evdokimov calls
the 'eschatological transcendence' of Orthodoxy and its emphasis,
shared with Methodism,[31] upon the eschatological nature of the
Eucharist, where, to quote from the Anglican–Orthodox dialogue
report of 1976, 'the end breaks into our midst'.[32]

Charles Wesley's hymns on the Incarnation mark a very interesting
conjunction of Western and Eastern emphases. Consider this verse:

He deigns in flesh to appear
widest extremes to join,
to bring our vileness near

> and make us all divine
> and we the life of God shall know
> for God is manifest below.[33]

Here we see conjoined the Western emphasis upon the alienated nature of sinful humanity and the Eastern one on theosis.

There is a breathtaking emphasis upon the utter prodigality of God's love and his incredible kindness in sharing with us creatures, by grace, those energies that are his by nature. Brian Frost, in his invaluable little book, *Living in Tension Between East and West*, a study in the relationship between the Methodist and Orthodox spiritual traditions, draws attention to the theme of 'fullness' in Charles Wesley's hymns, citing, in particular, one that I, personally, have always greatly loved,[34] 'Being of beings, God of love, to Thee our hearts we raise' with its lines:

> The sole return Thy love requires
> is that we ask for more

and

> For more we ask; we open then
> our hearts to embrace Thy will;
> turn and revive us, Lord, again,
> with all Thy fullness fill.[35]

The completeness of the 'divine exchange' at the Incarnation, from which all such 'fullness' is derived is proclaimed in the hymn 'Glory be to God on high' and especially in these concluding lines:

> Knees and hearts to Him we bow,
> of our flesh and of our bone,
> Jesus is our brother now,
> and God is all our own.[36]

The emphasis upon love is very significant. One cannot underline too strongly that, in sharing in it, we share in the highest attribute of the divine nature. In Scripture, many adjectives are used to describe aspects of the divine nature. God is holy, just, righteous, almighty, eternal, omnipotent, merciful, etc., but only one noun is ever used to describe him absolutely, and that is 'love'.[37] We

'The Saviour "Acheiropoietos"'
(*c.* twelfth century, Tretyakov Gallery, Moscow)

'The Adoration of the Cross'
(*c.* twelfth century, Tretyakov Gallery, Moscow)

cannot, as creatures, share in God's omnipotence and
omniscience, but we can share in that attribute which is most
primary to God himself, that which he elects in his eternal
freedom always and consistently to be 'pure, universal love',
as the Wesleys put it. It is interesting to note in this context that
they would have no truck with the mealy-mouthed Authorized
Version translation of *ekenosen* in Philippians 2.5 as 'made
himself of no reputation'. They translated it literally, as 'emptied',
as Wesley does in his hymn 'And can it be?'

> emptied Himself of all but love
> and bled for Adam's helpless race.[38]

God communicates himself most fully to us in his supremest
attribute, which, as Clément emphasizes, is only disclosed fully
in the abandonment of the Cross, the place where, paradoxically,
God is most fully hidden, yet also most fully revealed.[39]

Clément also says that human beings can only realize themselves
in turning to the 'unknown one' who both gives them life and calls
them. The human longing to realize the potential of the image that
can, alone, give us lasting satisfaction, is summed up in another
hymn of Charles Wesley:

> Loose me from the chains of sense
> set me from the body free.
> Draw with stronger influence
> my unfettered soul to Thee.
>
> In me, Lord, Thyself reveal
> fill me with a sweet surprise;
> let me Thee when waking feel
> let me in Thy image rise.
>
> Let me of Thy life partake
> thy own holiness impart.
> O that I might sweetly wake
> with my Saviour in my heart.
>
> O that I might know Thee mine
> O that I might Thee receive.
> Only live the life divine.
> Only to Thy Glory live.[40]

Inextricably linked with the emphasis on love are two of its necessary correlates, freedom and creativity. The ability to love necessarily implies freedom, since what is coerced or robotic cannot be real love, which, of necessity, involves free gift; as the present Pope put it in *Ut Unum Sint*, human beings can only realize themselves in the 'sincere gift of themselves'.[41] Modern biblical studies emphasize fertility and creativity as being of the essence of the original Hebrew concept of the image; human beings are to multiply and to harness all the fruitful potential of the earth both to their proper use and to the delight of the God who invites us into partnership in his very work of creation. Humankind is necessarily *homo faber,* man who makes and creates. Human beings are necessarily artists, celebrating creation, exploring in it and unlocking the potential that God has placed there for them to develop as an act of loving stewardship and celebration of all his goodness. Wesley's couplet.

> Thy gifts we render back to Thee
> in ceaseless songs of praise[42]

applies not just to worship in the formal liturgical sense. There is a very real sense in which we become co-creators with God, even of our own personalities. Many modern Eastern theologians, such as John Zizioulas, have emphasized the centrality of personhood for the Christian understanding of human nature and its vocation. Christians are never isolated individuals: they are always persons in relationship,[43] simultaneously with the trinitarian God himself and with all those whom the Father has given to the Son, 'the entire people that your Son has gained for himself', as the current Roman rite of the Mass puts it. Wesleyan theology and hymnody share this insight. As Charles Wesley puts it in his hymn 'See where our Great High priest before the Lord appears', Christ is 'never without His people seen, the Head of all believing men'.[44] We are people in relationship, constituted by the creating and redeeming grace of God, enlivened and given our complementary charisms by the Holy Spirit, constantly giving to and receiving from each other in the fellowship of Christ's Church.

We turn now to W. B. Pope, the greatest Wesleyan systematic theologian of the nineteenth century. Pope follows the Wesleys in giving prominence to the concept of the 'image of God' in humankind. He calls the image the 'first note and attribute of human nature'. He emphasizes 'self-conscious and self-determining personality' as central to it; he does not emphasize love as the central attribute to the same extent as the Wesleys. He adduces some important theologoumena. Firstly, he argues that it is precisely because of the 'divine image' that humankind can fall. 'The freedom of the human spirit is the purest reflection of the divine nature, but that same freedom involves the possibility of its excellence being lost.' However, he goes on to contradict the widespread Protestant view that the 'image had been totally effaced by the fall'; rather, he argues that it is 'essential and indestructible', asserting that 'from beginning to end the holy record regards this image as uneffaced and uneffaceable.' Secondly, he argues that, since the Eternal Son is, in the supremest sense, himself 'the image of God', Adam, as the representative of humankind was created in and after that image.[45] There is a natural symmetry between Pope's theologoumenon and that of St Maximus the Confessor, that God so loved his creation that he willed his own *ensomatiosis* (incarnation or embodiment) within it.[46] Pope also sees a very close relationship between our adoption and regeneration in the eternal Son of the status and eternal generation of the Son. Thus he says: 'Our regeneration answers to the eternally Begotten; our adoption to the eternally Beloved.'[47] Notice the extraordinary nature of this statement, which applies to humankind under the covenant of redemption: that our very restoration is related to the totality of the mind-bending self-gift and mystery of the Father who begot the Eternal Son from all eternity. When we consider the sheer wonder of divine love as it is refracted through an experience and contemplation of our nature as we are created and redeemed in Christ, we cannot but cry out with Paul, 'O the depth of the riches and wisdom and knowledge of God.'[48]

Let us finally turn to consider the bearing of our creation in the image of God upon some of the great questions of our time, most especially in mission, ecclesiology and ecumenism.

First, mission. The Eastern tradition has always spoken of the importance of *diakonia* or service, sometimes called the 'liturgy after the liturgy', and thus seen as the natural corollary of the latter, a further reflection of that divine *philanthropia* or, if we use the Wesleyan phrase, 'pure, universal love', which is celebrated in worship and, above all, in the Eucharist. It is service and loving care for all in a needy world.

The emphasis upon the 'all' is important in both traditions. The divine offer is for all: there is no limitation to a hypothetical 'elect', excluding others. In controverting such Calvinist views, Wesley was fond of quoting the Psalmist's 'His mercy is over all his works.'[49] St Isaac of Nineveh caps the Psalmist with his splendid and oft quoted: 'What is the heart of compassion? It is the heart that burns with compassion for all creation, even for the fallen angels, even for the reptiles.'[50]

Wesley told his preachers to go 'not to those who need you, but to those who need you most'. He encouraged the Methodists to be benevolent not just to the poor of their own community but to those beyond. He instituted his 'Strangers' Friends' Society' to do just that. He also encouraged the Methodists to pray for and support generously the missionary efforts of other churches.[51] Wesley asserted that God had 'appointed the poor' to receive all our surplus.[52]

Writing in 1840, William Shrewsbury insisted that 'disinterestedness' was the core virtue of Methodism.[53] One might see it very properly as the human counterpart to that divine 'undistinguishing regard' which, as Charles Wesley sings, was cast on all of Adam's fallen race.[54] According to Shrewsbury, Methodists were to esteem the good in every Christian church whether or not there was any reciprocity of sentiment towards Methodism.[55]

At the heart of both Eastern and Wesleyan ecclesial experience and ecclesiology is an understanding of the Church as *koinonia*/communion, as *sobornost*, to use the Russian word, or 'fellowship' to use the Methodist one. Wesley's comment on the practice of the first community in Jerusalem in 'having all things in common' is interesting. He says,

> How came they so to act, seeing that we do not read of any positive command . . . the command was written on their hearts.
> It reasonably and necessarily resulted from the degree of love that they had. Observe they were of one heart and soul.[56]

Effectively, one might add, they were the many persons in the One of whom Clément speaks.

James Rigg is also interesting on this. He relates how both
the first disciples in Jerusalem and the first Methodist converts
'instinctively' joined together. For Rigg, the Methodist revival was
at least as much a revival of primitive fellowship as of primitive
doctrine.[57] The action both of the first disciples, and later of the
first Methodists, is the most eloquent testimony to the existence
of the *sensus fidelium*, that supernatural capacity of the faithful,
whether or not they be in any way formally instructed in theology,
for recognizing and doing the truly Christian 'thing', the capacity
of which St John spoke when he referred to the anointing 'by the
Holy One' for discernment that the faithful enjoy.[58]

In recent years, the Western Church in general has recovered
koinonia as the key concept in ecclesiology, and rightly so, since
it gives us a common meeting ground for considering in depth
the mystery of the Church in the totality of God's design. What,
however, has not yet received sufficient attention is the bearing
of the understanding of the divine image upon this doctrine.
Until recently, much Western ecclesiology, most especially in
the Roman Catholic and reformed traditions, was primarily
concerned with the disciplinary functions of the Church. These
most definitely have their place, but they must be balanced by
an understanding of the charismatic nature of the Church. The
christological emphasis upon obedience to the Master and those
who are his authorized under-shepherds[59] must be complemented
by an emphasis upon the charismatic structure of the Church,
upon its role in fostering, liberating and granting 'space' for
charisms at every level, and, above all, on the fact, constantly
underlined by the Methodist ecclesiologists, Shrewsbury and
Gregory, that the mutual partnership of laity and ministry can only
be effectively maintained in an atmosphere of mutual trust and
love, based upon mutual respect for the varying gifts distributed by
the Spirit, both those given in formal ordination and those given
directly by the Spirit, which the leaders of the Church have a God-
given duty to foster and to use for the edification of the whole.[60]

Eastern tradition has always tried to balance the significance of
unity in the one Christ with diversity in the pluriform gifts of the
Spirit. One of the most interesting applications of this has been
in the work of Cardinal Willebrands with his concept of typol of
Christian life.[61] It seems to me that ecumenical progress can most
rapidly be made when we take this concept and relate it to our
understanding of how we, as Christians, made and renewed in the

image of God, discern within each other the mystery of the Church under many different forms. It has to be complemented by a recognition that, for continuing pilgrim Churches, there is a corporate counterpart to our personal pilgrimage from being made in the image of God to realizing, through the power of the Holy Spirit, the fullness of that likeness. All our Churches are still *in via*. None has arrived yet at that eschatological plenitude, which will come when Christ finally presents us 'without a spot or wrinkle'.[62] As those who are called to a totality of communion, we are in the process of constantly receiving from our fellow-Christians of every tradition. Such humble receiving and glad giving is of the very essence of what it is to be in God's image, delighting in each other's God-given gifts. As Charles Wesley sings:

> The gift which He on one bestows,
> we all delight to prove.[63]

That, I believe, is at the heart of the sharing to which God calls us. Increasingly, within the ecumenical movement, we are indeed 'proving' it and realizing the value of Wesley's dictum that Christianity is, indeed, the 'true, the experimental religion'.

I have only been able to scratch the surface of this important truth. In discerning the very real parallels between the two traditions discussed, I believe I have, in a very specific instance, lent credence to the valuable hypothesis of Cardinal Willebrands. I have also only been able to give you the merest taste of the riches of the two theological and spiritual traditions concerned, but I hope I have whetted your appetites a little.

Section Three –

But what if your experience makes you feel that you are not fully made in God's image?

Black people made
in the image of God

Arlington Trotman

This paper is my response to being asked to present my
understanding of what it means that a black person is made
in the image and likeness of God. Before dealing with this subject
I must immediately register a twofold disclaimer. First, I do not
presume to speak for black people in general, or the Black
Majority Church community in particular. The thoughts expressed
here will be merely individual, though many of the ideas will
almost certainly reflect much more widely held views among
British-Caribbean black people.

Secondly, I will resist any attempt to justify the existence and,
therefore, the redemption of black people, on the premise that any
such approach can only be artificial, and ultimately unscriptural.
The basis for this is rooted both in an anthropological and biblical
tradition that makes no attempt to justify ethnicity, but provides
a socio-cultural and Christian model of life, and a redemptive
eschatology for all people. I will try to reflect, however, some of
the issues that determine the modern cultural and religious reasons
that inspire the question, and assess some of the distinctive
cultural and *spiritual* features of life on which British-Caribbean
black Christians base their understanding of Christian truth.

Biblical foundations

The apologia put forward here rests on two basic tenets: the
distinctly biblical, and the socio-cultural realities. In the Genesis
account of creation God said:

> Let us make humankind in our image, according
> to our likeness . . . So God created humankind in
> his image, in the image of God he created them;
> male and female he created them. (Genesis 1.26-7)

In reflecting the unity of the race, Martin Luther King frequently
used the eloquence of the following poem:

Fleecy locks black complexion,
cannot forfeit nature's claim.
Skin may differ, but affection
dwells in black and white the same.
And were I so tall as to reach the pole,
or to grasp the ocean at a span,
I must be measured by my soul,
the mind is the standard of the man.[1]

These two traditions can be taken to represent the basis for the impression the black person has of being in the image of God, and is closely linked to his or her understanding of 'knowing' God.

The value of all human beings is rooted in the reality of having been made in the image of God, and is based on key beliefs. In Christ, God comes to be known in his self-revealing nature as truly God and truly human (John 1.1-14; 19.5; Colossians 1.15). In Christ exists the true meaning of covenant and destiny (Ephesians 1.22; Hebrews 2.6ff). In Christ the human race finds its fullest and truest meaning. Through him we are being changed into the likeness of God (2 Corinthians 3.18). To God, the human race is more valuable both in its individual aspect (Matthew 18.12) and its corporate entity (Matthew 9.36; 23.37) than the whole of the rest of nature (Matthew 8.36-7; 10.31). The individual, made in the image of God, represents the whole human race.

The image of God is manifested, therefore, in people's enjoyment of what is exclusively good, in the fact that human beings alone respond to God, and, as head of God's creation, in obedience to God. Our knowledge of this truth is our freedom, and the image of God cannot be erased since it is part of the constitution of the race. But disobedience and the Fall created the division, which is driven by selfishness.

The Holiness-Pentecostal tradition provides the context for some of the views expressed here. God, who created with equal intrinsic value all human beings to rule over the created order, is personally involved with, and determines, what experiences the individual (the human race) has every day. A firm belief in Christ's vicarious sacrifice, mediated through the Holy Spirit, enables us to see that God meets the social, spiritual and redemptive needs of the one human race, and will deliver it in his final eschatological victory.

This largely evangelical theological perspective is needfully balanced by the practical outworking of that theology in the socio-cultural and spiritual reality, which is historical.[2] But the socio-economic division of the race has emerged also as sin, and the present problem seems to have arisen in strong associations with the modern Western imperialistic culture.[3] This brought about critical polarizations among people of different ethno-cultural groups, widely reinforced by modern Western cultural activities.

The problem of modern culture

Modern culture embraces many different features, conflicts and nuances. Often, divergent culture ideas indicate something of the content and historicity of the problem, and tend to keep the race divided. Culture for some is viewed as godless and secular; for others it is based on a natural rational knowledge of God, in which Christianity is regarded as an integral part of its Western mode. H. Richard Niebuhr's understanding helps our case.[4]

Niebuhr stated that culture entails, first of all, 'the total process of human activity, and the total result of such activity to which now the name *culture*, now the name *civilization* is applied in common speech . . . the artificial secondary environment which man superimposes on the natural'.[5] This is perceived basically as social and non-private, and relates essentially to the character and nature of human existence on the one hand, but also purely human endeavours by which that existence is maintained, on the other.

Secondly, culture takes in 'human achievement . . . that proportion of man's heritage in any place or time which has been given us designedly and laboriously by other men . . .'.[6] The assertion that 'the world as far as it is man-made and man-intended is the world of culture'[7] reveals a poignant dialectical dimension; for it is clear that the modern world locates man (not women, minority ethnic groups, etc.) at its centre; it refers to man in his divided and marginalized modern contexts, which means social exclusion of members of the race.

Thirdly, there is the economic interpretation of culture, which is concerned with human achievements as ends in themselves. These ends are thought to be in the minds both of the designers and the users, but the inherent value-relation is for the good of 'man' who becomes the 'chief value'; all other values are directed towards human self-realization. Finally, Niebuhr insists that all culture is 'pluralistic'. He writes:

> The values are many partly because men are many . . . and societies are always involved in a more or less laborious effort to hold together in tolerable conflict the many efforts of many men in many groups to achieve and conserve many goods.[8]

This approach accentuates modern, Western, white-male-dominated society's preoccupation with material existence, but critical questions arise when existence is divorced from its divine source, one such being the artificial polarization of the race into the pseudo-scientific myth of Caucasian superiority and Negroid inferiority. The ontological characterization of modern culture, however, demonstrates the problem that leads to the need for the original question: *What it means that a black person is made in the image of God.* I move to consider the internal structure of culture as it determines critical outcomes, not least racism and discrimination against minority ethnic groups, and the related components, that have contributed to these divisions in society.

Oppression and knowledge of God

We identify here the concepts of language and technology as the 'hub' of some people's cultural activity. If its divine substance is taken as transcendent foundation, it is important to see that life can create itself through the dynamics of growth, the process by which intrinsic form is transmuted to another form, thereby preserving original reality. But language and technology are central to a modern person's calculating self-realization. It is in this, however, that cultural and ethnic difference is seen as a problem rather than a gift, and a fragmented identity results from this philosophy. Certainly, the language of oppression has been very different from the language of the oppressors, who, in collusion in the seventeenth and eighteenth centuries, for example, used its economic intent to empty African religious and cultural traditions in order to achieve economic ends. The African, said Martin Luther King, was brought against his will and used as 'a depersonalized cog in a vast plantation machine'.[9] The language used in the slave plantation culture was the constant cry for release from oppression and marginalization. Says King: 'Realism compels us to admit that the struggle will continue until freedom is a reality for all the oppressed people of the world.'[10]

Yet that language is evident in modern (or postmodern) times in different contexts. Oppressed people reject the isolation and marginalization that result, however, since their knowledge of God leads to the view that all human beings are valued as equal in humanity. This provides the basis of a strong self-knowledge as belonging to the single human race for many marginalized people. And repels the forces of racism and discrimination, particularly where the homogeneous extended family life affirms and supports the identity, in which the expression of subjective feelings is allowed as normative.

The enlightened rationalistic demand that all emotional elements be excluded from the culture did little to maintain the created goodwill and unity of the race. Yet the age of reason could still demonstrate a peculiar subjectivity and, as the work on culture in Paul Tillich's writings shows: 'people wept about everything which remained after the principles of reason were actualized.'[11] Emotions were thought to be irrelevant to control and production, and were considered a negative imposition on humanity's essential and existential situation; but emotion expresses an irrefutable dimension in humanity, and in no more appropriate place could emotional expression be expected than in the contexts of oppression and pain and in the evidence of exclusion.

Natural science and socio-religious exclusion

Modern science provides the vehicle for another attack against a Christ-centred world view that supports the concept of the oneness of the race *made in the image of* God. First, the philosophy of nature and the mechanical application of the categories of humanity's spirit to nature, produced the great empirical reaction. This development viewed the mathematical structure of nature as a presupposition for truth, and conjoined with Newtonian physics to produce the metaphysical framework within which all knowledge and truth would be ascertained. This is directly expressed in Darwinism, which reinforced the socio-cultural division, especially the concept of the survival of the fittest.[12]

Evolution advanced the idea of *change with time*, which spread to all branches of human thought, completely upsetting the well-established, previously accepted, inclusive patterns. Darwin's own belief in divine creation was radically overthrown, and he asserted: 'There is a force like a hundred thousand wedges trying to force every kind of adapted structure to the gaps of the economy of nature or rather forming gaps by thrusting out weaker ones.'[13]

Secondly, what it means as a black person to be *made in the image of God* would have been affected by the impact of Darwinism on the biblical view of reality. Evidently, it contradicted Scripture and substituted automatic natural mechanism for God's designed creation, giving credence to a dualistic view of reality. If God is considered the ground of being for, and creator of, the soul, it seems incoherent to suggest that he is not also creator of the material physical body of all human beings.

The great Scottish theologian T. F. Torrance is unique in his depth of knowledge of the philosophy of natural science and, unlike Tillich, embraces a biblicist tradition that objectively presupposes God as 'active' and known through his self-manifestation. His contention about what is proper to Christian theology and science, as 'the conviction that we must allow the divine realities to declare themselves to us, and so allow the basic forms of theological truth to come into view and impose themselves on our understanding',[14] is vital for maintenance of the unity of the race made in God's image. Torrance asserts that a truly Christian notion of reality must support the scientific notion and, if that is true, significant consequences ensue.

First, with critical Christocentric insight, he declared that empirical theories are transparent as 'disclosure models through which . . . the truth in creation as it has come from God . . . shines'.[15] God is the presupposition of the question about God, and the ontological solution to the problem of man. It is possible here, therefore, that truth derived scientifically also points in the direction of God, the affirmation of truth. The scientific revolution at the beginning of the modern period radically disjoined science from its ground and placed it exclusively in the realm of humanity's autonomous grasping for truth in the fashion of modern culture. This excluded the weakest from the accepted norms of socio-cultural reality, and limited that section to a subservient existence.

Secondly, at the centre of this philosophically-expressed theocentric model of life is the reality of existential disintegration, which is concerned with the importance of will and its place in the divine-human economy. It is a philosophy that undermines, but a theology that seeks to embrace, the unity of all human life.

What is being conveyed here is that there are 'given' or positivistic concepts, which tend to be stressed in their concrete structure without the commitment to any principles of what is taken as absolute in its fundamental assessment. Why has the 'merely given' law of the eighteenth century fallen short? It may be because 'it did not allow critical attacks from the side of the natural law, nor did it establish current positive law as eternal law.'[16]

On the other hand, atheistic relativism also manifested itself in philosophical relativism, which commenced with David Hume. Of relativism he wrote: 'Truth is relative to a group, to a concrete situation, or to an external predicament.'[17] But his philosophy also assisted the disunity of the race. He said:

> I am apt to suspect the negroes, and in general all other species of men (for there are four or five different kinds) to be naturally inferior to the whites. There was never a civilized nation of any other complexion than white nor even any individual eminent either in action or speculation. No ingenious manufacture amongst them, no arts, no sciences.[18]

This relativized the situation, and it may be said that even the relativizers in this context are themselves relativized, as in the description of 'cynical relativism'.[19]

In contemporary society cynical relativism and sceptical relativism are manifested in ways symptomatic of the humanist's existential predicament, not least in a radical form of modern individualism. Yet relativism at the level of personal choice can be affirmed, but it is choice that can be exclusive. It is here that Tillich usefully argues for the transcendence of relativism, which must be presented as *agape*: 'The principle of *agape* expresses the unconditional validity of the moral imperative and it gives the ultimate norm for all ethical content . . . But it is the source of moral motivation. It necessarily commands, threatens and promises because fulfilment of the law is reunion with one's essential being.'[20]

Thirdly, love here transcends law, for example, and can be expressed, as such, only paradoxically since the ultimate principle is constantly breaking through. The apartheid laws found their meaning in this flawed principle, which could not, therefore, be sustained. It is here that relativism and convenient exegesis lost their pervading power to negate the reality of the knowledge of God,[21] and lacked ontological foundation; hence they are essentially limited in meaning for the status and unity of modern human beings.[22]

I reiterate the truth that we do not justify the black person's being made in the image of God, or his or her existence, based on any sociological or philosophical criteria, since all people are made in the image of God. The development of the invisible institution within the plantation culture bears testimony to this.[23] That black, oppressed people in that culture expressed their innate need for spiritual fulfilment, and held to the belief that they would one day be free, is typified in the following Negro spiritual:

> Steal away steal away, steal away to Jesus,
> Steal away, steal away home,
> I ain't got long to stay here.

The black Christian, in particular, has been excluded from the mainstream in church life on the basis of nominalism, an intellectual distortion of divine reality and the denial of the reality and function of groups of things that have self-evident properties of universal truth. Nominalism inverted biblical unity and projected dualistic perceptions of the world, while stressing human beings' power of reason as, ultimately, the freedom from any other authority. Black people made in the image of God opposed this by virtue of their theological and cultural perspective, viewing the world as a single unity in which sin is the divisive reality that disrupted the unity of the race.

Alienation from the modern Black Majority Church community also came about through the classical argument about the existence of God, and the fundamental Christian dogmas that are still, for some distinguished ecclesiastical authorities, a matter of conjecture, confusion, and invariably the reason for disbelief and despair, and moral absolutes are either lacking or ill-defined.[24] The mainstream Church appears helpless to maintain unambiguously the standard that must be rooted in its essentially redemptive reason for being. The culture is pervasive in its decadence, injustice and the loss of meaning, having intellectually and practically split the world into two distinct individual and purportedly unrelated realities.

Moreover, the theory of progress, which has evolved into radical capitalism, has advanced humanity's pride in the purely mathematical and materialistic culture, and reinforced its race divisiveness. Such culture, however, may not necessarily be entirely inimical to ultimate truth principles Christocentrically established, as these apply within the black Church community.

The reality of positive black experience

The contributions of black people to every branch of scientific and theological knowledge, and every area of socio-political analysis, is almost common knowledge. The black American experience of contribution and oppression has been well documented, and the situation in these islands is developing despite contemporary evidence to the contrary. Black people have been active here for many centuries, mainly, but not only, as slaves.[25] Prejudice and discrimination based on colour or ethnic origin of black are still common features of life in these islands; this gives the question of what it means to be a black person in the image of God its currency.

The principles of justice, common sense and good biblical exegesis will show that we are required to stand in solidarity with people who are oppressed, marginalized, discriminated against, maltreated, and whose loved ones have died as a result. We are called to respect their humanity and cultural value, and to appreciate that cultural diversity enriches the life of a community. Difference is not to be regarded then as a threat, but an exciting aspect of new knowledge for life in the global village.

Scripture teaches that we are one highly valued human race, born without the labels of social exclusion. The barriers people build between themselves, therefore, are rather false. Angry resentment based on religious, cultural, ethnic, social and colour difference has been removed through the incarnational model of life, and we are really free truly to love and value one another.

Common sense shows us that it is less than the just dues of human intelligence to hate in general and, in particular, to deny common justice, or to injure or kill in order to make real the prejudices of the mind. But we must make real and take seriously the responsibility to fight racism, the evil that emanates from hate.

Conclusion

We must come to appreciate that, having been *made in the image of God*, all people must continue the fight against racism and xenophobia in British society, and make obsolete the question about what this means for a black person. We must challenge not only the cancer of racism as a historical reality, but also overcome it as a present actual reality that dehumanizes both the victim and the perpetrator.

In a sermon delivered in Montgomery, Alabama, in November 1956, King acknowledged the oneness of the race while advising black oppressed people:

> In your struggle for justice, let your oppressor know that you are not attempting to defeat or humiliate him, or even pay him back for injustices that he has heaped upon you. Let him know that you are merely seeking justice for him as well as yourself. Let him know that the festering sore of segregation [racism] debilitates the white man as well as the Negro [Black and Asian people]. With this attitude you will be able to keep your struggle on high Christian standards.[26]

We will all do well to grasp and practise this truth in the fight to overcome the evil of racism, which questions the fact that black people have their identity in the image of God.

'One ladies'; one normal': Made in the image of God – Issues for women

Zoë Bennett Moore

I went with a friend to the YHA shop in Cambridge to buy rucksacks for our daughters, who were off round the world. The rucksacks had been chosen and set aside already. 'One ladies' and one normal?' confirmed the young man pleasantly. I just grinned wryly at the woman standing behind him. 'Well, I mean, one ladies' and one standard?' he tried. I just smiled at him. 'Well, it isn't our fault; it's the manufacturers' – he started to get a little flustered. This amusing and apparently trivial incident hides within it an issue of the utmost seriousness – are women regarded as 'subnormal' human beings? And does the way we *talk* about people (and indeed about God) have any bearing on the realities of our lives?

An issue of the utmost seriousness

'More than 100 Million Women are Missing.' This is the title of an article by the economist Amartya Sen, written in 1990.[1] 'It is often said', writes Sen, 'that women make up a majority of the world's population. They do not.' We make this mistake because we generalize from the situation in Europe and North America, whereas 'in South Asia, West Asia and China, the ratio of women to men can be as low as 0.94, or even lower, and it varies widely elsewhere in Asia, in Africa and in Latin America.' The shortfall of women is over 100 million, and it is caused by unequal access to food and medical provision. The undervaluing of women literally kills them.

This is not just outside the Churches. The WCC *Living Letters* documents the feminization of poverty and the global increase of violence against women, within and without the Churches. The Churches are challenged to 'practise economic justice within the church in terms of equal salaries for equivalent work' and to recognize that 'often violence against women finds theological justification in the teachings of the church.'[2] One of the most urgent challenges to emerge from the ecumenical decade is the issue of violence against women in the Churches.

There is a global epidemic of physical, sexual, psychological, racial and cultural violence against women. It happens everywhere, including churches of all traditions and communions. There is also a growing body of research and evidence demonstrating religious collusion with and theological justification of gender and sexual violence against women and girls.[3] Gendered violence against women and girls is significant in a discussion about women and girls being made in the image of God. This is, first, because it makes clear just how serious sexism is. The undervaluing and devaluing of woman leads to suffering and even death on a global scale, through a whole range of practices including domestic violence, deprivation of resources, and rape in war. To suggest that sexism, or the feminism that challenges it, is just a Western, middle class, politically correct fad, is utterly immoral and takes no account of the realities under which so many people live and die.

Secondly, explicit gendered violence is a symptom of even more widespread underlying, often *implicit*, violence. This may appear as the threat of violence, or as simply the pressure to keep the established power patterns. Gender differences are used pervasively to justify differences of power and privilege between men and women. In this the churches are key players, as are other religious groups. 'Difference', writes feminist lawyer Catherine MacKinnon, 'is the velvet glove on the iron fist of domination.'[4] Women in many of our Churches would recognize that description – as women are denied leading roles in the Church by men, or are treated as the 'weaker sex', in need of anything ranging from paternalism to a bit of 'disciplining'. So violence as an issue raises for us the question of whether women are different from men. If so, in what ways are they different? And above all, why is what is 'different' about women so often allowed to be used to hurt them and to class them as of less worth than men?[5]

This leads directly to the connection between gendered violence and the image of God. Value is intimately linked to godlikeness.

Value and the image of God

That which is deemed to be more like God, closer to the divine, is valued most. The Christian doctrine that human beings are made in the image of God is indeed often linked with issues of human rights, of the proper valuing and the proper treatment of all human beings. It would appear that, in different ways in many of our Churches worldwide, women are less highly valued than men. Where they are, in theory, highly valued, that value is often linked to an explicit understanding that they have their own proper place and dignity, which must not be allowed to usurp the place and dignity of men. While this is a human problem that extends well beyond the Churches, it is also clear that such views and practices are given widespread theological justification. It is, therefore, important to explore how images of God and images of being human might be used in our Christian traditions and practices. These may, on the one hand, be used to reinforce the low value given to women or, on the other hand, to reinforce positive evaluations of women and girls in relation to God.

The God in whose image

The two key texts in the Bible for the Christian doctrine of the human being made in the image of God are Genesis 1.27:

> So God created humankind in his image,
> in the image of God he created them;
> male and female he created them

and Colossians 1.15:

> He [Christ] is the image of the invisible God.

The first of these texts points to the image of God as being of the essence of what it means to be created. Interpreters have differed concerning whether 'male and female' is implied as partaking of the image of God. The second text points specifically to Jesus Christ as the bearer of the image of God *par excellence.* Human being in the image of God is therefore in the Christian tradition intimately connected with being like Christ. For a range of interpretation of these verses in their textual context the reader is referred to the articles in Kari Børresen's excellent book *The Image of God: Gender Models in Judaeo-Christian Tradition.*[6] Here my concern is to point out that, in practice, our understanding of what it means to be made in the image of God as a human being inevitably depends on what our image of God is. Is our God (as I once heard a bishop say in a sermon) 'like a very big bloke'? Does the fatherhood of God have masculine overtones? In Genesis 1.27 humankind is made in the image of God; in Genesis 5.3 Adam becomes the father of Seth 'in his likeness, according to his image'. This should alert us to the sense in which we project onto God our patterns, our images, and make God in human image even as we assert that we are made in God's image.

One interpretation of Genesis 1.27 that has been very influential in the West is that of Augustine, who asserted that male and female together complementarily make up the image of God, but that man represents the rational soul whereas woman represents the lower bodily part. The rational soul is that part of the human that is most truly and most nearly the image of God. Subsequent definitions have excluded those whose rational powers are impaired (children, the mentally sick) or whose bodies are not perfect. All of these definitions of what it means to be made in the image of God assume a certain image *for* God. Women have been excluded from ministry and priesthood on the grounds of their not being able to represent fully God (or Christ, the Son of God). The defence of racism, slavery or abortion may employ arguments about who counts as human, who is fully made in the image of God. The questions must always be asked – what kind of God is presupposed? And who has decided what this God is like – in whose image is this God made?

Jesus Christ as the image of God holds up an ambiguous picture to women. Many women have found in the figure of Jesus a strength and a comfort, as he is seen to be on the side of those who suffer, of those who are outcast and devalued. The undervalued and oppressed are thus given value, and furthermore, are called and empowered to work for others who are undervalued or oppressed. Jacquelyn Grant, in *White Women's Christ and Black Women's Jesus*, writes of the threefold significance of Jesus: 'first he identifies with the "little people", Black women, where they are; secondly, he affirms the basic humanity of these, "the least"; and thirdly, he inspires active hope in the struggle for resurrected, liberated existence.'[7]

Other women have found the figure of Jesus more problematic: given that Jesus clearly was a human male, how much of the female human experience can we assert God shares in Christ? This question is especially poignant in the light of the issues with which this article began. Furthermore, it is difficult to take seriously the theological assertion that Jesus Christ represents all humanity when in some of our Churches not all humanity is permitted to represent Jesus Christ (for example in priesthood or leadership).

One problem, which often literally stares us in the face, is the figure of a male human being as the central symbol of the Christian faith. Jesus Christ, depicted in art work, on crucifixes, in statues, occupies centre stage in our Churches and our religious heritage. The story of Jesus Christ dominates our lectionary, our hymnody and our preaching. We worship *him* and tell *his* story. *He* is the centre of our religious life. Honour is given universally to a man in a way that it is not to a woman. From this stems a potential for imbalance in the honour given to men as opposed to the honour given to women. It is a potential that would matter less if it were not so often realized.

The problem is the problem of ideological distortion. The kind of God we believe in affects the way we behave and the way we treat one another. But, conversely, the values and practices we have in our human community are reflected in the way we describe God – the image of God we make, choose and respond to. A society in which there is male domination will serve a God who is thought of in male terms and who legitimates male domination. As Mary Daly said: 'if God is male then the male is God.'[8] While it is true that there is a strong tradition in the Bible and in Christian history of visions of God that *challenge* the status quo, it is also true that there are many examples of unchallenged ideology. Many Christian feminists who stay in the Churches do so because they believe that the feminist challenge to patriarchal religion has a real and historical place in the Bible and in Christian tradition.[9]

I will now examine three areas of Christian living and faith that show up the deep connections between how we see each other and relate as human beings, and the image we have of God – our pictures, our words, and our pastoral practices.

Our pictures

A student in a seminar I was leading gave the opinion that when he thought of God as male there were no sexual overtones, but when he thought of God as female the image became sexualized and difficult. I think he speaks honestly for many of us, men and women. Men are 'normal'; women are 'ladies'.

There is, however, another way of looking at this. Jo Ind writes of her experiences as a teenager suffering from an eating disorder.[10] She had been brought up with conventional twentieth-century, Western middle class images of father as distant and unemotional and mother as emotionally close. She had also been brought up to consider that referring to God as 'mother' was blasphemous. But, as she struggled with compulsive eating and found more pain than help in her 'father' image of God, she played with another possibility.

> When I imagined that God was my heavenly mother, the context in which I had an eating disorder changed. It is not an exaggeration to say the whole world became a different place.
>
> I realised that God was close, not distant. She was as close to me as I had been to my earthly mother in the womb . . . When I came to my heavenly mother and told her about my eating disorder I did not have to explain. I could rest in the presence of the one in whose image I was made. Worries about stretchmarks and thighs had a place – I pictured her as being on the round side herself . . . nothing I had experienced was alien to her. I rested in the love of one who knew.[11]

Our picture of God and our self-image are inextricably bound up. A fatal combination of the patriarchal social structures we live in, together with the male-centred pictures of God we have inherited in the Christian tradition, conspire to damage and devalue women and deny them access to this way of relating to God.

There is a quite specific nervousness of female imagery for God amongst Christians. Not only does this encompass envisaging God as mother, but also extends to the imaginative depiction of Christ as a woman on the cross – the Christa figure. While a whole range of depictions of the crucifixion, many of them far from realist, are welcomed, the Christa figure often stirs deep-seated anger and disturbance. When recently, in our Theological Federation, slides from the collection *The Christ We Share* were shown, the slide of Edwina Sandys's 'Christa', which is part of the collection, was conspicuous by its absence.[12]

This pragmatic aversion to the association God/female, which is not paralleled by a similar resistance to a God/male association, conspires against a real (rather than a merely theoretical) commitment to seeing and treating women as if they were as fully made in the image of God as men are.

Our words

As with our pictures, we cannot dissociate words used for humans from words used for God. And, within the Christian tradition, male language about God is considered normative, authorized.

Take for example that use of the word 'father' for God. Classic Christian doctrine has asserted that God is beyond gender. Whatever we say about God's fatherhood, we do *not* say that God is our biological father, and thus the use of the term father is a metaphor. (In spite of this I was roundly told by an apparently orthodox Anglican clergyman that God is indeed the biological father of Jesus, because God created a sperm in Mary. Thus far may the language of God's masculinity be stretched, at least in popular clerical piety.) Even as a metaphor, however, the language of God's fatherhood is given a particular validity. Thus a very significant masculine way of talking about God carries a special authorization and normativeness in the Christian way of thinking, and careful theological assertions about God being beyond gender are often subverted in common thought and speech about God.

There is an exercise I frequently conduct in teaching. It comprises drawing a line on the whiteboard and inviting those present to identify themselves anywhere on a line that has four marked points. At one end are those who feel that there is no problem about the use of generically masculine language for the human community ('man', 'his', 'mankind' – meaning to include both men and women) and also no problem with predominantly masculine language for God. Then there are those who feel we should change (as many Churches have in their official liturgy) the language for the human community, but leave the language for God alone. Next come those who feel we should explore the possibilities of adding to current imagery for God, perhaps from biblically based feminine images for God (God as a mother bird, God in labour). Finally come those who feel we should challenge the traditional images for God as well as adding to them, examining the in-built sexism, as they see it, of God 'the Father', or of the trinity of 'Father, Son and Holy Spirit'. Although actually understanding how religious language works is complicated, and although symbols and images can change in meaning in different contexts, it will always be inadequate to stop at the mid point on the line – changing the language about the human community but leaving language about God untouched. This is because of the phenomenon identified earlier, that the use of predominantly or exclusively masculine language about God both *demonstrates* and *reinforces* the way in which the society that uses the language values the masculine in different ways from the feminine, and, crucially, values it as more 'godlike'.

Our pastoral practices

Riet Bons-Storm's book *The Incredible Woman*[13] tells of how women are rendered silent, unable to tell their story. In looking at the pastoral care of women she demonstrates 'unstory' – those places where women say nothing or even make things up because they have no words with which they can tell the truth in a way that could be understood. She writes of the 'rhetoric of uncertainty' with which women haltingly tell their stories –'I don't know if I'm putting this right' . . . 'maybe' . . . 'I'm probably not making sense' . . . 'it's sort of like this . . . but . . .'. Bons-Storm goes on to analyse the dominant socio-cultural narrative that keeps women silent – the philosophical narrative, the psychological narrative and even (*especially* in churches) the theological narrative. It is impossible to escape the roles written in the narratives we all take for granted, whether they be good or bad roles. To tell a different story is to disturb normality. Among many others, she tells of 'Lucy', who hates her disabled son and can find no one in church to accept her as she is. 'I hate my son' cannot be heard, except to be instantly 'sorted out'. And she writes of Eva, struggling to find her identity and to articulate her story – 'God was a stranger to me because he was behind this "Christian woman" stuff.'[14]

There has been a particular story about women prevalent in the Churches at many times and in many places and in various guises. It concerns women's sin – weakness, sexual depravity, irrationality, irresponsibility – and how women's salvation is achieved – through marriage, virginity, self-sacrifice, or submission to men.[15] So while there is 'ladies'' and 'normal' there is also 'normal for ladies'. What is normal for ladies may be construed as abnormal for normal people (that is men) – hysteria, depression, tears and irrationality. Furthermore, if women try to tell stories that contradict the dominant narrative they are regarded as rebellious, strident or even 'dykes' (women who refuse to accept the choice of heterosexual femininity or virginal purity). Because women are positioned differently in the social and theological narratives, they have not been in a position to say what is 'normal for women' *let alone* to claim their own experience as 'normal', full stop, normal for humans.

Hence the question of what it might mean for a woman to name herself as made in the image of God is one that is only just beginning to be extensively explored. As women's experience increasingly becomes the subject of theological reflection, and as understanding increases of how our images of God and the divine are inseparable from our images of what it is to be human, the debate about God and female experience can be expected to intensify.

Some concluding questions

There has not been space here to do more than set down some initial problems concerning women made in the image of God. In conclusion I suggest two questions that I regard as significantly raised by this article. I do no more than raise them here for future consideration, as implications of the line of thinking represented in this paper. They concern the implications of what has been said for what it means to be human, and also for what we want to say about the nature of the God in whom we believe.

1 Single or dual anthropology?

In the light of all this, do we have to say that women's and men's experiences are so different that we can no longer speak of the category 'human' in a way that is meaningful? Can we speak of the human being made in the image of God in a way that includes all – across gender and also across cultures? Is there a single anthropology?

Dual anthropology has been the material condition under which we have lived and is still our experience. Single anthropology has been an idealist projection – an unreal pretence of equality – where talk of complementarity and difference has served to cover up materially unjust and sinful conditions for women – even fatal conditions. Yet the vision of full humanity in the image of God for both men and women is an eschatological vision – a vision of hope for the future – which should act as a thorn in the side of the present reality and inform all our pictures, our words and our practices.

2 Sexuality in God?

We have seen how closely images for God and images for human beings are tied together. Looking back at Genesis 1.27 we have at least three possible interpretations of the final part of the verse – 'male and female he created them' – open to us. In saying this I am aware that there are two quite separate issues. One concerns the best interpretation of the meaning of the text when it was written. The other, which is my interest here, concerns the way in which Christians down the ages and still today do, in practice, interpret the text, and set it in the context of their attitudes and practices. Some consider that that which makes us sexual beings is not part of the image of God. Others believe that man and woman together complementarily make up the image of God. Yet others assert that man and woman individually are completely in the image of God.

If the third of these is how we see the matter (or even if we take the second seriously) then female images of God, as well as male, are of the essence of the matter. What is more, our assertion that God is beyond gender has, at the very least, to be seriously qualified. Our pictures, our words and our practices have to be brought in line with this theology.

Conclusion

Men and women are valued differently in significant ways in the world today and, where that valuing is related to religious beliefs, it is inextricable from the question of perceived 'godlikeness'. That which is like God is valued. In a Christian context we have some searching questions to ask ourselves about the pictures and images we have of God and of ourselves, about the words we use for people and for God, and about practices within our communities. These practices may be to do with roles and expectations put on women, or they may be to do with the toleration and even the encouragement of implicit or explicit violence against women. In fact, the distinction here is blurred, as one does violence to a person by forcing her or him into a role. The discussion concerning what it means for women to be made in the image of God has raised questions about what it means to be human and about how we might envisage and understand God more truly.

Made in the image of God: A womanist perspective

Lorraine Dixon

I was recently invited to give a talk at a church. The publicity information that had gone out about me included the statement that one of my keen academic interests was in black and womanist theologies. A white woman approached me and asked 'Why a womanist and not a feminist?' I replied that, although women the world over have shared similar struggles in terms of their oppression on the basis of their gender, there are also differences in terms of the nature of that discrimination. There may be differences in terms of our experience of racism, imperialism, where we are located in the world, how poor we are. So many things can limit or endanger our lives as women apart from sexism. I said that the African American author Alice Walker made a famous statement 'Feminist to Womanist is as lavender to purple',[1] to emphasize the similarities but also the marked differences in our lives as black and white women. Womanist theology speaks to me because it says that my life as a black woman is of merit to God, to myself and to the world. My personal resonance with womanist theology has developed because it has given voice to my experience as a black woman who, too, is made in the image of God.

At this juncture, it may be helpful to outline some of the main developments in this field. It owes its genesis as a self-aware and named discipline to African American theologians such as Kelly Brown Douglas, Delores Williams, Katie Cannon and Jacquelyn Grant. They themselves have been influenced by Alice Walker's definition of womanism in her book *In Search of Our Mother's Gardens.* Reflecting on that definition has given womanist theology its pattern or canvas; an opportunity to explore the complexities and depth of black women's existence and their understanding of God. Walker's definition includes the following:

> Committed to survival and wholeness of entire people, male and female. Not a separatist, except periodically, for health . . . Loves music. Loves dance. Loves the moon. Loves the Spirit. Loves love and food

and roundness. Loves struggle. Loves the folk. Loves herself. Regardless.[2]

Walker explains that the term 'Womanist' arises from

the Black folk expression of mothers to female children 'You acting womanish,' i.e., like a woman. Usually referring to outrageous, audacious, courageous or willful behavior. Wanting to know more and in greater depth than is considered 'good' for one . . . Being grown up . . . Responsible. In charge. Serious.[3]

Black women were, until recently, noticeable by their absence in the theological project – both black and white. Hence, black Christian women have had to reflect on what it means to be black and a woman before God in alternative areas of expression, for example, in music and storytelling. Womanist theologians have begun to weave these sources into an integrated theological project with diverse strands.[4] Jacquelyn Grant, in her major work and key text *White Women's Christ and Black Women's Jesus: Feminist Christology and Womanist Response*, reminds us that 'professional' theology has mainly been exercised by white men and subsequently white women in European and American universities. In recent years, black American and third world voices have joined this project. Central to their understanding, according to Grant, is that 'there is a relationship between Western articulated theologies . . . and Western supremacist ideology which tends to perpetuate the oppression of the oppressed. Specifically, one who does not challenge the concept of a God and Christ who allow the evils of a socially unjust society is merely a tool of white supremacist ideology.'[5]

Womanist theology is marked by its holistic nature that connects it to other liberation struggles such as those of the white feminist movement for equality as well as the black liberationist struggle against white supremacy. What has often been missing, until very recently, from the feminist platform has been a widening of the agenda to include all women and not just the agenda of white, middle class women. At the same time, what has been missing from black theology, until recently, has been the experience of black women. For when black male theologians reflected on the black human condition, black women's voices and understanding

of the world were left out.[6] Black people, according to such
theologians, thus are black men. The freedom agenda is for them,
and black women better tag along to show they are 'down with
the programme'. Womanist theology has been one response to the
sexist silence of black theology by saying that true liberation is for
all and not for some. All have to be included in the programme
including their knowledge. Womanist theology probes black
women's experience to reflect on their particular oppression as
black women. This has a multidimensional landscape relating not
only to 'race' but its interaction with gender, class and so on: a
fact highlighted by African American thinkers such as bell hooks
and Angela Davis. They engage in a tri-dimensional analysis of
black women's lives that explores how racism, sexism and
classism can form a web that entangles and thus limits them. Such
thinking has fed womanist theology, enabling it to seek to affirm
'Black women's resolute efforts to survive and be free from that
oppression . . . also affirms black women's faith that God supports
them in their fight for survival and liberation'.[7] Further, womanist
theology 'begins with the experiences of Black women as its point
of departure'.[8] Black women's lives are brought from the shadows,
invisibility and the margins to the centre. Their opposition as well
as contribution to an unjust society and Church are central
features of their theological story.

Womanist theology in Britain could be said to be a new discipline.
Yet womanist themes have been worked out in poetry, prose and
non-fiction since the mid-1980s in the work of women such as
Joan Riley, Buchi Emecheta, Jean Binta Breeze and Grace Nichols.
Womanist theology makes a self-aware appearance in the 1990s
with essays in two joint publications of Racial Justice and the
Black Theology Working Group, edited by Paul Grant and Raj
Patel.[9] However, it could be argued that Sybil Phoenix's book
Willing Hands, a series of reflections for Lent, was a womanist
theology text.[10] Although 'womanist' is not used in the text, the
themes she explores reflect womanist perspectives. These include
Phoenix expressing her deep faith in an ever-present God. She has
tapped into the deep well of spirituality that exists within the black
community, a legacy of their African heritage, including a belief in
the interaction of the Lord (High) God in the affairs of the world,
through the working of the Spirit. The book also testifies to her
commitment to the wholeness and liberation of her people. She
involves herself in the struggle for black people's equality, as well
as the freedom to be whole and truly perceived as human in

Britain. Subsequently, *Black Theology in Britain: A Journal of Contextual Praxis* has provided a forum for the development of a black British womanist theology.[11]

The central issue of this essay is being made in the image of God from a womanist perspective. This issue is not unlike black people's struggle for validation in the theological project and in the Church, for it involves recognition of our black humanity as of worth and consequence. The Christian faith has, for a large number of black women of the African diaspora, provided a vehicle for their spirituality with its dual dynamic of survivalism and liberation. I remember growing up in a household where my mother would quote Scripture or sing spirituals or gospel hymns. My mother would also talk of her faith sustaining her and helping her to carry on when she had to face the harsh lick of racism in her workplace. I grew up in the Anglican and Pentecostal traditions. In the Pentecostal Church, the 'mothers' there enabled me to grow in the faith I had been baptized into at the Anglican church. They possessed a deep faith that spoke of being somebody in the presence of God, a faith that said that I too was created in the image of God and thus equal to everybody, despite how I was treated as a black person in the wider society. In this discriminatory society, these women could find employment only in low-paid and unrewarding jobs in factories or as nursing auxiliaries with few prospects. Yet, in church, they spoke with power as they testified of their love of God and what he had done for them. In this church the women were not treated like dirt but had their personhood validated. It was in the faith, hope and the humanity of these women that God came to life in my soul. It was their understanding of Jesus as God with us (Emmanuel) as well as Jesus as co-sufferer (a term I have borrowed from African American womanist theologian, Jacquelyn Grant) that helped me to realize I too was made in the image of God, I, Lorraine, in all of my black womanness. I came to have faith in Jesus who inhabits our troubles with us; who we can call on by name when we are at our lowest. This Jesus who helps us survive oppression and shares our burden when it is too heavy. This Jesus who also gives us strength and the hope in our struggles for life free of prejudice, life in its fullest. It was in the faith, hope and the humanity of these women that Jesus came to life in my soul.

Much womanist discussion has centred on Jesus. The maleness of Jesus is not perceived as a problem central to womanist thought because gender issues have been only one aspect of the struggle for liberation and personhood for the black woman. Jesus as God with us in the struggle for personhood has been a key issue. In this respect, womanist theological perspectives share much with black theology, a discipline brought to the fore by James Cone who wrote the book *Black Theology and Black Power* in 1969.[12] This was followed by the book *A Black Theology of Liberation* in 1970.[13] In these and subsequent volumes, Cone seeks to explore some of the problems Christianity has to face up to regarding its uneasy relationship with people of colour. Cone asks 'Is there a message from Christ to the countless numbers of blacks whose lives are smothered under white society? . . . Must black people be forced to deny their identity in order to embrace the Christian faith?' Further, he has made a severe critique of racism and how this has been internalized and manifested by white theology, Church and society. He has also argued that, for one to attempt to understand God's revelation to the world, one has to start from the concrete, from context, and interpret God talk from that perspective. Cone states that '[t]heology is contextual language – that is defined by the human situation that gives birth to it.'[14] The location of theology in context has implications concerning the sources used for the construction of such a theology. Black theology as a contextual theology reflects on the place of God in the black experience. It is a way of affirming black humanity in a hostile and racist society such as Britain. Liberation is its central hermeneutic with its aim being the emancipation of black folks from white racism and 'freedom for both White and Black people . . . Freedom IS the gospel. Jesus is the Liberator . . .'[15] for oppressor and oppressed. There is therefore a serious theological attitude to black identity and its importance in relation to spiritual and psychological liberation. It is seen as central to claiming one's humanity in a context that negates that by racism and other forms of oppression. It is about claiming who we are before creator God and stating 'I am somebody'; a co-created being in the image of God. Womanist perspectives have broadened out the discussion by revealing a knowingness about how societies such as in Britain devalue not only blackness but 'womanity' as well. These are societies where to be white is esteemed as the norm and to be woman is scrutinized from the viewpoint of maleness. The road to recognition of self and worth as a black person is an occupation that includes reclaiming stories that give us a sense of presence in time and space. For the womanist theologian, that entails considering God in Jesus as co-sufferer in the struggles of black women.

In a book written by the Chapeltown Black Women's Writers Group, Katie Stewart writes this:

> Is there anyone out there? Yes, there is a God out there. Is there someone out there who can help me? Yes, there is someone there. God is there. Can religion help? The answer is no, but God can. How will I know he hears me? You will feel his presence. Just trust him and he will come into your heart and into your life.
>
> What is God like? God is a spirit. You won't be able to see him with natural eyes but you can feel him when you let him close to you.[16]

Stewart and the other writers wish to encourage their readers that, even if the journey of life might be rough, God is in the mix. The God Katie Stewart writes of is one who is ever present, the one who is immanent. God is imaged in the suffering of oppressed communities as sustainer. God comes close in love and as comforter, someone who has known suffering (through Jesus) and is able to give solace. Jesus connects us with God because he is one of us but, at the same time, he is other, he is the Lord, he is God. However, if Jesus is involved in black human existence then he must 'en-gender', be intimately connected to, the black woman's experience(s) and not just the black man's. Christ needs to be made incarnate in the guise of black womanhood. Kelly Brown Douglas says on this very point a 'womanist Black Christ avoids myopic concern for White racism. At the same time a womanist Black Christ enables Black women and men, girls and boys, to see themselves in Christ and Christ in themselves . . . as they fight for life and wholeness.'[17] If Jesus is to be Jesus he has to be seen as part of their struggles. The struggle for racial justice has been focused on the powers and structures that have oppressed, whether in terms of education, employment practice, racialized violence or white majority churches. However, the struggle is also an internal one, the struggle to love oneself in an environment that teaches people of colour to think themselves inferior. It is about being free truly to be oneself. The business of worship has enabled black folks to maintain their sanity when oppression might have sent them over the edge. The struggle then:

includes the emancipation of mind, soul, and spirit
from psychological, spiritual, and cultural tyrannies
from within a dominant society . . . [It] is an interior
affair of the mind and spirit as well as an external
venture of the body and soul from physical bondage.[18]

The Jesus who en-genders our experience enables us to find God
imaged in ourselves as black women. It is to free ourselves from
Western images of beauty, which are tied up with visual images
in magazines and newspapers of thin white women. It is also,
ultimately, to free ourselves from a representation of God as a
white, grey-haired male with his white, blond, blue-eyed son and
to see ourselves as part of the rainbow God. To connect with the
divine one within is to have our black womanity affirmed and
valued and to love her dearly as God does – not because we are
more than anything or anyone else but because we are a part of
God's creation too.

God may be imaged through Christ as co-sufferer in the struggles
of black humanity but womanist theology holds within itself, often
in tension, a dual concern not only with survivalism but also
with liberation. The picture of God that seems to be painted by
Scripture is God who is imaged in the struggle for liberation. The
Exodus narratives tell the story of how the people of Israel become
aware of their oppression in Egypt, and name it as slavery. They
cry out to God and God hears them and sends them Moses to
work out his purpose for the people, that is, liberation from their
bondage. For centuries this story has been used as a model,
especially for those who have been victimized by oppressive
systems of one kind or another. Black Christians have taken this
story very much to the heart of their experiences of discrimination.
In the Exodus account we see a God who is concerned about
those pushed to the margins of life. We see a God wholly
committed to the freedom of his people. God is the one who
liberates such people from the pharaohs of this world, through
women and men the Spirit of God makes a stand for justice. The
story of God's imaging in the struggle for liberation does not end
with the Exodus narrative: it is repeated in the prophets as well as
in the story of Esther, who worked within an oppressive system to
effect the liberation of her people. The liberator God then chose to
dwell among us in the person of Jesus. The Gospel stories reveal
God in Christ concerned for those on the margins of life and
community; many of these people were women, including the

Syro-Phoenician woman, the Samaritan woman, the woman bent double, the woman with a heavy bleed as well as the woman caught in adultery. These women were not given a name in the retelling of the stories; women are often anonymous participants in his-story. Yet, their activities and what God was able to do in their lives through Christ has left us with an indelible impression of the nature of God. According to Luke chapter 4, the Spirit in Jesus' life compelled him to be involved in the activity of God in the world to enable those oppressed to gain a sense of freedom from their bondage. This had socio-political as well as spiritual implications. Jacquelyn Grant explores Jesus' demand, in Matthew 25, to his followers to have a care for him by caring for the 'least of these'. She says to her readers that, in modern America, 'the least of these' are often women. Poverty stalks their lives especially among women of colour. This is a phenomenon that is repeated in many societies around the world and highlights how the tri-dimensional nature of oppressive forces can limit the experiences and lives of such women. Grant states that 'Christ among the least must also mean Christ in the community of Black women . . . for me, it means today, this Christ, found in the experiences of Black women, is a Black woman.'[19] To identify with the 'least of these' is to see God in Christ imaged in the struggle against the processes of dehumanization in our churches as well as society and thus actively engaged in the struggle against discrimination.

Despite the use of the Bible as an instrument of oppression, black women have continued to utilize it because, as Renita Weems states, 'of its vision and promise of a world where the humanity of everyone will be valued'.[20] Black women have 'read' the Bible in creative ways that are liberative. It is a way of reading the biblical narratives that privileges inclusion: the inclusion of people of colour who have been and are denied their humanity. Reading Scripture in this way challenges us not to lose hope; the present situation does not define what is possible for God. The multidimensional narratives of the Bible question the way things are, and dare us to live, hope and struggle for what might be, what should be, what must be. We need to struggle for communities where inequalities because of 'race' or because you are a woman or because you are poor do not exist. For such a community would indeed be an expression of the image of the God of love, peace and justice.[21]

Disabled and made in the image of God

Elisabeth Davies-John

The film *The Elephant Man*[1] gives some insight into attitudes
towards disability a century ago. John Merrick (who had a physical
condition that distorted his face and body) was an exhibit in a
peep show. He was admitted into hospital in sickness, but then
was housed there as a continuing patient. He could not be placed
on a general ward, as 'he would alarm the patients'. Those who
came into contact with him reacted in different ways. Some of the
medical staff treated him as a specimen, some visitors saw him as
amazingly special, some shied away, one porter saw him as a
source of income as a curiosity.

I can remember very similar reactions among staff and patients
from my years of midwifery. When a baby was born with
monstrous disabilities incompatible with life, there was a
voyeuristic tendency about attitudes to the baby and a rejection
of the mother.

Freak, devil, saint, the possessor of special wisdom, subhuman,
supra-human . . . sometimes the overt statement that the person
is not created by God – all these attitudes have been attached to
people with disabilities in what little history can be discovered. If
feminist theologians think that the history of women has been one
of hardship then that of the disabled has been much worse. There
has been fear, revulsion, fascination, awe. Disabled adults or
children who were born into families with some money were
often kept hidden at home or in a private institution. For many
others the only options were the workhouse or a freak show.

One frequent way of dealing with disability, particularly in the
newborn, has been to place the person outside the community
and 'allow the gods to decide'. Their fate was either death from
exposure or life as 'lepers'. In Nazi Germany, the killing of people
with disabilities and the sterilization of mothers and sisters
preceded the 'final solution' for gypsies and Jews. Disabled
people were viewed as *untermenschen* (subhuman).

We deal with the issue more clinically today. Screening tests in pregnancy and the option of abortion allow the disposal of the problem before birth. Medicine or surgery attempts to make the person as normal looking as possible, even though the actual functioning of the person with a disability might be compromised. The primary model of care is just beginning to shift from a medical model to an educational or a social one.

People with disabilities live with a hidden history of rejection by or separation from society and the current approach is to reduce the incidence of the birth of disabled babies by clinical methods. We all live with it.

What has all this to do with the image of God? It relates to the way in which we communicate at a human level. It is a matter of how we accept or reject others.

Fairly close to the surface we probably all have some sort of a ranking order of what we can accept and for what we feel rejection or revulsion when we face the theoretical idea of disability. This may be worked through in our behaviour towards someone with a disability when we actually encounter that person. We may have some mediation of our instinctive feelings through social learning in politeness, religious conviction or the miracle of human contact. Our acceptance of 'made in the image of God' may then expand. 'Search me, O God, and know my heart.' When we are honest about the 'yes' and 'no' of accepting others, we can work on it.

Each one of us is affected by the culture in which we live. One current cultural movement lies within political correctness. Part of this is showing by our language, attitudes and behaviour our acceptance of people for who they are. As Christians, we also have the commandment to love, care for and accept our neighbours as ourselves. When the prevailing culture and the Christian urge to acceptance meet up with our subterranean attitudes and the 'other than' history surrounding disability, what happens?

One thing for Christians is to turn to theology, Scripture, tradition and prayerful reasoning. Scripture is somewhat 'iffy' about disability. There is a huge link made between disability and sin in both Testaments. Where the visible grace of God for individuals and groups is health and wealth, those who are without one or both must be sinners. The book of Job explores this in depth. It is present as an underlying assumption in many Psalms and in the work of the prophets. There are rules about who and what are acceptable in the priestly and sacrificial system in Leviticus. People (and animals) with disabilities are specifically excluded (see Leviticus 21.14, 22, 25).

When David invaded Jerusalem, prior to attack he was mocked by the Jebusites who said 'Even the blind and the lame can ward you off.' After Saul died, that same David killed all potential rivals from that family. Mephibosheth was saved and given a home at court – after all, as a disabled person, he could never be a rival, could he?

In the Gospels we read of healings, some of which have a definite 'sin link' in the words of Jesus. Did Jesus heal so that people unacceptable to God could be rendered acceptable?

We read in the Gospels about lepers and are taught that this group of rejected outsiders included others than those with Hansen's disease. I speculate that 'leper' is a catch-all word in the New Testament. I believe that people like the elephant man, those with facial birthmarks, those with conditions such as cerebral palsy and spina bifida were included with those with skin disease.

Church tradition has continued the 'sin link'. However, the injunction to care for the sick was taken seriously through monastic dispensaries, hospices and hospitals. People with disabilities seem to have been cared for in such institutions, because they do not appear as a 'problem' in society until after the dissolution of the monasteries.

In the Church of today there are a number of ways in which this classical theology works in practice. In some traditions, the 'sin thing' seems to be inextricably linked to healing. If only a disabled person would turn from sin, have a deeper faith or pray harder, he or she would be healed (that is, will be made normal, like me – perhaps even made into the image of God!). Let us blame the victim! Much spiritual abuse both of disabled people and of the wider church community can occur when healing does not happen. The fallback position is often that healing will occur in heaven. One friend, disabled from birth, says, 'I hope not. No one will recognize me!'

Many Christians still see people with disabilities as ammunition for the caring impulse. They can be part of the church fellowship, as long as they continue to be cared for. But heaven help us all if they offer any form of leadership, skills, gifts or talents within the work or worship of the Church!

Some church communities are very accepting in theory, but there is no point in doing any of the expensive work for access, because no disabled people ever come to church anyway! A ramp, disabled loo, large print books, an induction loop system are not necessary just for the odd person who comes or who stays away from church now they have become disabled.

We come to the reason part of doing theology. Apart from access questions, which are now urgent due to the Disability Discrimination Act, we need urgently to work on a theology. Deep within this is that question about what being made in the image actually means. Are some people, those with disabilities, not actually human at all and so rightly rejected from the community of real humans who can be acceptable to God? Where do people like me stand? I became disabled – so was I once in God's image, but am no longer? Do we have to grow a new leg or whatever before we are acceptable? Are we so sinful that we must be rejected?

I do not accept this view. I am proud of myself as I am, confident that I am made in God's image as fully as anyone. On behalf of my fellow disabled people who are not so confident I say, 'Please, allow us into the Churches to hear the gospel preached, to worship God and to explore whatever ministry God calls us to fulfil.'

Gay and lesbian and in God's image

Martin Hogg

As we meet in Sheffield in December 1998, the World Council of
Churches meets in Zimbabwe. Among the other issues likely to be
discussed by the representatives from the Churches gathered there,
is the issue of human sexuality, particularly the sexuality of gay
and lesbian people. Whether the issue causes as much heated
debate and anger as it did at the Lambeth Conference of Anglican
Bishops this summer past, remains to be seen. At Lambeth there
was little real discussion of the subject as such, more angry words
thrown by people on both sides at each other. Most of the bishops
who voted for the motion on human sexuality passed by the
Conference seem to have come with their minds made up:
homosexual practice was sinful and, while the Church should be
compassionate to gay and lesbian people, it could neither tolerate
their sexual desires nor accept them into Christian ministry if they
committed themselves to a same-sex relationship.

Where can we begin to start our thinking about the sexuality,
indeed the humanity, of gay and lesbian people? With the Bible?
With Christian tradition? With modern psychology and medicine?
I would suggest that we should begin our thinking by remembering
that it is not really an 'issue' at all. It is about the Church's
theological pronouncements on the lives of *real people* – people
with feelings, hopes, fears, lovers and friends; people who are
parents, and children, and brothers, and sisters; people who might
be sitting next to us in the pew in church or working next to us
on the factory floor or the office; people, moreover, for whom
sexuality is *only one part of their lives*, but who are forced to think
of themselves *only* as sexual beings because of their rejection
by the Church on the grounds of their sexuality. If we treat our
statements about gay and lesbian people as just more theology
about disembodied concepts and ideas, we shall run the danger
of saying things that bear little relation to the people we are
talking about, and that have the potential for hurting and scarring
our brothers and sisters in Christ.

We must begin our thinking about gay and lesbian people by
listening to them, rather than just talking about them – by hearing
their stories of pain and rejection by the Church; their stories of

refusal of communion at the altar, of being told to throw their partners out of the house if they want to avoid damnation; their stories of rejection by family and friends and congregation; their stories of being compared to people with hereditary illnesses or child molesters. We must listen to the life experiences of gay and lesbian people and of their relationships with God for, if we do not begin by doing this, we shall be hopelessly lost in our struggle to understand our own humanity.

Only in listening to gay and lesbian people, as I hope everyone here has the chance to do at some point, can we approach the question: are we all made in the image of God, or are some human beings made corrupt and flawed? For that is what the traditional theology of homosexuality says. Homosexual persons are 'disordered', to use the terminology of the Roman Catholic Church. That is the polite way of putting it. There are less polite ways of putting it, and most gay and lesbian people have heard these less polite ways. The practical manifestation of such attitudes is seen in various ways, such as attempts like that of Bishop Chukwuma at the Lambeth Conference to 'heal' a gay man of his homosexuality. Movements offering to convert gay and lesbian people to heterosexuality are on the increase, with differing rates of claimed success.

Only if we listen to gay and lesbian people can we then begin to work out how to tie in this listening to our view of God and humanity, to our understanding of what the 'image of God' means. My thoughts on our shared humanity and the interconnectedness of all life begin with the belief that *all* creation was made in the image of God. It is an outpouring of God's creative goodness – his love of variety, his love of physicality. We see, in the creation story, that God saw all that he had made and *it was very good.* Of course, to say that all creation is flawed through sin is also a strong tradition in certain strands of Christian theology. But it does not detract from creation's inherent goodness. Nor does it mean that some parts of creation are more flawed than others. It is not right to say that homosexuality is part of 'disordered' nature, but that heterosexuality is not, for there is no reason for us to believe that God intended all human beings to be heterosexual and to procreate with a member of the opposite sex, unless one takes the most literal view of one of the Genesis creation stories. Nor is there any reason to believe that the only purpose of sex is procreation. Christianity is finally beginning to shed itself of the view that people should not enjoy sex, or, if they do, that they should feel guilty about it. God delights in our sensuousness and physicality. God enjoys the erotic side to our being, whether that eroticism occurs in the context of procreation or not.

To argue that homosexual people are *not* made in God's image, or at least that their sexual orientation is not so made, is necessarily to argue that their sexual orientation did not originate from God, but from somewhere or something else. Suggestions for the 'other' provenance of homosexual orientation have been given variously as: one's nurture; an absent father or mother; biological mutation; or, in the less charitable words of Bishop Mityana of Uganda at the Lambeth Conference, 'by Satan'.

It may well be the case that sexual orientation is affected to a large extent by nurture and by the effect of our peers, but my experience of human sexuality and my relationships with gay, lesbian and straight people from a wide variety of social backgrounds, leads me to believe that most people experience their sexuality as innate, and that sexuality is a spectrum from the out and out heterosexual all the way across to the solidly homosexual. It seems to me that this wide variety of sexuality is something to be rejoiced in and embraced, as part of the wonderful variety of God's creation, rather than condemned and contorted. If we try to 'heal' another of his or her God-given sexuality, we are not only going to warp and damage that person, but we are failing to respect an essential part of that person's humanity and failing to respect and adore the image of God revealed in his or her nature. It is as foolish to try and convert a gay person to heterosexuality as it would be to try to convert a straight person to homosexuality. Both attempts would be equally laughable and equally likely to end in failure, unless the person's purported sexuality was uncertain to begin with.

The real healing that is required is a healing for us *all* from fear about our sexual nature, both sexual orientation and sexuality in the widest sense: healing from a fear of our nature, into a joy at having a physical body and having sexual desires. This healing is needed for so many people who have been hurt by Churches that teach them that sex is wrong and that their sexuality is disordered. Furthermore, the Church as a body needs to be healed from its obsession with sex and from its need to pry into the sex lives of adult human beings who wish to share their love with each other.

There are those who would accept that gay and lesbian people are made in God's image, but would not accept that they should be allowed to practise their sexuality with their partners, though this does seem rather odd if gay and lesbian people are supposedly fully made in God's image. But this view is taken, it is said, because the Bible is quite clear about homosexual practice. It is probably fruitless today to get into this complex discussion. I do wish to make three brief comments on this view, however.

First, gay and lesbian people, indeed, all of us, are entitled to require that those who present such arguments are *consistent*. It cannot be correct to say of biblical passages dealing with sexual practice that they require absolute adherence, but then to blatantly ignore other passages of Scripture merely because they are thought to be awkward or outdated. So, gay and lesbian people may require of those that demand celibacy of them because the Bible says so, that such people should also forbid women from speaking in church or from having their heads uncovered when they pray, both of which are required in the New Testament. However, I have yet to find one Christian who condemns homosexual practice who has required women to behave that way!

Secondly, beyond the issue of sexuality, there is a larger issue about how we view Scripture and revelation. Do we see Scripture as a rule book, designed to be applied rigidly? Or do we try to see the diverse books of the Bible as a record of how the people of God witnessed to God in their own time and place? If we have the courage to explore this latter view, then we may be drawn on by God into finding our own voices and into witnessing to God's will for her Church today. This will only be possible if we do not see God's revelation as a dead letter, as something that ended when the last verse of the Bible was written. This will be possible only if we are still open to God, ready to receive his Spirit afresh. If we had *not* been open to that Spirit, we would never have reassessed the Bible's view of usury, of divorce, of the role of women in the Church, and of the evil of slavery. But we did. And now it may be that God is asking us to look again at that modern day group of people consigned to be lepers by the Church, her children who are gay and lesbian. Do we have the courage to be open to such a question, to such a Spirit? Perhaps not. Openness to God is a dangerous thing. The Spirit of God can surprise and frighten us. It can creep up on us with startling revelations. Like Mary, sitting alone, we can be confronted with life changing decisions that can appal us with their possibilities. For many Christians, I suspect that is too much. They want the certainty of a religion that tells them the rules and which draws lines in the sand: on this side of the line you are saved, but not on that.

I thank God that there are some prophetic leaders in the Church today who *are* willing to be open to that new revelation of God in our time and to lead to freedom those who have been shackled by their love for other human beings.

Thirdly, there is a pay-off here for those who require celibacy of gay and lesbian people. The pay-off is in what such a stance must mean for their view of God. If God has made some people gay or lesbian – planted within them an attraction, physical and spiritual, for others of the same sex but is then requiring them to remain celibate, in effect he is playing a cruel game with them. What kind of God gives human beings an overwhelming desire to share their lives in a loving way, including a physical, sexual way, but then simply says 'But you cannot do it'? He does not even justify his decision, he just says 'thou shalt not'. Such a God would be a tyrant and not worthy of our love or obedience. But it is such a view of God, foisted on many Christians and churchgoers, that has driven so many gay and lesbian people out of the Church. The God they have been shown is not one they want to know. The tragedy is that the real God, in whose image they are made, is their friend, lover and source of being.

Men and women

I want now to say a few words about men and women. Strangely enough, it is usually men, often celibate men, who are most vociferous in theological condemnations of homosexuality, and usually about the sexual practices of other men. In the eyes of many fundamentalist Christians, homosexuality is about men having anal sex with each other. Never mind that the majority of anal sexual acts are practised by heterosexual men upon their female partners, often as a means of contraception in the developing world. The more I see of that strand of Christianity that is unaccepting of gay and lesbian sexuality, the more it seems to be about an obsession with men's sexual practices, as if God were as worried about these as some men seem to be. I think Dr Freud might have something to say about the homosexual obsession displayed by many male Christians.

Women don't feature in their discussion very much, just as they don't feature in any of the few biblical discussions of homosexuality. Women's sexuality is forgotten. We have yet to hear fully the silent history of women's sexuality, though more and more women are now exploring the sexual side to their being, a side that was for so long suppressed by society. Even today, there are still some cultures that seek to repress women's sexuality, as a *dangerous* thing. Long live dangerous things!

I believe that, until we see more women in leadership roles in the Church, we shall continue to have a warped theology of sexuality. No theology about such a deep aspect of our human nature can be healthy if it has been largely formed by only one half of humanity. I am not saying that all women have a wonderful, holistic view of sexuality, but I do believe that, when the insights of women's sexuality are brought into the mainstream of Christian theology, we can expect a deeper and more rounded view of the nature of sexuality, and a less paternalistic and obsessive attitude to the sexual practices of others.

What can gay and lesbian people offer the Church?

I wish to conclude with some remarks about what gay and lesbian people can offer the Church.

So far, most of what I have said has been about the acceptance of gay and lesbian people. But this is perhaps to view things the wrong way round. Indeed some gay and lesbian people don't want to be the grateful recipients of grudging acceptance, while other gay and lesbian people often feel that their sexuality is being talked about without their being consulted, or without seeing what they have to *offer* the Church. The lesbian theologian, Elizabeth Stuart, has compared gay and lesbian sexuality to a football, being thrown between different people in the Church, until the anxious liberal thinks to ask of the owners of the football: 'well, what *do* you want from the Church?' To which the uniform reply from the gay and lesbian Christians standing on the touchline is: 'may we have our ball back please?'[1]

When the football is given back, wonderful fruits have come from gay and lesbian Christians doing their *own* theology. Most of these fruits are, I suspect, not known to the wider Church. Gay and lesbian Christians have been discovering new models for the basis of our relationships, described by some as the model of 'friendship', rather than the old patriarchal model of dominance so ingrained in Christian thinking about marriage. The insights about the nature of relationships is one gift that can be offered to the whole Church, but only if it is willing to receive them.

There are other gifts, and they flow from insights gained from being rejected. I have already mentioned 'sexual healing'. There are others that are not offered to the Church exclusively by gay and lesbian people, but by them among others. Among these, one might number the following:

- being rejected by the Church, gay and lesbian people can identify with the suffering Christ, the Christ rejected by his own people, and can challenge a Church that is comfortable;

- having been unjustly treated, gay and lesbian Christians can remind the Church of its need to do social justice;

- most gay and lesbian people, not being parents, can remind the Church that its members' contributions are more than the merely procreative;

- in being deemed 'social outcasts', lesbian and gay Christians remind the respectable Church that Jesus was also a social misfit;

- importantly, lesbian women and gay men, together with transgendered people, and *all* women who have empowered themselves, challenge the Church on gender stereotypes. As a gay man, I have offended against the 'male role' – but I ask the Church, should there be a 'male role' or a 'female role'?

Building relationships

I wish to end by saying that I am very pleased to have been able to share these thoughts with you. If you take nothing else away with you, you will at least be able to say, if you weren't able before, 'I have met a gay Christian'. How paradoxical that seems to so many outside and inside the Church. But it is through building relationships between gay, lesbian, bisexual and heterosexual Christians, between black and white, between men and women, that the barriers of ignorance and misrepresentation will come down. Through building such relationships, people begin to free themselves from belief in the myths about gay people. Myths such as that (and I quote) 'a homosexual lifestyle reduces life expectancy by 25 to 30 years' – that statement comes from the Internet site of a parish church in the Church of England. I hope you will return to your various Churches with the hope of building new relationships and understanding with those dispossessed by the Church of Christ.

I look forward to the day when I can join you, not as a second class person in the Church, as a flawed imperfect human being, but as a full member of the Body of Christ and a beautiful and valued child of God.

What do I want to say to the Churches about my God-given sexuality?

Colin Coward

I am a gay man. I am a Christian. I am an ordained priest in the Church of England. I live with my partner in Wimbledon. I worked originally as an architect and, in more recent years, I have trained as a psychotherapist, of which more later. I want first to tell you something of my story, because I think we understand one another better when we understand each other's stories.

My Christian story and my story as a sexual person, a gay man, will be different from yours. Of course, because we are each unique, and our experiences may be quite similar to one another's in some ways, and almost bafflingly different in others. But my story, for me, is normal, ordinary. It is made abnormal by reactions to it, from other people, other Christians especially, by the Christian Church here and around the world, and also by Muslims and Hindus, Jews and Rabbis, atheists, and agnostics.

I was born in Wimbledon in a family that had strong church connections, but my parents weren't attending church at that time – perhaps because of the effect of the war (I was born in 1945) and almost certainly because of my mother's depressive nature. I have a brother who is four years younger than me. About four months into the pregnancy, my mother had a major breakdown and was hospitalized through the pregnancy, taken to St Helier's Hospital to give birth, and returned to the institution for another six months. My baby brother was looked after by friends down the road, I was looked after by my maternal grandparents, and my father was teaching in Ripley, Surrey, and spending his evenings and weekends visiting us in three different places. I remember nothing of this time but, of course, it affected me deeply.

I was baptized at three months, sent to kindergarten Sunday school when I was three, graduated to the main Sunday school at five, and to a class run by the vicar when I was eleven. The vicar was gay, though I wasn't aware of that (he would have called

himself homosexual), but I did find him an extraordinary person –
cultured, musical, independent, free-thinking, and interested in
me. He was the first person to inspire some degree of awareness
in me about what it could mean to be a Christian. I was confirmed
when I was twelve, became a server (it was a highish church), was
elected to the PCC at eighteen, and became a youth club leader.
In my twenties my whole social life revolved around the church.

I'll break off there for a moment to introduce the sexual strand
of the story. When I was in my final year at primary school, aged
eleven, a boy arrived from another school. He was blond with a
beautiful smile, and I 'fancied' him. I found him deeply exciting
and persuaded my parents to invite him to my twelfth birthday
party. He bought me a present I didn't like and, because we were
going to different grammar schools and didn't live in places where
our paths crossed, I never saw him again. But I knew then that I
had feelings for him that my male peers were having for girls, and
my feelings were different and they weren't going to change. This
was how I was attracted in love to another person, and this was
my sexual nature.

I also knew by then that it was dangerous. If people knew I loved
and desired other boys, they would have been embarrassed; they
would have been disgusted by me, especially the other boys; they
would have rejected me and humiliated me. I had to keep myself
hidden, to disguise my true feelings and attractions. You can
imagine, perhaps, the effect that has on a person. I had no idea
whether anyone else around me was gay. There were no role
models around with whom I could identify. On television, the
homosexual characters were people like Larry Grayson, Kenneth
Williams and the man from 'Are You Being Served?', and I
certainly didn't identify with any of them. And I knew perfectly
well that to have sex with another man was illegal.

I knew all this perfectly well, though I'm not sure how. Family and
church and social and school culture all worked to communicate
that sex per se was dangerous, and to love another man was
totally perverted and disgusting. One thing I wasn't taught. I wasn't
taught that the Bible said that to be homosexual was a sin.

When I was 16 I was seduced by a young clergyman who also
had a girlfriend. I had no idea how to protect myself and the sex
continued for about six years. I hated it, but found it impossible to

escape from the situation in which I found myself. I dealt with my disgust with him physically by splitting and cutting off, being there and not being there. Allowing him to be physical while, emotionally, I was absent. This also had a profound and long-lasting damaging effect on me.

Now to weave both stories together. Later, aged 21, I went on a series of three weekends for young adult Christians run by the Diocese of Southwark. They were led by Derek Tasker, the Diocesan Director of Ordinads, tall, aesthetic, homosexual but celibate, deeply spiritual, profoundly present when he presided at communion; and Gwen Rymer, youth officer, a smoker who liked a drink, somewhat chaotic, down to earth and very real. The huge contrast between these two, their wonderful working relationship, and the ideas they introduced, showed me that it was possible to be a Christian and be absolutely real and true to myself, true both to my Christian convictions and true to my sexual self. Southwark at that time was also the diocese of South Bank religion, Mervyn Stockwood, John Robinson, *Honest to God*[1] and Nick Stacey experimenting socially and liturgically at Woolwich. This was my culture of church, in a diocese where there were clearly gay priests who were treated as ordinary and welcomed, even if it was never talked about. But it was another eight years before I found myself for the first time in an environment where I could be open about my sexuality, at Westcott House in Cambridge.

I have had good experiences and bad experiences. This is normal for any human being. Some of us are fortunate enough to be born into very healthy, loving, stable families. Some of us are born into deeply damaged, dysfunctional families. It isn't our fault, but it has a profound effect, for better or worse, on us. It isn't a question of sin, not ours nor our parents'.

So the first thing I want to say to the Churches about my God-given sexuality is that, for me, it is normal and ordinary, and it has been formed from a complex matrix. I am sure my sexuality was with me at my birth. I am also sure that the particular version of my sexuality has been formed by my childhood and parenting and the traumas of life.

Secondly, I want to say that my sexuality *isn't* ordinary. Growing up as a minority in a culture that is strongly sexualized and deeply prejudiced has an effect. Being gay, I think, means that you have to explore your inner world far more than if you are a male heterosexual. It means that gay men often have much greater levels of self-awareness and sensitivity than straight men. We are often creative, imaginative, sometimes flamboyant, person-centred, feeling individuals. We can also be narcissistic, dysfunctional and ill-equipped to sustain relationships.

Thirdly, as you can tell, I work from experience. I am deeply intuitive, though I have had to recover trust in my intuition in recent years. I have strong emotions, and I think through things all the time. I am clear that this me is *the* me God has made and delights in and loves. God rejoices in the gay me and in my struggles to seek love and intimacy and sexual expression.

Fourthly, we are all the product of our culture, in time, country of birth, family, society, education, faith tradition. There is no pure, perfect, unadulterated human being. Some would give the word 'sin' to this state. I would simply see it as normal. It isn't wilful or chosen. It is an intrinsic part of who we are. We have a birth identity that then develops into personality through all these experiences and accidents. It is from this context that we develop the other things that will be of interest to us here: a theology, a code of ethics, an understanding of the gospel and the call to lead a Christian life. But everything we experience is mediated through our mind and heart and feelings. Everything.

My starting place is clearly different from those who would begin either from Scripture as the authoritative source of Christian teaching, or those who would add tradition and reason to Scripture. To these three some might add experience, but experience isn't always accepted as a fourth authority. Why not? My answers would come from my training and experience as a psychotherapist.

I chose to train in what is called a body-centred therapy school. I chose it because I realized that I had an uneasy relationship with my body, out of touch with my emotions, distrustful of my body symptoms and of my intuition. I think my Christian tradition had taught me to be suspicious of my body, and the culture of hostility about my sexuality, my mother's depression and breakdown and the sexual abuse by the curate had all reinforced a high level of detachment from my body.

I now know that our bodies and our emotions are God-given resources for experiencing the divine. They have a great wisdom of their own, in addition to our mental capacity. I meditate every day. I have learnt to breathe, to listen to my feelings, to root myself in my body, to trust that God communicates with me, is present within me, nourishes me, here inside my body.

I also learnt about anxiety and defence mechanisms in my therapy training. We all live with anxiety. It is a normal, universal human characteristic. We all develop different ways of dealing with our anxiety, depending on its strength. We split, cut off, project, deny, become neurotic, fundamentalist. Fundamentalism is just one way among others of defending ourselves against extremes of anxiety, living in a culture of rapid change and complexity, globalization, insecurity, relativism and uncertainty – the postmodern society. Fundamentalism is an effective way of dealing with this, but damaging when our fundamentalism supports prejudiced attitudes towards other people or groups – in my case, lesbian or gay people.

Understanding fundamentalism is one way for me of understanding why many Christians believe that either God does not create lesbian or gay people – it is a wilful, deliberate life choice made by individuals in opposition to the will of God – or it is an unfortunate fact of some people's lives. But, because of certain passages in Scripture, people who are attracted to the same sex are not allowed by God to act on their feelings, but must live celibate lives or seek 'healing'.

I am clear that God *does* create lesbian and gay people. I am also clear that God creates us to be drawn to loving, intimate relationships. So if the Bible really does teach that sexual relationships are only permitted in marriage, then I have been created by a very perverse, tyrannical God. Living in relationship with a perverse God, who looks at me and disapproves of what he has created is extremely damaging for my self-image and well-being. Parents look at their children and adore their offspring. If they don't, they risk damaging them. Why would God be a bad parent, creating children he disapproves of? This would be contrary to the teaching of Jesus about God's relationship with us – the lilies of the field . . .

So here's another bit of my theology. God created a world in which he delighted. This is the teaching of the first chapter of

Genesis. Original blessing rather than original sin is the story of God's creation. In the beginning, God created human beings, male and female, in his own image, and God blessed them and saw everything that he had made, and behold it was very good. To me, the Fall is our human way of understanding and interpreting why we find life so difficult, why things go wrong, why there are natural disasters and disasters of human origin, and men and women who are bad or evil.

And another bit from my therapy background. We are all wounded. We all have the capacity for good and evil. We all have an amazing capacity to be creative and to love. We are frightened of the dark, murderous thoughts we find within us. If we are reasonably healthy, we acknowledge these thoughts and feelings and integrate them in a broad awareness of who we are, good and bad. If we do not successfully integrate the good and bad in us, we are more likely to project the bad out of ourselves onto others, to develop prejudices and phobias, to be afraid of gay people, or Jews, or Muslims, Arabs, liberal Christians, fundamentalist Christians, Catholics, Evangelicals, whatever. You get the picture.

Why are there such strong feelings and prejudices in the Church about lesbian and gay Christians? The answer has to be more than, simply, because the Bible and the tradition of the Church teach that it is wrong. My answer would be that our sexuality is one of our strongest drives and our strongest source of fear and anxiety. We can be afraid of simply being sexual, anxious about being sexually successful, being a good lover, good at sex, having a good body, but mostly, just being sexual, wanting not sex, but touch, intimacy, hugs, cuddles. I know people who long to be simply held or hugged safely, without sexual expectation, but with their sexuality present, and I suspect there are many more like them, who do not feel able to express what they really desire, and may not even be aware of their feelings.

A fifth thing I want to say to the Churches. What about the Bible? I think the problem for the Churches and for lesbian and gay Christians is not the seven or so texts from Leviticus, Romans, etc., which seem to refer to same-gender sexual contact in a critical way. I think the Churches need to think about hermeneutics in general and in particular the nature of Scripture, why it was written and how it is used theologically. An awareness of the history of hermeneutics would be of value here, so that we have a better grasp of how Christian theology and ethics have developed through the Christian centuries in response to changing social and cultural experience. Changing attitudes over the centuries towards food laws, Gentiles, Jews, usury, slaves, women and divorce spring immediately to mind.

I realize that there will be a wide difference of Christian attitudes and opinions in this Conference about the place of lesbian and gay people in the Church. There will be a difference between those who would want the Church to welcome lesbian and gay people and our partners and bless our relationships, those who believe that being lesbian or gay is OK, but sexual intimacy is prohibited by God, and those who believe that to be lesbian or gay is not how a person is created, but a disorder from which the person can be healed. For our Churches to be able to live with difference is important, though they don't always find this easy. But how do lesbian and gay people live in the Church when it judges or condemns gay people at worst, and often, at best, fails to understand lesbian and gay experience or fully welcome us into the Church?

So, sixthly, be aware of the terrible pain and damage some Christian groups and individuals are inflicting on lesbian and gay people. In the name of their Christian beliefs, some people think they are justified in expressing extremes of prejudice and judgement against us. I've developed a thick skin, and I've learnt to accept that people say these things. But they hurt and undermine my confidence. They attack my very personhood, my friendships, my Christian identity and my relationship with my partner. If such things were being said about black people or people from other cultures, they might now be subject to legal action. But to say such things against lesbian and gay people is understood to be doing the will of God and saving our souls.

Secular society is leading the way in changing attitudes. Here is another contrast. Conservative Christians are more likely to see the Church of God as set against the world, upholding divine principals and teaching against a godless, secular culture. Radical, open, liberal Christians might see the world itself, secular society, as the place of God's presence and action, demonstrating to the Church the nature of the kingdom. Of course, it isn't one or the other. But, as our present Government legislates for equality for lesbian and gay people in law, and as those in secular employment experience the effect of equal opportunities legislation and employment policy, those who are also active Christians in local churches will bring their experience to bear on church teaching and attitudes. They will have learnt that prejudice against lesbian and gay people is just that, prejudice, and is as unacceptable as prejudice based on race, gender or disability. This does mean that lesbian and gay people should expect absolutely equal treatment under the law, in employment, sickness, housing and partnerships. Eventually the Church will catch up, discovering that what it justified on the basis of biblical teaching is no longer tenable.

A final insight from my psychotherapeutic background. Why this current fascination with what lesbian and gay people do? And the ideas that go with it – that gay men are prone to be paedophiles, are sexually promiscuous and have a very high sex drive, are unable to form long-term, stable, committed relationships. I would suggest that it is another form of projection, projecting much that is uncomfortable for heterosexuals on to lesbian and gay people. The sexual abuse of children is far more common in heterosexual families. It is heterosexuals who are choosing to live together rather than marry, who display evidence of promiscuity and a fascination with all things sexual. One look at the tabloids or the top shelf of many newsagents or the profusion of sites on the Internet demonstrates that this is true.

So this gay man says to the Church, examine your general attitudes towards sexuality, and the experience and lifestyles of your heterosexual members. Work needs to be done by the Churches to develop a much better, more adult and mature understanding of human sexuality, heterosexual, gay, lesbian, bisexual, transgender, rather than projecting all the failures and problems and disgust on to lesbian and gay people.

The problem isn't the sexuality of lesbian and gay people. The problem is human sexuality. The Church of England 1991 report by the House of Bishops at least got the title right *Issues in Human Sexuality*[2] – the trouble is, this was a pretext for talking almost exclusively about lesbian and gay sexuality.

So this is what I want to say to the Churches.

- Grow up in your attitude towards human sexuality.

- Recognize the integrity of lesbian and gay identity.

- See that, first, we love one another. Then we may seek a sexual relationship.

- You are willing to bless so many other things in God's name. Bless the loving relationship of a gay or lesbian couple.

- Continue to work at developing a mature theology of human sexuality.

- Take a proper look at the nature of heterosexual sexuality and activity.

- Respect God's creative activity and intention, even if it seems at first to be at odds with what you have been taught.

- Learn to love first rather than judge first.

Section Four –
Back to the Bible

Gone fishing or *Saussure* or *not so sure: Why we need a methodology to read the Bible*

Alastair Hunter

Introduction

The punning title of this paper is *intended* (if I may for the moment assume the prerogative of authorial intention) to alert the hearer/reader to what some perceive to be the fundamental instability of the process of interpretation, and others see as a glorious opportunity. In the context of a possible ecclesiastical[1] use of the Bible to define theology, policy or ethics, this health warning is equally (if not more) valid. The two gurus (I dare not write 'authorities') indicated stand at opposite ends of one possible hermeneutical spectrum, that which runs from the objective nature of the text as a given at one end to the subjective nature of the text as the preserve of the interpretive community at the other.

There is a naïve view of interpretation that sees its task as recovering either 'the author's intention' on the one hand or 'the meaning of the text' or its effect on the reader (as though it were an independent object with affective powers) on the other. The classic discussion of these issues is to be found in two essays by Wimsatt and Beardsley, 'The Affective Fallacy' and 'The Intentional Fallacy'.[2] The former describes 'the error of judging a text in terms of its effects, particularly its emotional effects upon the reader' while the latter 'is an appeal to the supposed intentions of the author in the reading of a poem or other literary work'.[3] While few professional critics today would dissent from the consensus, based on Wimsatt and Beardsley's work, that 'intention' and 'affect' are profoundly flawed approaches to interpretation, they remain primary motivating principles in much popular and church-based biblical exegesis. I do not propose to discuss them directly here, except to say that the quest for authorial intention is peculiarly fraught in the case of the Bible. For most of its books we do not even know the name of the author; even when we do, the name is about all we have. Some scholars have resorted to the process of reconstructing the author from the text and then interpreting the text in terms of the intention of that hypothetical construct – an enterprise whose circularity is even more vicious than is the norm in the traditions of biblical interpretation. I take it as read that supposing the author to be God is equally futile, given the inaccessibility of the mind of God to human reason.

1 Two theories of reading

In his epochal *Is There a Text in This Class?*[4] Stanley Fish addresses the idea that the text is a fixed and objective reference point which 'only' [*sic*] requires to be interpreted. His starting point is the work of Wimsatt and Beardsley to which I have briefly referred, and what he takes issue with is the privileging of an objectified concept of 'the text', which is implicit in their position. For, if the text is not *intended* by an author or the sum of its *effects* on a reader, what is left floats freely, independent of both. As we shall see, this harmonizes nicely with the tradition of interpretation founded on the work of my second guru, Saussure. For Fish, however, the Wimsatt/Beardsley conclusion that '[o]nly the text [is] both indisputably there and stable' is itself problematic, since the self-sufficiency of the text is predicated on a spatial physical object which 'belie[s] the temporal dimension in which its meanings [are] actualized'. To quote him at length:

> I substituted the structure of the reader's experience for the formal structures of the text on the grounds that while the latter were the more visible, they acquired significance only in the context of the former. This general position had many consequences. First of all, the activities of the reader were given a prominence and importance they did not have before: if meaning is embedded in the text, the reader's responsibilities are limited to the job of getting it out; but if meaning develops, and if it develops in a dynamic relationship with the reader's expectations, projections, conclusions, judgments, and assumptions, these activities (the things the reader *does*) are not merely instrumental, or mechanical, but essential, and the act of description must begin and end with them.[5]

There is a problem with this approach, namely the 'danger' of fragmentation of interpretation into an uncontrolled diversity of idiosyncratic and purely subjective readings. One way to control this unwelcome fecundity is to appeal to some kind of normative 'level of experience which all readers share, independently of differences in education and culture'.[6] Fish admits that, in using this controlling device, he 'was practising a brand of criticism whose most distinctive claim was not to be criticism at all but a means of undoing the damage that follows in criticism's wake'.[7] In effect, the recognition of the reader's responsibility comes with a danger warning – we cannot trust the reader! The solution Fish appeals to is one that is peculiarly pertinent to the Churches: he argues for a community dimension to the problem of determining which has priority: text or reader, reader or text. Thus

> it is interpretive communities, *rather than either the text or the reader*, that produce meanings and are responsible for the emergence of formal features . . . An interpretive community is not objective because as a bundle of interests, of particular purposes and goals, its perspective is interested rather than neutral; but by the very same reasoning, the meanings and texts produced by an interpretive community are not subjective because they do not proceed from an isolated individual but from a public and conventional point of view.[8] (emphasis added)

At one level this is, of course, uncontroversial: a statement, perhaps, of the blindingly obvious. But its subversive or revolutionary aspects emerge on closer inspection, when we realize that what Fish has done is to deprivilege *both* the text *and* the reader. The community contains the reader and creates the text in so far as it is anything other than a meaningless succession of marks on a page. A rather obvious example of the truth of this is the canon, which is clearly meaningless without the Christian community, and diversely defined in different branches of the Church. How the principle might operate at a more detailed level is something for the community itself to work out. Let me remind you in the meantime of the 'canon within the canon' and the existence of treasured phrases that are carried (metaphorically) in the Christian's pocket and lovingly rubbed from time to time to keep them shiny ('the Lord's my shepherd', 'underneath are the everlasting arms',[9] 'by grace are you saved through faith').

The second of my exemplary gurus is Ferdinand de Saussure, the man who may be held responsible both for structuralism and its much derided alter ego, deconstruction. I shall not engage with the latter in this paper, not because I believe it to be irrelevant to the task of applying the Bible to the work of the Church, but because there is scarcely as yet a significant body of practical deconstructive work that might serve to exemplify the theory. Let me say only this: that where Fish prioritizes the community, and Saussure the text as signifier, deconstruction reminds us that a fundamentally unstable text has a part to play in defining the reader, who in turn rewrites the text in what is potentially an unending iterative process. The conclusion may well be that institutions like churches might find this unendingly daunting, in that it would seem to be impossible to offer any sort of compelling opinion (whether individual or collective) on such a theory of interpretation.

Saussure, however, and his epigones in the structuralist movement, constitute an interesting alternative to Fish's interpretive community, in that their fundamental starting point, however they may later diverge, is to accord to the text a form of complete objectivity, on the basis of which meaning may be either excavated or constructed (to use two contrasting metaphors from archaeology and architecture). The former sees the text as a kind of skeletal framework, the ruins that survive the death of the author and the loss of the historical perspective.[10] All we have is what we see, and the most useful thing we can do is to place a grid over it and describe it in formal detail. While this is essentially a minimalist approach to meaning, it may be that the cathartic effect of such a regime might be something of a relief in the face of the reams of over-interpretation to which the Bible has been subjected in the two and a half millennia of its use by religious communities. To be able to say no more than that 'the bones of the text are thus and thus, its meaning is no longer present' might be a blessed relief. I recall the story of the Buddhist who engaged in study with some Christians.[11] They began with John's Gospel, and read 'In the beginning was the word.' The Buddhist sighed, and said wearily, 'Even in the beginning was there no silence in your religion?' The trouble is that, just as nature abhors a vacuum, so do clerics disdain silence. I suppose that an ethics based upon absence might be hard to practise. Still, since so much ethics is noisy, intrusive and domineering, there may be something seriously to be said for interpretation as a modest exercise in archaeology.[12]

The architectural model could be explained as more expansive, constructive and generous in its nature. Here the text is regarded as the foundation of many possible superstructures. The text is a necessary element, a given, and the superstructures are not independent of its objective reality. Nevertheless, the text (the ground) does not wholly predetermine what may be built upon it. I have in mind, in using this analogy, Barthes' approach to structuralism.[13] He regards the act of reading, of perceiving structure, as creative. The text is mute until, by reading, we shape it and give it organized form. This might be as simple as paragraphs, sentences, pauses and phrasing, or as complex as the 'discovery' of a detailed system of parallels and patterns, allusions and references, puns and ambiguities: the whole apparatus, in short, of literary criticism. The truth of this is easy to demonstrate: as regards the former, we have all been irritated at some time by what we heard as an inappropriate oral performance of a text (those scriptural readings in church, for example, where the reader emphasizes the first person pronoun whenever it appears); the latter is evidently creative from the wide disagreement that almost any non-trivial analysis of a public text receives. I would imagine that such a philosophy of interpretation would have much to commend it. The structures discerned would not be merely idiosyncratic, since they would have a shared context; the material reality of the text is assured, since it is at the heart of Saussure's work that language ultimately refers – the only problem is that we cannot ever reach the conclusive end of the work of understanding the signified through the signifiers. But that is not so far away from many traditional conceptions of the mysterious nature of the 'word of God'. The difference that it does build in (to return to architecture) is freedom from the illusion (or perhaps delusion) of having once and for all constructed the perfect edifice. What I build on the ground of the text will sooner or later give way to something better: there are few List A protected buildings in the structuralist economy. Think, for a moment, how many once popular exegeses have been demolished on the grounds that they were now rather ramshackle, requiring more energy to repair than was justified by the likely results. The complex allegorical interpretations of the Church Fathers, for example, are mostly a curious relic now, to be visited on the biblical equivalent of National Trust tours.

2 Some reasons for reading

2.1 To approach some ideal of the original text and meaning

Perhaps the most familiar of modern approaches to Bible study is that of *historical criticism*, by which is meant the process of asking – and seeking answers to – a whole range of, broadly speaking, historical questions. When was this or that text written, and by whom? What social or cultural context does it belong to? Can it be related to known historical events, or to events that can be plausibly reconstructed?

Attempts to answer these and similar questions have generated a huge literature. What they all share is the characteristic of being external to the text itself. The answers, should they be forthcoming, will not enable us to read any particular passage, though they might provide contextual material that will shape a particular reading. Thus if (as some would argue) the Deuteronomistic history and theology is post-exilic, it follows that the material in the Torah about the conquest of the land and the defeat of its indigenous peoples has a political resonance at the same time more appropriate to the creation of modern Israel, but also deeply disturbing as to its genocidal elements. In effect, this *historical* reading leads to a highly charged *political* assessment: does modern Israel have the right to practise ethnic cleansing in order to define a state that – far from being part of a genuinely ancient divine promise – is in reality the late invention of an antiquity to justify a takeover supported by a friendly imperial power (in the one case Babylon, in the other, the USA)?

2.2 To approach some ideal of the meaning of the text as a Christian (or other religious) authority

The great debate between the liberals and the fundamentalists in the nineteenth century centred on the twin questions of authority and truth. The two are inseparable, and arise ultimately from the Reformation destruction of the simple equation Church = authority = truth. For a considerable period the destructive nature of the Reformation was concealed by the substitution of papal authority with that of Geneva, the English crown, or the General Assembly. In short, the Reformation was a staged revolution whose consequences became apparent only with the eighteenth century and the beginnings of an independent scholarly approach to texts that refused to accord special protection or privileges to Scripture. The result was historical criticism (see above), and what that enlightenment project gave rise to was a dilemma as to the definition of truth. The fascinating result was that both liberals and fundamentalists agreed over what truth meant – it was effectively reduced to a matter of scientific or historic actuality – but disagreed as to whether such truth could be found in the Bible. The argument between them, in short, is largely constrained by the culture of the Enlightenment and scientific rationalism. For the purposes of the contemporary project of making *religious* sense of the Bible, this debate is, in fact, quite sterile. It can only ever lead to a stand-off (irresistible force versus immovable object), and is intellectually wearisome. As anyone who teaches theology in higher education will confirm, there are few things more dispiriting than the annual encounter with first year student angst about the historicity of the Bible and 'evolution versus creation'.

On the other hand, the link between the text and the Church is both organic and traditional, and the distinction between liberal and evangelical, radical and fundamentalist, is far less sharp than our lazy polemic would suggest. Surely here there is a place for the application of Fish's concept of the interpretive community. The Church owns the Bible, the Bible configures with the Church's experience, and the intersecting interpretive communities of the Church work sometimes together, sometimes in opposition, and sometimes in uneasy alliance, to make sense of this reciprocal relationship. We cannot, therefore, expect a consensual outcome; what we must concede is the right of each community interpretation to coexist with others and to make its own way in a sort of free market of opinion. Even the CTBI – even Rome – has to accept this reality.

2.3 To employ the text in the service of some prior demand

By this I mean that very few readings are disinterested. More often than not what we have in mind when we open the text has the character of a leading question. What has the Bible to say to me about this or that *doctrine*? Can it provide me with appropriate *ethical* guidance? How can I read the Bible in the light of modern *social* or *cultural* concerns? Can I be a Conservative and a Christian (or a Marxist and a Christian, or a member of the British National Party and a Christian)? – the application of the Bible to *politics*. We might loosely categorize these as interpretations based on relevance criteria, in that none can even claim objectivity (since it is, I would argue, self-evident that the Bible is not primarily or principally devoted to any one of these areas of interest): each requires that we have a pretty clear and full agenda to start with. It is this agenda which is then used to interrogate the text – and rightly so, since we are the product of and producers of a variety of communities and cultures that cannot, no matter how we try, be set to one side while we debate meaning on some hitherto unknown planet. If the deep misunderstandings following the attack on the World Trade Centre have taught us anything, they have surely brought home to us the truth of the profound enculturation of everything we hold dear. I cannot imagine the psyche of a suicidal fanatic, but it will do me no good simply to consign him or her to some psychotic limbo reserved for those who have excluded themselves from rational debate.

2.3.1 Doctrine

I suspect that one of the structuralist modes is best suited to understanding the link between Scripture and doctrine. Theologically, the Bible is like one of those complex archaeological sites in which successive layers have eaten into each other, partly destroying what went before. The result is a puzzling, and often contradictory, body of fragmentary evidence. What we may make of this depends on how determined we are to create (or recover?) a single coherent story.

For example, many theologies of the Old Testament in the scholarly world are content to describe the evidence, with a certain amount of creative restoration (not unlike the physical restoration of buildings and works of art) in an effort to let the reader wander freely around the museum that is ancient Israel. Like its physical analogues, such restoration more often than not proceeds from an ideal truer to the mind of the restorer than to any likely original!

The New Testament has prompted a more architectural approach, in which the ground is cleared of unnecessary detritus (references to 'presbyters' for example) and unwanted finds stored in a damp cellar (James and his awkward gospel of deeds is a good example). Once complete, this clearance permits the creation of fine new structures, such as the Chalcedonian doctrine of the Trinity, or Calvinist double pre-destination, without the fear of awkward bits of rubble spoiling the building.

2.3.2 Ethics

I have to confess to a particular prejudice on the subject of ethics. I am not persuaded that, where ethics is understood as a matter of rule or authority, it is *in principle* any different from law, though, of course, *in practice* we impose ethical laws by different means – the power of the community, convention, peer pressure, and public humiliation (once the preserve of the priest from the pulpit, but now more often carried out by the secular priests of the fourth estate). The same reservations apply, even more so, to the notion of a global ethic, which I suspect to be little better than a neocolonial attempt to impose largely Western middle class values in the guise of a noble and worldwide enterprise.

The trouble with the Bible as a pre-text for ethic is that much of what might be so described in its pages is actively repulsive. From relatively inoffensive injunctions to beat your children in order to teach them discipline, through a range including the practice of polygamy, divinely enjoined lies, the death penalty for failing to pay your dues to the Church, and a deeply unsympathetic view of alternative sexuality, to such gross practices as genocide and ethnic cleansing in the name of God, the Bible poses problems that suggest that it might be better viewed as a grim warning than a mentor in matters ethical.

All of this brings me back to my starting point: ethics is not a set of rules to be discovered or delineated. It represents a *process* from which none of us can resile; and, in so far as the Bible has a role, it is surely in the processual exchange of views between reader-in-community and text, and not in any 'reading off' of rigid rules. Further, because there can be no definitive statement resolving ethical dilemmas, the model of the creative and ongoing dialogue with the text is surely the more appropriate.

2.3.3 Social and cultural issues

This is perhaps the realm where the most striking misfits between the biblical world and our own are to be seen. There are good grounds for the claim that the Bible has more in common with contemporary Afghanistan than with Britain or North America. We ought to reflect on that uncomfortable probability: the Bible's assumptions about women, gay men, ethnic minorities, blasphemy, slavery, war and capital punishment are decidedly pre-modern, and must be offensive to every liberal, democratic, inclusive-minded Christian. Yet, ironically, the Bible is seen to be the West's book!

What is usually done in response to such difficult facts is to combine a progressive modern stance with two hermeneutical devices. First, the more 'advanced' parts of the Bible are held to have superseded the more 'primitive' – the Bible is allowed to be self-critical. I believe this is appropriate to the sort of community of interpretation envisaged by Fish, for it constitutes a clear example of the text being shaped by the community in the light of a progression in thinking that has, it could be claimed, in its turn been stimulated by certain attitudes previously read from the text. The famous rabbinic saying quoted by Jesus, to the effect that the Torah may be summed up in the aphorism 'love God, and your neighbour as yourself', is a leading example of such a potentially challenging text. But this amelioration is not purely the consequence of a closed system of text and community. It is further influenced by developments – either in the secular world or in other interpretive communities – which themselves have a bearing on the matter. And where the logic of love might point in a direction the community is not ready to take, it will be resisted. This is the reason for the highly selective nature of modernity's appropriation of enlightened readings.

Accordingly, a second device is required: that of the subversion of the text, the re-inscription of marginalized or rejected options into a reluctant Scripture. This is where the process I have not specifically dealt with – that of deconstruction – might prove most fruitful, in its insistence both on the importance of marginal readings, and in its understanding of the place of absence, negation and contradiction as we go about the business of interpretation. Thus the *marginalized* can be recovered from the *margins* of the text and allowed to speak against the dominant authoritative word that seeks always to control and to impose its illegitimate power. The specific way in which this is often made to work is the recognition that the few passages that speak positively of the oppressed, and those that conceal their presence (Genesis 22 never refers to Sarah during the whole story of the Akedah – the binding and would-be sacrifice of Isaac), take on a significance that goes beyond the mere volume of words. Words may speak volumes, but silence is often more powerful.

There is, of course, a place for traditional interpretation in this area. Once the subversive text has begun to work on the collective prejudices of the community, it can begin to see more clearly that some silences were never in fact *biblical* silences, but rather those of the community imposing its prejudice on the text. Hebrew speaks of Wisdom always in third person feminine – why have male scholars frequently used the pronoun 'it' to refer to her in translation? The Song of Solomon 1.5 begins with a statement that used always to be rendered, 'I am black but beautiful.' The 'but' is not a necessary interpretation – in Hebrew the word used equally often means 'and'. You will find that most really modern translations read 'I am black and beautiful.' These are but two straws in the wind indicating the kind of change of perception that results from the process of interaction in interpretation, which has been the subject of this paper.

Conclusion

I would like to say more, I could produce many more words on this subject. I have not taken up the last of my examples in 2.3 – the way we use the Bible politically. There are many obvious points of interest that could be further explored: the just war, which has become an urgent item in the context of the crushing of the Taleban and the attack on Iraq; theories of race and ethnicity, which have historically been derived from biblical genealogical legends, and which never fully leave the stage of human affairs; was the Good Samaritan an entrepreneurial success, and does it matter? (the Thatcher reading); the Pauline passages on authority and how we respond to it; the kingdom of God – socialist paradise or free market heaven?

But enough, already, as they say. Whether we go Fishing, or are Saussure of our readings as to be able to build on them, the challenge remains, and the fascination of an interaction between text and reader, Bible and community, that will never exhaust the possibilities of interpretation.

Homosexuality and Scripture

David Hilborn

It must be granted that direct references to homosexual activity in the Bible are relatively few. However, these more explicit texts belong to a much broader biblical discourse on creation, love, holiness and human relationships – a discourse that goes to the heart of God's purpose for humankind and which, as I shall argue, flows in continuity with such texts rather than in discontinuity from them. I shall briefly outline the contours of this broader discourse first, and shall then move on to discuss those passages that refer more specifically to homosexual practice.

The early chapters of Genesis do not go into great detail about the distinctions between female and male – but they do emphasize that each was a separate, intentional creation, and that they were made distinct rather than 'two of the same'. It is these chapters that provide the basic context for human sexuality, procreation and marriage (Genesis 1.27-8; 2.18-24). They are foundational for the classical Judaeo-Christian teaching that sexual intercourse is designed for expression solely within the lifelong, marital relationship of a man and a woman.[1]

Plainly, biblical models of sex, marriage and reproduction must be related in turn to the essential quality of love. The concept of love in the Bible extends far beyond sexual love. God's love defines our love, not vice versa: 'We love because he first loved us' (1 John 4.19). God's creation of the human race extends this love outwards and opens the way to a covenant of mutual trust and care. When God sees that it is not good for Adam to be alone, he creates an 'other' – a woman – to be his companion (Genesis 2.20-25). The complementarity inherent in the resultant relationship is expressed at least partly as a physical complementarity: the two who are clearly distinct and different are nevertheless intended to become 'one flesh' (Genesis 2.24). As is well known, traditional Jewish and Christian interpretation has accorded this complementarity a unique and exclusive moral status: it has been taken to mean that man and woman are created anatomically for each other – and that, since they correspond genitally and procreatively in a way that two men or two women cannot, homosexual activity lies *ipso facto* outside the realm of divine sanction.

This historic view of the creation narrative has, of course, been
dismissed in much recent lesbian and gay liberationist theological
writing as a 'naturalistic fallacy' – a leap of logic from 'what is'
to 'what ought to be'; a flawed inference of exclusive divine
intentions from particular biological consequences.[2] Rowan
Williams even goes so far as to call this same inference
'nonscriptural', apparently on the basis that, while Genesis 2 may
describe a relational norm, it should not be read as *proscribing* all
exceptions to that norm.[3] Certainly, it needs to be recognized,
quite apart from the current debate about homoerotic sexual
practice, that heterosexual sex is *itself* hardly confined to penile-
vaginal penetration and reproduction. Still, however, it would take
an extraordinary evasion of the plain sense of the biblical narrative
on men, women and sex to suggest that the link between
heterosexual activity and procreation is merely incidental.
Granted, the vast majority of such activity is not finally
procreative; granted, the advent of artificial contraception has
made it even less so; granted, God gave us sex for pleasure, too;
granted, large numbers of men and women, who for whatever
reason cannot produce children, continue to enjoy intercourse.
But there can be little doubt that Scripture takes the procreative
capacity of heterosexual interaction per se to be a distinguishing
mark of its explicit divine endorsement – something that validates
it over against other, intrinsically non-reproductive modes of
sexual relating (Genesis 1.28; 9.1-15; 15.1-21; Psalm 127.3).[4]

Admittedly, the complementarity of woman and man is more
than simply physical. Genesis 1.27 emphasizes that God created
human beings in his own image – male and female together. The
context shows that this divine image is expressed in a relationship
that may be sexual, but which is also spiritual, emotional and
psychological. Their being joined together in marriage becomes
a fundamental expression of all this: 'Therefore a man leaves his
father and his mother and clings to his wife, and they become
one flesh' (Genesis 2.24). This becomes the definitive biblical
paradigm for human sexual love. Granted, like everybody else,
evangelicals need to remember that the application of this
paradigm was not immediately confined to *monogamous*
heterosexual marriage in the Old Testament; still, there can be
little dispute that, in biblical-theological terms, heterosexual
monogamy emerges from it teleologically, as its purposed end.
Certainly, the Genesis creation narrative is later taken as the basis
for monogamous heterosexual marriage by both Jesus and Paul

(Matthew 19.4-6; Ephesians. 5.31).[5] Moreover, it also serves as the ground of various laws and obligations designed to reinforce the singular validity and social status of such monogamy (Matthew 19.4-12; 1 Corinthians 7.1-40; Colossians 3.18-19; Titus 2.4-5; 1 Peter 3.1-7; Hebrews13.4).

While so much current debate centres on sexual activity, we should be careful to reiterate the key place in God's purposes of other forms of non-erotic love, for example, sisterly and brotherly love (*philadelphia*), and love expressed in friendship (*philia*). A classic biblical example that illustrates both is that of David and Jonathan. Nor should we forget that Jesus chose friends whom he regarded as 'family' (Mark 3.33-5). The closest of these were Peter, James and John, the latter of whom was distinguished as 'the disciple whom Jesus loved' (John 21.20). These examples confirm that we need not be fearful of same-sex friendships. They should also spur us to reject insinuations that such friendships must be homosexual in nature. It has become a staple of pro-gay exegesis, for example, to present David and Jonathan in homoerotic terms – despite the fact that the text offers no credible evidence of this.[6]

It is important to note in this context that many homosexual people, for Christian or other reasons, are committed to chastity – that is, to abstention from genital sex. In this they resemble many heterosexuals (whether single, divorced or widowed) who believe it right to refrain from sexual relations – however much they may long for the physical bond of marriage (cf. 1 Corinthians 7.11; 1 Timothy 5.9). In addition, of course, there are those of both orientations who have chosen the equally hard way of celibacy, that is, a lifelong, rather than a provisional, commitment to sexual abstinence. Not only did Jesus himself live a single, abstinent life; he seems to have recognized and commended others who observed this pattern, even making a distinction between those (probably impotent but possibly with a strong same-sex orientation) who had been 'born' to observe it, those (probably castrated courtiers, but possibly others) who had been 'made that way by people', and those called to renounce marriage 'because of the kingdom of heaven' (Matthew 19.12; cf. 1 Corinthians 7.7). These points should not be lost as we approach those texts that deal more directly with homosexual activity.

In what follows, it will become clear that, while a number of biblical passages bear on the debate about homosexual practice, it is those from the Pauline epistles that offer the clearest and most directly relevant guidance to us as we struggle to address this issue in the present-day Church. This balance of focus is very much reflected in the length and detail of my contributions on the various biblical texts that may be adduced in respect of homoerotic sexual activity.

Old Testament

Genesis 19.1-29

The story of Lot and Sodom clearly entails a gross breach of hospitality. According to justice and tradition, the men of Sodom should have protected Lot's visitors (cf. Ezekiel 16.49). Instead, however, they abused them. Lot is keen to act as an upright host towards those who are 'under his roof', and as such he reflects the typically high standards of hospitality that pertained in ancient Near-Eastern cultures. The men of Sodom, however, contravene those standards severely. Indeed, as the text suggests through its report that God aims to destroy the city (19.12-14) and, as Jesus later confirms when he denounces Sodom in Matthew 10.14-15 and 11.20-4, the men's actions constitute more than an isolated breach of domestic etiquette; they are, in fact, a manifestation of much deeper-seated sins of idolatry, pride and rebellion. These, rather than homosexuality per se, are undoubtedly the overriding themes of the passage. They cannot, however, mask the fact that the abuse in question does appear to have strongly sexual connotations.

Among others, Derrick Bailey, John Boswell and John McNeill have claimed that, in verse 5, the verb *yāda'*, which is usually translated 'know', means simply 'get acquainted with' rather than 'have sex with'.[7] Admittedly, this verb is used in a sexual sense on just 15 other occasions out of 943 uses in the Hebrew Bible. Yet the context here is one in which Lot himself seems to have viewed the intentions of the men of Sodom as sexual, by offering them his daughters instead of guests whom he believes to be male (even though they turn out to be angels). The further detail that these daughters have not yet 'known' a man, would seem to bear with it the strong contemporary cultural attractions of female virginity to a sexually mature male. Moreover, there are compelling semantic and narrative parallels between this account and that of the rape of the Levite's concubine in Judges 19.22, 25, which quite explicitly uses the verb 'know' in a sexual way.[8]

From a Christian point of view, it is also relevant that in the New Testament, both Peter (2 Peter 2.10) and Jude (7) seem to regard Sodom's sin as at least partly to do with disordered sexual behaviour. Peter presents God's punishment of Sodom as a salutary reminder of God's impending judgement on the unrighteous – especially those who, like the men in Genesis 19, 'indulge their flesh in depraved lust'. Likewise, Jude casts the same 'sexual immorality' and 'unnatural lust' as 'an example' of sin prone to merit the 'punishment of eternal fire'. As Robert Gagnon points out in his exhaustive study of this and other relevant texts on sexual immorality, it is noteworthy that Peter and Jude highlight the sin of lust here, rather than any failure to provide social justice or hospitality.[9]

Having said all this, it must be stressed that the intended sexual act in this passage is actually one of gang rape, which, as in the parallel incident at Gibeah in Judges 19, renders it less specifically relevant to the headline, present day theological issue of non-violent, consenting homosexual practice. For an Old Testament source that might apply more specifically to this, we must turn to Leviticus.

Leviticus 18.22; 20.13

These verses could conceivably refer to cult prostitution, and would thus not be pertinent today. But the orientation of both chapters 18 and 20 is against *all* forms of ungodly sexual behaviour – incest, adultery and bestiality as well as homosexual practice. All such activities are viewed as a threat to marriage and the family, each of which plays a pivotal role in Hebrew culture and religion. They are deemed wrong not simply because pagan Canaanites indulged in them, but because God has pronounced them wrong as such.

It is significant that when Leviticus 18.22 declares 'You shall not lie with a male', it would seem to prohibit men from taking the 'active' role in homosexual intercourse, even though this was deemed to be comparatively respectable in several contemporary cultures, as compared to the effeminate 'passive' role. The same root text also deploys the generic term 'male' rather than any more specific word for 'man' or 'youth' – a detail that also points to a more comprehensive understanding of homoerotic activity. Furthermore, the death penalty in Leviticus 20.13 applies equally to the active and the passive partner: there is no implication of rape, in which case the rapist alone would have been executed (cf. Deuteronomy 22.22-5). Nor is there any hint of coercion. The context, rather, would seem to include homosexual intercourse by mutual consent. Comparative literary study has revealed that the Assyrians outlawed forcible same-sex intercourse; it has also shown that the Egyptians banned pederasty; Israel, however, appears to have stood alone in viewing homosexual acts *in general* with this degree of severity.[10]

Gospels

Matthew 15.19; Mark 7.21

It is often pointed out by apologists for lesbian and gay sexual relationships that Jesus himself does not pronounce explicitly on homosexual practice. Yet arguments from silence are notoriously suspect in theology, and Jesus hardly commented in direct terms on every ethical issue under the sun: slavery and capital punishment, for instance, are not matters on which he taught explicitly. Having said this, his condemnations of *porneia* or 'sexual immorality' in Matthew 15.19 and Mark 7.21 would almost definitely have been meant, and been taken, to include homoerotic sexual activity. Certainly, as Michael Saltlow has shown, such activity was typically condemned by the rabbis of the time whenever they considered it.[11] Having said this, at least following the exile, there is very little evidence of, or extant comment on, such activity among Jewish men[12] – so Jesus' not mentioning it in specific terms is hardly surprising.

Epistles

Romans 1.18-32

This is by some distance the most important biblical reference for the homosexuality debate. As such, I shall deal with it in considerably more depth than the other passages being considered here. It is important, first and foremost, because it provides by far the fullest theological reflection on same-sex sexual relations in the biblical canon. It is also significant for being almost certainly the only reference in Scripture to lesbian sexual activity – something contemporary Graeco-Roman sources hardly ever mentioned in the same breath as male homosexual practice.[13]

After an opening salutation and prayer (vv. 1-15), Paul begins to establish the context for what he will go on to teach about

homosexual behaviour. First, he affirms that the gospel is for both
Jew and Greek alike (v. 17). This is fundamental for a Roman
congregation that appears to contain members from both
communities (1.13, cf. 4.1; chapters 9-11). More specifically, it
underlines the equal status of Hebrew and Gentile Christians with
respect to salvation (v. 16), while at the same time implying their
equality with respect to divine 'wrath' (v. 18) and 'judgement'
(2.3). On both counts, there is a universality in Christian
experience: the righteousness of God is available to everyone
who has faith (v. 17), but by the same token, all who spurn God's
benefits are subject to what Paul later calls God's 'righteous
condemnation' (2.5). Indeed, as the apostle sums it up, 'God
shows no partiality' (2.11). It is crucial to realize that this
impartiality applies just as much to the 'wickedness' of v. 18
as to the 'righteousness' of v. 17.

This avowedly comprehensive, non-partisan soteriology frames
the ethical analysis developed by Paul in vv. 18-32. Here, we
learn that the global scope of salvation history has been made
manifest not only in 'the gospel of God's Son' (cf. v. 9), but also
in the very 'creation of the world' (v. 20). Some commentators
(notably William Countryman) have suggested that Paul in these
verses is rehearsing a stereotypically self-righteous Judaic account
of Gentile depravity, precisely in order to debunk that same
account in 2.1ff, where Old Covenant notions of 'impurity' are
(supposedly) contrasted with genuine sins, and where homosexual
'impurity' is shown to be no more threatening to Christ's New
Covenant order than the consumption of pork.[14] This 'set up' is
inferred from an apparent switch to 'us and them' rhetoric, as
denoted by the third person plural personal pronouns of vv. 18ff
('they', 'their', etc.). While such a reading is just about
conceivable, we should be careful not to dismiss the various
definitions of 'wickedness' cited in vv. 21-31 simply on the
grounds that those who apply such definitions happen in this case
to be smug and sanctimonious. Indeed, the fact that Paul declares
such hypocrites to be guilty of 'the very same things' (*gar auta*,
2.1) as the sinners they attack, only confirms that those 'same
things' are nonetheless to be viewed as *consistently* and
intrinsically wrong. As Thomas Schmidt has put it, our exegesis
here must not throw out 'the baby of righteousness with the bath
water of self-righteousness'.[15] Besides, Countryman's tortuous
attempt to recast the vocabulary of chapter 1 wholly in terms
of a superseded Levitical holiness code hardly reflects Paul's

more complex handling of the Law in the rest of the letter
(cf. 3.19; 7.7-25; 7.28, etc.) and, as Schmidt shows, would
collapse immediately if only *one term* in vv. 24-8 did actually
connect with 'sin', rather than mere ritual purity.

But what precisely are the 'things' Paul has in mind – the things
that violate God's creation order and thereby undermine
righteousness? In general terms, we may say that they go under
the heading of that 'godlessness' (*asebeian*) to which he refers in
verse 18. More specifically, they are exemplified first by what
might be called the *apathetic neglect* of God – a failure to honour
his purpose as revealed in the world. This, says Paul, leads to a
numbing of the spirit and a dulling of the mind (vv. 21-2). Beyond
such plain 'lukewarmness', however, lurks the more active and
more sinister threat of *idolatry*. Above all else, it is this that
provides the key to interpretation of verses 26 and 27.

In verse 23, Paul presents the first of three vital 'exchanges'.
He states here that the wicked characteristically 'changed (*ēllaxan*)
the glory of the immortal God into images resembling a mortal
human being or birds or four-footed animals or reptiles'. One
thinks readily of the Israelites' golden calf (Exodus 32) and the
Ephesians' shrines to Artemis (Acts 19.26). Obviously, the second
of the Ten Commandments – that prohibiting on 'graven images' –
looms large here (Exodus 20.4). However, Paul quickly broadens
his conception of idolatry to take in the first commandment, too:
'they exchanged (*ēllaxan*) the truth about God for a lie and
worshipped and served the creature rather than the Creator'
(v. 25, cf. Exodus 20.1-3).

Vitally, for our concerns, it is this more general conception of
idolatry that prompts Paul to cast homosexual practice against
the backdrop not only of Mosaic law, but also of 'natural' law –
that is, not only in relation to Exodus 20, but also in relation
to Genesis 1-2, with its picture of humankind made 'male and
female' in God's image, and its portrayal of their complementarity
as 'one flesh' (1.27; 2.24). Granted, John Boswell may have been
right to note that no full-blown juridical system of 'natural laws'
was institutionalized in human society until 'more than a
millennium after Paul's death',[16] but the absence of such a system
does not, in itself, denote the absence of any natural *theology*,
or any ethic based on 'general revelation', and it is these to which
Paul is clearly appealing here.

I have already emphasized the centrality of God's creation design
in Paul's thinking (v. 20). Indeed, it is probably significant that
the idolatrous exchange of creature and creator in v. 25 here is
described literally not just as *a* lie, but as *the* lie (*tō pseudei*) –
the defining distortion or 'perversion' of God's purpose for the
world, from which other distortions and perversions must
inevitably follow (cf. Genesis 3.5).[17] It is as archetypes of such
'consequential' distortions and perversions that we must approach
the bodily 'degradations' (*atimadzesthai ta sōmata*) described
generically in v. 24, and illustrated specifically in relation to same-
sex intercourse in vv. 26-7. No doubt, such degradations belong to
a much broader catalogue of evils – not least those listed by Paul
in vv. 29ff as including covetousness, malice, jealousy and the
like. Even so, within the structure of his argument, it is clear that
such bodily degradations are marked out for special attention
because they constitute a *particularly* vivid paradigm of 'creation
gone wrong'.

Although we may assume from v. 24 that Paul is thinking of
heterosexual as well as homosexual depravities, the third
'exchange' in vv. 26-7 suggests that Paul sees homoerotic activity
as almost iconic of what he is condemning. Richard B. Hays bears
this out vividly when he writes of homosexual behaviour being
for Paul 'a sacrament (so to speak) of the antireligion of human
beings who refuse to honour God as Creator. When human beings
engage in homosexual activity, they enact an outward and visible
sign of an inward and spiritual reality: the rejection of the
Creator's design.'[18]

From what has been said so far, it can be seen that a creation-
theological reading of verses 26-7 derives from the *broad contours*
of Paul's discourse, and not, as is often alleged by 'pro-gay'
apologists like Victor Paul Furnish and Michael Vasey, from a
dogmatic eisegesis of the single words 'nature' and 'natural'
(*phusin, phusikēn*) in vv. 26-7.[19] No doubt, these particular
terms do carry other meanings in Scripture, sometimes culturally
specific (as in 1 Corinthians 11.14), and sometimes even negative
(Ephesians 2.3). But, given the pervasiveness of Paul's wider
'argument from design' here, it would take a quite extreme
form of special pleading to divorce *phusin* from the apostle's
understanding of God's eternal intent for humans (cf. v. 20).
Besides, the notion of homosexual practice as *para phusin* and
thus immoral is found in several contemporary Graeco-Roman

sources, and especially in that Hellenistic Jewish tradition with
which Paul himself was associated.[20]

In the midst of all this, we should not lose sight of a somewhat
surprising theodicial 'twist' in Paul's reasoning, namely, the
identification of God as actively 'giving people up' to the lusts
of their hearts. This concept is mediated no fewer than three times
by the use of the verb *parēdōken* (vv. 24, 26, 28), and implies that
sexual perversion has about it an innate, and even unconscious,
compulsiveness – a compulsiveness which, after a time, hardens
itself even against the will of the creator. In such circumstances,
Paul envisages what Mark Bonnington and Bob Fyall describe as
a 'terrible divine "hands off"', or what Hays sees as the 'irony of
sin [playing] itself out' – an irony in which the creature's original
instinct for glorification is wrathfully loosed by the creator into
doomed self-destruction.[21] In this way we realize that the sexual
misconduct abhorred by Paul is in a very real sense the *result* of
divine judgement rather than the cause of it. The homosexual
practice abhorred by the apostle is, therefore, as much to be
regretted as castigated: it is a presenting symptom of a world
estranged from its maker. As such, it is a mark of that universal
'fallenness' in which we all share, and should not be singled out
for particular scorn, even while it cannot be condoned. This point
is made explicit by Paul in 2.1ff.

Discerning the theological superstructure of Romans 1-2 as we
have done is a necessary prelude to closer semantic analysis of
verses 26-7 themselves. Few serious scholars doubt that, when
Paul here condemns the use of human bodies 'against nature'
(*para phusin*), he has in mind sexual acts performed by men with
men, and by women with women. Admittedly, Derrick Sherwin
Bailey and Vern Bullough have suggested that, since Paul insisted
elsewhere that women subordinate themselves to men (Ephesians
5.22; Colossians 3.8; Titus 2.5), he could be referring to women
who adopt the dominant position in heterosexual intercourse,
rather than to lesbian sex *per se*.[22] Conversely, it is just about
imaginable that the 'unnatural use' of women's bodies that Paul
has in mind is their indulgence in anal sex with men. Both
interpretations are, however, unlikely. The second ignores the clear
rhetorical and grammatical parallels that the apostle is drawing
between women and men, the latter of whom are explicitly said
to have abandoned heterosexual practices (*krēsin tēs thleias*) for
homosexual ones (*orexei autōn eis allēlous*). Moreover, both this

and the first reading disregard the universal sweep of Paul's natural theology, focused as it is on sexual relations as such, rather than on specific sexual techniques. Indeed, the fact that Paul uses the more generalized vocabulary of 'male' and 'female' here (*arsenes; thēleias*), rather than the terminology of 'men' or 'women' (*gunē; anēr*), may well bear this out.[23]

Given that Paul is concerned to categorize homoerotic sexual practice as a 'shameless' activity (*askēmosunēn katērgadzomenoi*), the next question to be asked is whether that category should be taken to include all forms of physical relationship between people of the same gender. Those who seek to argue against such a 'blanket' condemnation usually do so on the premise that the homosexuality to which Paul is referring here is in some way distinct from the sort of 'faithful, stable, loving' same-sex partnerships that many would now commend as authentically Christian.

One suggestion, mooted by Furnish and others, is that Paul is, in fact, describing a quite particular form of pagan temple prostitution.[24] This, they argue, would hardly equate with the lifestyle of modern gays and lesbians. Certainly, Paul would have known about the temple of Aphrodite in Corinth (the city from which Romans was probably written), with its thousand priestesses and 'sacred slaves' known colloquially as 'the sailors' delight'.[25] But, as even Boswell admits, this explanation falters as soon as one realizes that the parties involved in the sexual activities defined by Paul are 'burning with lust' for one another (v. 27) – a description unlikely to fit the more dispassionate prostitution associated with such religious ceremony and ritual.[26]

Another increasingly familiar interpretation holds that Paul is concerned here primarily with pederasty – a practice restricted to the upper echelons of society and indulged in by basically heterosexual males. This was indeed the most common manifestation of homosexual practice in ancient Greece, but it was by no means the only recognized form of same-sex relationship. For example, the 'Sacred Band' of Thebes institutionalized the pairing of soldiers as lovers to foster their courage in battle, as they fought to the death for their 'faithful, stable, loving' partner. A similar arrangement pertained in Sparta, while longer-term homosexual partnerships were accepted in Elis and Boeotia.[27] Granted, these partnerships were often maintained side by side with heterosexual marriage, but it is not even true, as many gay and lesbian exegetes claim, that the Greeks and Romans had no recognition of what we would now call 'homosexual orientation'. The extensive researches of Kenneth Dover in this area in fact reveal a much more complex situation than many appreciate.[28] Notwithstanding all that has since been discovered in genetics and biology, the Anglican Bishops' report *Issues in Human Sexuality* rightly concludes on this basis that the world of the New Testament did in some cases recognize phenomena 'which today would be interpreted in terms of orientation'.[29]

We cannot, of course, know for certain the full range of homosexual relationships and practices with which Paul was familiar. His virtually unprecedented yoking of lesbianism with male homosexuality does, however, suggest that his perspective is unusually broad for his time. It certainly rules out the restriction of his words to pederasty alone. Nor is it likely that, as an educated Pharisee, he would have been ignorant of the subtle ethical reasoning of Plato, Aristotle and numerous other ancient philosophers, who had condemned homoerotic sexual practice while nonetheless venerating same-sex friendships. Indeed, when linked with all that we have said about the universality of Paul's vision of divine salvation and divine judgement, and when placed in the context of his cosmic creation-theology, these points compel the conclusion that the most authentic reading of Romans 1.26-7 is that which sees it prohibiting homosexual activity in the most general of terms, rather than in respect of more culturally and historically specific forms of such activity.

1 Timothy 1.8-11 (and 1 Corinthians 6.9)

Our consideration of Romans 1 confirms that crude law–grace dichotomies are hardly commensurate with Pauline teaching. This point is also borne out by 1 Timothy 1.8-11. Indeed, the need to integrate legal/doctrinal rectitude ('the law is good', v. 8) with 'love that comes from a pure heart, conscience, and sincere faith' (v. 6) is the keynote of this passage.

Paul is, apparently, dealing on one flank here with fanciful Gnostic speculations about the Hebrew Scriptures – particularly those practised by sects (like the Ophites) who mythologized and allegorized the genealogies of the Pentateuch (v. 4).[30] Such speculations are criticized by Paul precisely because they are not 'legal' enough – i.e. they focus on religious marginalia rather than

on the heart of the law (v. 7). On another flank, Paul is faced with
more routine contraventions of 'sound doctrine', and it is as part
of his list of those who commit such contraventions in vv. 9-10
that we encounter the word *arsenokoitais* – a word that appears
also in a similar Pauline list of vices at 1 Corinthians 6.9.[31]

Most translations and commentaries associate *arsenokoitais*
in some way or other with practitioners of homoerotic acts.
G. W. Knight suggests very plausibly that the sins catalogued
by Paul in 1 Timothy 1.9-10 are cast as 'a deliberate echo of the
order of the second part of the Decalogue'.[32] Hence, after the
ultimate dishonouring of parents in matricide and patricide, and
after murder in general, Paul can be seen to focus on those who
undermine the seventh commandment as 'fornicators' (*pornois*)
and *arsenokoitais*. In this way, both homosexual *and* heterosexual
dimensions of sexual immorality are dealt with, and *both* are seen
as undermining the sanctity of marriage.

But what of the word *arsenokoitais* itself? At first sight, precise
interpretation appears difficult, since there is no record of its
use in pre-Christian literature. Yet it is a compound of two terms
which, in their own right, carried familiar sexual connotations:
arsēn was a specific word for male, but was often used in
connection with male sexuality; *koitēs* usually meant 'bed',
but functioned as a widespread euphemism for sexual intercourse
(cf. our term *coitus*)[33] Paul's yoking of the two therefore points
strongly to a homoerotic denotation.

Of course, this still leaves us with the same problem we faced
with Romans 1.26-7 – namely, what *kinds* of homosexual practice
are in view? As with that text, John Boswell, Michael Vasey and
others argue for a restriction of Paul's thinking only to the
dominant Graeco-Roman models of pederasty, male cultic
prostitution and slavery.[34] But this reading ignores the crucial
context of 'the law', and the probable origin of the compound in
question within the Torah: *arsenokoitais* seems most probably to
have been coined by Paul in response to the vocabulary of the
Septuagint version of Leviticus 18.22 and 20.13, where its
constituent terms appear as a translation of the Hebrew *mishkav
zakur* ('lying with a male') – a phrase that rabbinical texts routinely
take to refer to homosexual intercourse.[35] As we noted above, the
purview of Leviticus 18 and 20 is remarkably comprehensive:
it takes in a *whole range* of sexual sins, including incest, adultery

and bestiality – and it does not appear to make any moral differentiation between 'active' and 'passive' homosexual activity, as the law-codes of other contemporary societies did. It is also worth reiterating that, in drawing on these sources, Paul is echoing a preference for the generic term 'male', rather than any more particular word for 'man' or 'youth'. It is significant, too, that the death penalty in Leviticus 20.13 applies indiscriminately to the active and the passive partner, and that there is no implication of rape, since the rapist alone would then have been executed (cf. Deuteronomy 22.22-5). Given that Leviticus 18 and 20 are the most logical source for Paul's thinking here, it therefore seems most unlikely that his reference would be as restricted as Vasey and Boswell suggest.

Importantly for current debate, the context of Paul's remarks in both 1 Timothy 1 and 1 Corinthians 6 is eligibility for God's kingdom in general, and for church membership in particular. As in Romans 1, homoerotic sexual practice here belongs to a catalogue of sins: it is apparently no better, and no worse, than fornication, adultery, theft, greed, drunkenness, slander and robbery. This surely confirms that the Church is a community of sinners, and disallows the singling out of homosexual sin for special condemnation. It also, incidentally, suggests that Early Church congregations contained homosexual people. Indeed, some of these may still have been sexually active. The clear teaching of Paul, however, is that continuing attachment to this, as to the other sinful practices he mentions, is incompatible with authentic participation in the community of God's people: 'And that is what some of you *used to be*. But you were washed, you were sanctified, you were justified in the name of the Lord Jesus Christ and in the Spirit of our God' (1 Corinthians 6.11, my emphasis). In this, as we have seen, Paul is nothing less than consistent with the witness of Scripture as a whole.

Interpreting the biblical texts on homosexuality

Michael Williams

When I taught practical theology at St John's College, Durham, our New Testament tutor, when he came to Romans Chapter 1, would always refuse to say what his views on homosexuality were. In each generation of students there were always some who took great exception to this. 'Tell us what the text says', was their demand and, when it was not forthcoming, they were disillusioned with New Testament studies. What the tutor went on to say also infuriated some. He said that he would do his best to interpret the text within its context, but that they would have to ask the ethics tutor what the significance of the text was for today. While I don't necessarily accept such a rigid distinction, it makes a good point.

New Testament studies, which works with a 2,000-year-old text, cannot tell us what is right and wrong today unless we explore the significance of the 2,000-year gap and apply it in our own day and in our own generation. My approach here will be to try to be that present day ethics tutor. For this reason I will primarily appeal to the discipline of ethics in my remarks.

In their book, *Bible and Ethics in the Christian Life*, Birch and Rasmussen make a similar point.[1] They see it as their task to take the 2,000-year-old text and see what directions and pointers it gives as we face our modern day questions. They are convinced that the Bible *does* speak to us today and that it is a primary source of Christian ethics, but they insist that there are no short cuts in this process.

In committing themselves to the authoritative function of the Bible in ethics, they put themselves at a considerable distance from the classic liberal tradition. Liberalism sees only a symbolic role for the Bible in current day ethics at best, or it regards the book simply as an antique to be left behind in favour of a 'common sense' or a Spirit ethics. We had a practical example of such a stance in our church recently when the archdeacon came to preach for a civic service. The first part of his sermon was an exhortation for Christians to be engaged in the public task and to work for justice in the political sphere. Towards the end of the sermon he linked his thoughts with a passage from Joshua that had been read as our first lesson. As one of our senior church members put it crisply, 'The first part of the sermon was good, but the second half was a waste of time. What could a 3,000-year-old Joshua know about Bolton today?' Like Birch and Rasmussen, I cannot share this general liberal view. For me Christian ethics must be ethics guided by the Bible and the New Testament in particular.

But before we turn to the so-called standard texts on homosexuality I must add some words of caution. The first is that, by beginning with Genesis, then moving through Leviticus, Romans, and Corinthians to the Pastoral Epistles, may be heavily to prejudge the issue. To choose this set of texts, as conservative evangelicals tend to do, may be to prejudge the question completely.

For example, Michael Vasey (another of my colleagues from Durham days), in his book *Strangers and Friends*,[2] suggests a completely different list such as 2 Samuel 3.9; Matthew 8.5-13; 2 Samuel 1.17-27; Mark 3.13-14; John 13.23; 15.15; 19.26; 20.2 and 21.20; and 1 John 4.16, and it could well be that, on this selection, gay relationship might be seen as a wonderful fulfilment of part of God's varied creation.

Perhaps the best way, then, would not be to start from any particular short list of texts but think about the Bible as a whole. What about thinking of those great themes that run through the Bible and applying them to our modern day dilemma in connection with gay and lesbian sex? How would it be if we analysed our questions against the background of the grace of God, of Covenant, of the eschatological work of God in bringing creation to its fulfilment and, above all, as Paul puts it, through the Cross? What would we think of homosexuality if we took this broader brush approach? My own feeling is that we would have a far more open view of committed gay relationships. Be that as it may, I won't run away from these suggested texts.

There is also a problem with starting with the Genesis text. It seems obvious to begin at the beginning but beginning here can so easily silence further texts if we rush to premature conclusions.

These Genesis texts are undoubtedly about the shape of an originating vision within the will of God. It is in this sense that Jesus appeals to them when he quotes Genesis 2.24 in Matthew 19.5 and parallels. But, in his book on New Testament ethics, Wolfgang Schrage points out that the original will of God is only one theme in Jesus' ethic.[3] The two other great themes are love and the kingdom. If we began our discussion of homosexuality with either love or the kingdom (where there is no marrying or giving in marriage) we might come to a quite different conclusion than the one usually deduced from Genesis. Schrage's point is simple: Jesus' ethic is three pronged: if you simply rely on one theme standing on its own you will invariably go astray. To begin with Genesis, as if this is somehow foundational, misses the fact that, for Jesus, it was one starting point alongside two others.

Before proceeding to Genesis 1 and the other texts before us, I need to make another point about the nature of texts. The modern hermeneutics movement in theology and philosophy encourages us to see texts as having depth and not just a surface value. Although this is a modern insight, it reminds us that, prior to the nineteenth century, the Church always regarded biblical texts as having significant depth. It was said that there was one layer of meaning on top of the other. The literal meaning was a kind of surface meaning, with other meanings, such as the allegorical, the analogical, and the mystagogical, lying beneath them. It was this approach that led the ancient writer, Origen, to be so scathing about the simpletons who took the surface meaning only and insisted that God created the world in six days. From our perspective, Origen went too far in the allegorical and mystagogical direction but, even those in the Early Church who were more conservative still understood texts as having layers of meanings, which meant that they were a rich source to quarry. Modern biblical interpretation must not forget this, otherwise we slip into a historical and legal fundamentalism.

Let me give an example. The New Testament is, on the surface, quite clear in its support for slavery. Indeed many people in the eighteenth century were strongly pro-slavery on biblical grounds. Such a biblical approach to slavery persisted into the present day in the Southern United States. To go for the simple and straightforward meaning of the text of the New Testament would be to reintroduce slavery forthwith! Slaves obey your masters. But when we look at the depth of the New Testament, and Paul's writing in particular, we see, underneath this endorsement of slavery, a deeper truth about the brotherhood and sisterhood of all people in Christ. It is this deeper truth that challenges the traditional institution of slavery. The gospel itself means that the social institution of slavery is not the last, or the most fundamental, word. In the ancient world in which Paul lived, slavery was thought to be a natural order of creation. Paul, in his practical teaching, didn't ruffle the feathers. But, at a deeper level, his conviction about brotherhood and sisterhood in Christ was a revolutionary insight. Today we would say that it is that deep insight that is paramount and that is why the command 'slaves obey your masters' no longer troubles us. As Ogletree puts it, in a very arresting way, 'to say the same thing as the text we must say something different.'[4] Those who wish to insist on a surface meaning of Romans 1 would have to work for the reintroduction of slavery if they were to be consistent.

Let me say, therefore, at the outset, that the texts we will consider do seem to give us a clear prohibition of homosexual sex. I do not wish to deny that, but my argument will be that this is not the deeper meaning of the texts, nor is it the teaching of the Bible as a whole.

Keeping these introductory remarks in mind, let us now turn to the selection of texts that are before us. First to Genesis. Genesis 1.27: 'And God created the human (*adam*)[5] in his image, in the image of God he created him, male *(zakar)* and female (*neqebah*)[6] he created them.' Just two things to note about this before we look at wider considerations. First, the word translated human is *adam* and it is a generic term not a proper noun or name of the first man. Second, when the text says God created him, the *him* is grammatically masculine but not anatomically masculine. Now to wider considerations.

I have come to an understanding of this text from my reading of Emmanuel Levinas who was, until 1974, professor of philosophy at the Sorbonne, and a Talmudic scholar.[7] He sees this text as having depth. On the surface it refers to the creation of gendered being. It means that from the one, the *adam*, the two, the male and the female, are created. But Levinas wants also to appeal to a deeper level as he sees it. This text doesn't simply refer to gender differentiation, it refers to all differentiation.

For Levinas, when we encounter another person we encounter another who is wholly other. Every genuine personal encounter means that we have to encounter the mysterious otherness of the other, their essential difference. Every marriage, every friendship, every encounter between parent and child, is an encounter with another person who is wholly other. Their otherness means that we can never capture them, never pigeonhole them, we can never sum them up. It means that, even in a lifelong relation, we engage with ever-widening horizon as to who the other is. And this applies to our relationship with God. God is wholly other, God is transcendent. We cannot control God or pigeonhole him and, when human relationships are genuine, they too have this feature of glorious mystery. For Levinas, otherness, difference, is the beginning of his understanding of God and of all other people. The Algerian Jewish philosopher Jacques Derrida, following Levinas, puts it this way, 'tout autre est tout autre.'[8] Every other is wholly other. This otherness is the image of God in us and woe betide us when we diminish it.

From this perspective, gay relationships can be just as much encounters with otherness as can straight. While Levinas does not directly comment on this, it is a clear implication of what he is saying. Genesis 2.24: 'Therefore does man (*ish*) leave his father and mother and cling to his wife (*ishah*)[9] and they become one flesh (*bazar*).'[10]

Our problem in reading this text is that we have an almost irresistible temptation to read it as the foundation of the modern capitalist nuclear family. It is the one man married to the one woman who becomes the beginnings of a family. But let's try to put these spectacles aside for the moment.

What does one flesh mean? We assume that it means the union between a man and women initiated and symbolized by sexual penetration. Such thinking lies behind the idea that a marriage is not consummated unless there is sexual penetration and emission of semen. We also assume that the physical sexual imagery of a penetrating penis and a receiving vagina means that there is a fundamental complementarity implied in this text. Read in this way it gives rise to a social complementarity of roles in society where the man is the master and breadwinner and the woman is the carer and nurturer who looks after the family. But this is to let our imaginations run away with us.[11]

Notice that the rest of the Bible does not see any contradiction between this text and polygamy.[12] Perhaps our rush to one man and one woman for life is premature. It is interesting to note in this regard that Jesus quotes this text in the context of divorce. At least in polygamy a wife and her children are cared for and protected. It is also interesting that, after Jesus quotes this text, he goes on to his kingdom ethic where marriage is transcended. Jesus himself is single for the sake of the kingdom, which represents a high goal. Perhaps our modern Western reading of this text and other biblical texts has it the wrong way round. When the New Testament talks about the union between Christ and his bride, the Church, we take this to affirm traditional marriage. Perhaps, on the contrary, we should read these texts as taking us beyond the secondary and temporary social construction of marriage.

Perhaps, too, we are premature in linking the one flesh with physical sexual imagery. Perhaps it means something like one new clan, one new social kinship group. In other words, the deep meaning of the text is about the nature of sociality not about a particular idolization of the nuclear family.

There is also another modern Western assumption that we tend to make when reading these early chapters of Genesis, namely, we see them as falling under the Perfection, Fall, Perfection motif. But this motif is not so fundamental to Jewish or to Orthodox Christian interpretation. What we call the Fall is, in these two traditions, seen more as the developing work of God in dialogue with his creation. To go back to Levinas. Levinas sees the story of Genesis 2 as giving some priority to the man. There is a sense for him in which the man and woman are not created equal and that there is a complementarity in their roles. But he suggests that God created in this way precisely so that the human vocation would be to work towards equality. Feminist philosophers were, of course, furious when he said this, but it corresponds to a more realistic view of the world. Our vocation as human beings is to work with God for the fulfilment of his creation, which moves beyond the so-called perfection of Genesis 1 and 2. It gives human beings a profound dialogical role with God as he works towards his goal.[13]

Before leaving Genesis, let me return to the point about sociality. In our modern capitalist culture we have grown used to the idea that the two great social institutions are the family and the State. But such a way of thinking about sociality leaves out the great theme of friendship. For Aristotle, it is friendship that is the fundamental good of society; the family and the State only have any value for him provided that there is an undergirding of what he calls the friendship of the good. And it is not just in ancient philosophy that this theme comes to the fore. Starting with Aristotle there is a long tradition that runs right through the Church to the present day about the centrality of friendship in sociality. One of the high points of this tradition is Aelred of Rievaulx's *On Spiritual Friendship*.[14] For Aelred, Genesis 2.18, 'it is not good for man to be alone', is not just a text concerning the relationship between men and women, it is a text about sociality. God's plan here is for friendship. This is why Aelred can think about friendship in the wider context as being about the promise of God. And this friendship can exist between human beings independently of gender. So, although he comes to this text in a very different way from Levinas, one could draw the same conclusion that the deep meaning of the text is wider than gender and it gives a vision for what could be most profound in same-gender relationships as well as heterosexual relationships. In this sense, it is not at all far fetched to say God is friendship. Nor should we miss the significance of the great high point of St John's Gospel being, 'I do not call you servants any longer . . . I have called you friends' (John 15.15). Viewed from this perspective we can see how Genesis might apply to gay and lesbian relationship as well as to straight.

Leviticus

Let's move on now to the Leviticus texts. In doing so I will draw heavily on Countryman's thesis in his book, *Dirt, Greed and Sex*.[15]

> You shall not lie with a male as with a woman; it is an abomination. (18.22)

> If a man lies with a male as with a woman: both of them have committed an abomination, they shall be put to death; their blood is upon them. (20.13)

(It is worth noting in passing that the Hebrew, and, we shall see later, the Christian New Testament, has no word for homosexual. It cannot therefore talk of homosexual actions. Instead it uses a euphemistic description of anal sex.)

Countryman argues that, far from being a jumbled list of
independent commandments and punishments, Leviticus, in
company with Hebrew ethics elsewhere, is run along two great
themes – purity and property. Our two texts against a man lying
with a man as with a woman are, for him, purity texts. I won't go
into the detail of his argument because it is well set out in his
book, but he explores the way in which uncleanness in Hebrew
thinking actually works. Certain foods, certain bodily actions,
particularly those connected with bodily fluids, touching dead
bodies, etc. are all governed by what is deemed to be clean or
unclean. Holiness is interpreted here as cleanliness, and it is
opposed to that which is unclean. The abomination is the
uncleanness because it contaminates those who practise it.
That this is so is made quite clear by two other verses taken
from the same chapters of Leviticus:

> You shall not approach a woman to uncover her
> nakedness while she is in her menstrual uncleanness.
> (18.19)

> If a man lies with a woman having her sickness,
> and uncovers her nakedness, he has made naked her
> fountain, and she has uncovered the fountain of her
> blood: both of them shall be cut off from among their
> people. (20.18)[16]

It therefore becomes clear that, if we use Leviticus 18.22 and
20.13 to say that practising gay and lesbian people are an
abomination, we should also still implement these other two texts
about men and women having intercourse during menstruation.
We cannot take the clear meaning of some texts in Leviticus and
apply them directly to current ethics without taking other similar
texts in a similarly literal way. And a further reading of Leviticus
will show that there are many other cleanliness texts that we no
longer apply today.

And the reason that we do not apply these texts today is that,
in Christian theology, they have been transformed by the life
and teaching of Jesus. To put it very simply, Jesus and the New
Testament *keep* the theme of cleanliness but transpose it to a
matter of the heart. It is not what we do with our hands or body
parts that matters but what flows out of our hearts. This is the
fundamental reason why Jesus declares that all foods are now

clean. In making this declaration Jesus is taking us to a deeper level of cleanliness, he is not abandoning the idea. He is saying that what matters most fundamentally is the spiritual cleanliness of the heart.

And this is where I stand with the texts about male anal intercourse, for that is what I take the texts in Leviticus to be about. Like all the other texts on cleanliness, these too need to be transposed into teaching about the cleanliness of the heart.

Looking at these texts in this way could lead us to say that gay and lesbian sex is no longer a physical taboo but has now become a matter of the sincerity of the heart. If those relationships bear a sincere sociality of friendship, if they are crowned by fidelity and honour, then the question of physical cleanliness has been transcended.

Romans

If my argument is true, why is it that Paul in Romans 1 returns to these Levitical texts and even expands them to include lesbian sexual acts, and holds to the condemnation?

> Their women exchanged natural relations for unnatural, and the men likewise gave up natural relations with women and were consumed with passion for one another, men committing shameless acts with men and receiving in their own persons the due penalty for their error. (1.26-7)

Surely he would see that cleanliness is now a matter of the heart? But, as in the case of Genesis, I want to appeal to the depth of Paul's text and not just to its surface. The surface of the texts does excoriate certain sexual actions, but what of the deeper meaning?

Paul's argument here must be taken as a whole. It is what I call an entropy thesis. Paul takes up an argument that is almost a duplicate of that found in the Wisdom of Solomon chapter 13. The basis of it is that as soon as human beings lose the focus of the worship of God, their selfish desires take hold and human society and human history begin to crumble and disintegrate. If there is nothing at the centre of human society then selfishness, greed, and desire of all kinds, including sexual desire, will run rampant and the glory of God's creation will be lost. In Paul's argument 'men committing shameless acts with men' is a symptom of this deeper tragedy. When human beings cease to worship God they worship the idol of desire and fall into a frenzy of self-gratification.

The background to Paul's text here is illuminating. What he is doing is taking some traditional Greek philosophical ideas about the danger of desire, especially sexual desire, and putting them into a Hebrew format. He is taking over, lock, stock, and barrel, arguments that he would have been familiar with from Greek culture. Many traditional Greek moralists also saw it as a perversion of human life to let rampant desire take hold.

If this is Paul's argument, then he is saying nothing about the sensitive, thoughtful, loving, gay and lesbian relationships that we are familiar with today where friendship and fidelity can be just as strong as in the marriage bond. What he is condemning is desire run wild. And this running wild of desire is precisely what gives him his long list of vices in verses 29 and following. There all manner of wickedness includes evil, covetousness, malice, envy, murder, strife, deceit, malignity, gossip, slander, insolence, haughtiness, boasting, and so on.

So, what Paul offers us here is not only a list of vices that would have been familiar to secular and Jewish moralists alike, he offers us the list in the context of a pathology of desire which, again, would be familiar to anyone in his own culture.

My conclusion is simple: follow the deeper logic not just the surface of the text. Look below the surface to find the centre of the argument. Just as Paul endorses slavery, so he reiterates and expands Leviticus on sexuality. But, just as we have moved beyond an acceptance of slavery for gospel reasons, we should move beyond Paul's particular examples of sexual practice to grasp his deeper argument.

His deeper argument is that disordered sexuality is the result of idolizing human desire instead of worshipping God. This idolization of desire, either in heterosexual relationships or in homosexual relationships, is what we should guard against, not particular sexual actions.

Loving homosexual relationships and loving heterosexual relationships can both be places where sexual desire finds proper expression instead of rampant self-indulgence.

Before we move on we need to say something about one particular facet of Paul's argument. Another feature of secular ethics that Paul picks up in Romans 1 is his use of the terms natural and unnatural. Anyone familiar with Stoic ethics will know that these two terms were fundamental to it. The ethics of natural law which, in Western theology, has been taken up in a major way in Roman Catholic tradition, have their origin not in the New Testament but in Stoic ethics. What Paul does here is to import these terms into his argument. As Schrage[17] points out, this is somewhat uncharacteristic of Paul. By and large Paul's ethic is an ethic of grace, it is not a virtue ethic based on natural law.

In this uncharacteristic way Paul uses the terms *phusis* (nature) and *para phusin* (against nature). What I simply want to point out is just how rare this is for Paul. The only other place where he uses this kind of natural law argument is in 1 Corinthians 11.14 and following, where he teaches that for a man to have long hair is unnatural and for a woman to have short hair is unnatural.

It is quite clear from this usage that the term natural, for Paul, included cultural and local elements and not just what we might call eternal elements. In our culture today long and short hair is no longer a matter of moral concern. I have also argued elsewhere that we should be able to sit just as loose to his use of the same concept in Romans 1.[18]

Incidentally, it is quite interesting to me that it is evangelicals who today want to insist on Paul's use of these terms natural and unnatural. It was not so long ago that evangelicals fought very hard against the natural law ethics of the Roman Catholic tradition in favour of an ethics based on grace. As one who is old enough to remember those debates, I feel that evangelicalism has sold out somewhere along the line and reinstated what we all fought so hard against. What I would like to do is to call evangelicals back to their roots and to an ethic based on the gospel, not an ethic based on law or natural law. 'All things are lawful; though not all things are helpful' would be a good starting place.

1 Corinthians 6.9-11 and 1 Timothy 1.8-11

> Do not be deceived; neither the immoral, nor idolaters,
> nor adulterers, nor sexual perverts . . . will inherit
> the kingdom of God. (1 Corinthians 6.9-10)

> The law is not laid down for the just but for the
> lawless and disobedient . . . For immoral persons,
> sodomites . . . and whatever else is contrary to sound
> doctrine . . . (1 Timothy 1.8-11)

Let me now run together the next two texts, from 1 Corinthians 6
and 1 Timothy 1. In the first, Paul warns against what is translated
'sexual perverts' in the RSV, and in I Timothy against *arsenokoitais*,
which is translated 'sodomites' in the RSV. Much has been written
about these two key words. It is worth looking at some dictionary
definitions first.

Malakoi, translated as sexual perverts in the RSV, means,
according to Liddell and Scott,[19] soft, a grassy meadow, gentle and,
in a negative sense, effeminate. According to *The Analytical Greek
Lexicon*[20] it means soft, delicate and effeminate. It is because the
term is so loose that many different English Bibles translate the
word differently. My general conclusion is that it is so difficult
to pin the word down that it would be hard to make absolute
prohibitions based on it.

Arsenokoitais means unnatural offences according to Liddell and
Scott, and the *Analytical Greek Lexicon* breaks the word down
into its two constituent parts: *arsen* is a normal word for male,
and *koite* is a word meaning to lie, or a bed. By extension from
this ordinary meaning of *koite*, the word is extended to mean
the conjugal bed. So perhaps, and only perhaps, it could mean
something like the Leviticus texts, which talk of a man lying with
a man as with a woman. My own judgement is that there would
not be enough agreement about the meaning of the word to base
any absolute ethic upon it.

But there is something more fundamental to say about these two
texts. Schrage[21] makes the point, once again, that Paul often pulls
into his ethical writing lists from secular moralists. The lists in
1 Corinthians and 1 Timothy do not come from his Hebrew
tradition, they come from his current secular context. Such lists

can be found, almost word for word, in the secular moralists of Paul's day. Schrage goes on to make a more telling point. He suggests that Paul pulls in these lists not so much to make them formal absolute commands as to take them on board as rules of thumb. Just like so much of Paul's ethics, he is not afraid to give particular precepts for particular times. In doing this he is not betraying his more fundamental ethic of grace, but is saying that such lists are meant for day-to-day guidance within the overall picture of the grace of God as revealed in Jesus Christ. Given this analysis of Paul's lists, I would want to exercise some caution before I made them absolute commands.

Given the fact that we cannot pin down the use of the particular words Paul uses (for example, some commentators see them as referring to prostitution), and because these lists only function as rules of thumb in his ethics, I would want to say that the Church should feel free today to work towards its own ethics of sexuality in line with our context here and now. We ought to take Paul's detailed comments into account and struggle with them, but we must not make them into absolute law.

Concluding remarks

In my reading of these texts I have not made any great appeal to the question of culture. The standard argument here is that we have to place the biblical texts within their own cultural context and, because our context is so different, we must be wary of a direct appeal to them today.

One standard argument along these lines is that, for the biblical writers, there was no concept of homosexuality as we know it today. The idea of a settled sexual orientation of a gay or lesbian kind had simply not been discovered in the ancient world. Following this line, neither Paul nor Leviticus could have been condemning the gay and lesbian relationships we know today because they did not know about them.

It is interesting that some liberal Jewish interpretations of the Leviticus passages run along these lines.[22] The argument is as follows:

We now know that some human beings have a natural sexual orientation towards their own sex. While it is true that Leviticus

calls men lying with men as with women an abomination, this
is only an abomination for those for whom it is not natural. The
ancient world did not know that sexual orientation worked in
the way we know it does today, hence the text does not forbid
homosexual relationships and sexual actions where that is part of
the orientation of the persons in themselves. It is worth noting in
passing that this argument is stronger for Jewish scholars because
there is less of an emphasis on the Fall. In other words, it would
be disordered sexuality for a homosexual man to lie with a
woman more than it would be for him to lie with a man. This
kind of argument by Jewish scholars is interesting, though
I wouldn't want to put too much emphasis on it.

In terms of a wider understanding of culture let me return to
Michael Vasey's book, *Strangers and Friends*. There he makes the
point that we need to listen very carefully to what gay and lesbian
culture is saying to us about our understanding of friendship and
sexuality. It is not that this will lead us into simple arguments like
the one above. What it does mean is that, before we come to any
ethical judgements at all, we need to be absolutely sure that our
reading of the biblical text is not being done from the kind of
modern day prejudices concerning sexuality that are deep within
our culture. In this way it is right to bear in mind, as Michael does,
the kind of persecution that gay and lesbian people come up
against. Is our traditional reading of these biblical texts not just a
cover for the hostility that our modern culture feels towards gays?
One of the myths on which we build much reading of these texts
today is that the Church has always condemned gay sex. The
question then becomes, 'why change now?' The answer might be
that such a reading of Christian history is simplistic. It is well
known that John Boswell[23] puts the opposite point of view. He
argues that, before the late medieval period, same-sex unions were
not only accepted but celebrated liturgically in church. He even
claims to have found texts for the blessing of gay friendships in
this early period. To bless homosexual unions in church today
may be to return to ancient church practice.

Michael Vasey's treatment of friendship certainly gives us a way
of extricating ourselves from the so-called traditional picture that
is so powerful in our modern understanding. This brings me back
to my treatment of the Genesis texts in that it suggests that the
fundamental question we must address is the question of sociality.

Section Five –
Pushing Out the Boundaries

Made and remade in the image of God

Anne Primavesi

Reading through the papers from the previous consultation, of particular interest to me was John Rogerson's conclusion that 'being made in the image of God is an empty concept which works negatively.' While I agree that it works negatively, I think that the fact that it does work shows that, far from being empty, it is a negatively *loaded* concept, full of potentially degrading content in regard to various categories of human beings, notably women, the disabled, blacks, homosexuals and lesbians. The vexed question for me personally of whether or not I am made in God's image was comprehensively treated by Zoë Bennett Moore.

And yet it is still a question. This was brought home to me last month when I attended a conference in Geneva entitled 'Women's Rights are Human Rights!'. This is the title of an ongoing campaign that began, I believe, in 1993. My immediate, resigned response to it was to ask why, today, there is any question of whether or not women are human: why it still needs to be *said* that we are *human* in order to claim our rights. Because, women involved in the campaign answer, the assumption that human rights, which serve as standards for justice, rule of law and respect for human dignity, first of all are universal, and have no gender, has had to be questioned time and again throughout the world.

I am emphasizing this point because, as I shall explain, one of the bases on which we in the Western Christian traditions supposedly claim and respect human dignity is on the grounds that 'man is made in the image of God'. And, as the previous papers have asked, why 'man' or 'human' has been interpreted as 'not woman, not black, not lesbian, not homosexual, and not disabled', so I shall ask why the dignity of every living being created, we would say, by God, is comprehensively denied once they are classed as 'non-human'.

Most of the comments in the previous papers referred to Genesis 1.26-8. To answer my question I shall take a later use of the image, in Genesis 6–9. The salient features for me are as follows.

a)　　Earth, its resources (such as the waters and the wood) and its creatures feature solely as the stage on which human beings act out their relationship with God.

b)　　We are reminded that earth is the place where God created Adam, Noah's ancestor, from whom, through Noah, the story implies, all human beings are descended.

c)　　In the case of both Adam and Noah, God's wrath is roused by human sin but its punishment is not confined to them: it embraces all living creatures. All are to die by drowning. What image of God does this give us? One less just than a county magistrate.

d)　　However, because Noah finds favour with God, some humans have their sentence of death suspended. The male human person is the focus of God's wrath or love: the decisive figure in God's relationship with the world. We are not told anything about Mrs Noah finding favour with God.

I was reflecting on this text when the foot and mouth epidemic broke out in the United Kingdom. I saw, as you did, Noah's descendants, in the person of government scientists, deciding which animals would be sacrificed, although the distinction between clean and unclean was rapidly abandoned in favour of a scientific policy which, as time went on, was summed up as follows by one letter-writer to *The Guardian* in August 2001: 'if the animals have had the disease (i.e. developed antibodies) and recovered: kill them. If they have it now, kill them. If they have not had it and are not likely to get it but cannot be exported, kill them.'

This policy was conceived and carried out as a rational, scientific, non-emotive response to the outbreak. The biblical parallel plumbed new depths when the pyres burning day and night were discovered to be burning to placate the God Mammon. For the vaccination policy was abandoned when commercial firms objected on the grounds that it would ruin their export market.

e)　　In response to Noah's sacrifice of clean animals, God promises not to curse the earth again because of human misdeeds; promises Noah many descendants and delivers all earth's creatures and produce into his hands. He is given absolute power, power of life and death over every living

being. He is, to use a familiar phrase, licensed to kill –
by God.

f)   With one exception: his fellow men. Human life, he and
       we are told, alone is sacrosanct, *because man is made in
       God's image.*

This is where the negative loading, the exemption clauses in the
concept of 'man' being made in God's image, starts to kick in.
One of the deadliest of those clauses to date has been that used
against 'not-Christian' man throughout Christian history, from
the time of Constantine to today's 'crusade' led by George Bush.
A rather less obvious exemption clause, but one that has
functioned lethally in regard to our relationship with other species,
was that formulated by Augustine.[1] He endorses the absolute
power over all living creatures given to Noah and his descendants
by God because, he says, 'we see man [sic], made in God's image
and likeness, ruling over all the irrational animals for the very
reason that he was made in your image and resembles you, that
is, because he has the power of reason and understanding.'

Here we have a doctrine of human supremacy based on man's
rationality as an image of divine rationality. As all other animals
lack God's image, they are deemed irrational. And vice versa.
Human rationality, which is an image of the divine, is, therefore,
necessary and sufficient cause for our ruling over them. The power
of reason is equated with human power to control. Therefore we
have (apparently) divine sanction to use that reason to control
and use the earth and all its creatures for our 'rational' purposes.

This conclusion, whether overtly legitimated on theological
grounds or not, was and is the imputed authority and justification
behind the monumental chemical, physical and biological
changes in the earth's surface and biosphere brought about by
Western industrialized nations, belonging to and/emerging from
Christian traditions, up to and throughout the twentieth century
and continuing apace. Those changes are documented in an
interdisciplinary study with the biblically allusive title *Something
New Under the Sun,*[2] which records the fact that humanity without
(as the editor charitably says) necessarily intending it, over the
course of the past century, to a degree unprecedented in human
history, has refashioned the earth's air, water and soil along with
the composition of the biosphere on which all life depends. We

have become, he says, a geological force rivalling wind erosion, glaciers, volcanoes and water; we have recast global nitrogen and phosphorus cycles; and through these activities have altered and polluted the earth's crust and atmosphere chemically, biologically and physically.

Is that rational? What kind of rationality are we talking about? Who wins and who loses as a result of its being exercised? Yet that is now the Big Picture, the contemporary landscape in which Noah's descendants have assumed power over the lives and deaths of all living creatures. That is how the implementation of the claim to a rationality imaged on that of God has actually functioned.

So what image of God are we talking about when we equate it with a human rationality that is commonly seen to exclude any kind of emotion or empathy with our non-human fellow creatures? One official reaction to some people's distress at the culling policies in the foot and mouth crisis was to dismiss it as 'irrational/emotional' and therefore suspect or non-tenable. And what image of ourselves does this support or endorse?

Our reason is held to give us a unique status within creation: one which, as in the case of Noah, makes us the focal point of God's relationship with the world. This claim is assumed to isolate us from all other life forms in our being governed, and governing, by reason alone. But what an impoverished view it is of both God and ourselves that empties both of all faculties other than reason! And what a burden we place on that faculty alone! Can it really do all we claim for it?

The hollowness of this claim was surely dismissed once and for all by the image of God recorded in Job 38-42. Exasperated by Job's assumption that he and his affairs are the sole subject of concern to God in the world, God responds by reminding Job of the glorious history of earth and of all the creatures living there for billions of years before we emerged, and of Job's ignorance of them and their history. It is ignorance, not reason, that marks our relationship with them.

> Who is this that darkens counsel by words *without knowledge*?

> Where were you when I laid the foundation of
> the earth?
>
> Tell me, *if you have understanding*?
>
> Have you *comprehended* the expanse of the earth?
> Declare, if you know all this.
>
> Do you *know* the ordinances of the heavens?
>
> Do you *know* when the mountain goats bring forth?
>
> > *(Job 38.2, 4, 18, 33; 39.1 – my emphasis)*

In this comprehensive fashion, God exposes Job's ignorance of
the earth's marvellous evolution into the complex reality of life
and environment that we have tinkered with on an unprecedented
scale. The wise biblical writer goes on to sound a warning about
the theological implications of justifying our conduct on the basis
of a claim to be made in God's image. Are we not doing a massive
injustice to that image when we use it to justify our violence
against other living beings? Are we not, so to speak, shifting the
blame for our violence onto God? God challenges Job:

> Will you even put me in the wrong?
>
> Will you condemn me that you may be justified?
>
> > *(Job 40.8)*

That, I fear, is precisely what the history of our use of this concept
shows us to have done.

Human nature and image of God – Social and biological factors

Chris Sunderland

The narrative of creation in Genesis 1 would suggest that humanity was both created as an integral part of the whole creation and is therefore creature, yet at the same time it speaks of us as made in the image of God, as if special. Much theological and social thought has been focused on defining our specialness, looking for qualitative, all or nothing, distinctions from animal nature. The tendency of this approach has been to define an area such as reason, conscience, religion, moral capacity as if it were itself free-floating and separable from the rest of our humanity. Such abilities are then understood over against a 'lower' animal nature, which is to be repressed or otherwise overcome.[1] Our language reflects this thinking as we use humane as a good word, and brutal, beastly, bestial as bad words.[2] The extraordinary importance of the Fall in Christian theology may also reflect this sort of process.

In secular thought, the twentieth century saw enormous divides over the issue of human nature. Schools of sociology and anthropology arose that decreed, at an almost ideological level, that there was nothing given about human nature. Human society was constructed from a mind that was at birth a *tabula rasa*. Humanity could create any sort of societies that it chose. The anthropologist Ashley Montagu declared confidently, 'Unlike all other animals, man has been freed of all those biological pre-determinants which condition the behavioural responses of other animals to the environment – the instincts.'[3] The sheer variety of human cultures was declared to prove the plasticity of human society. Nothing was given. Any type of society was as likely as any other. Yet hidden beneath the apparent rationality was a fierce commitment that had political repercussions. In part this was evidenced by similar *tabula rasa* doctrines being promulgated by Marxism and existentialism. Even more crucial, however, they were an attempt to distance academic thought from theories of racial superiority. This tended to set up a dichotomy in the academic world. Any branch of study, such as ethology, that studied animal behaviour and made deductions about deep level motivations, talked the language of instinct, and made generalizations into human society, was viewed as highly dubious and potentially fascist. The struggle that resulted from these ideological commitments was an important one at a social and political level, but may have been a block to more subtle and careful understanding of these questions.

The advent of socio-biology twenty-five years ago raised yet further spectres. Popularist accounts of 'selfish genes' caused much misunderstanding. Here was a new 'science' that claimed to offer a truly objective approach to understanding animal and human societies. By referring everything back to the propagation of genes, this new breed of biologists claimed to be able to provide a unique and certain reference point for understanding. Those of a more philosophical outlook were deeply suspicious and pointed to the extraordinary reductionism in the whole approach and the absence of proper discussion about human motivations.[4] Worse still, the new discipline found it very difficult to talk about the social in any other than highly individualist tones. It was dubbed 'biological Thatcherism' for its implicit support of free market ideology.[5]

By contrast, sociology was coming to terms with the fact that its own strong rationalizations were consistently leading it to methods of thinking that could only see collective realities and failed to give adequate consideration to the freedom and creativity of the individual.[6]

The good news is that postmodern criticism has enabled many to expose the ideological undercurrents in our previous approaches to the subject of human nature and allowed us to work with a new humility that genuinely crosses disciplines and builds a more complex and subtle view of our humanity.

For example, in socio-biology, the study of animal behaviours in which an exchange of favours occurs over a period of time has demanded the inclusion of psychological, social and even moral factors into the explanatory frameworks of the discipline. Such 'delayed tit for tat' mechanisms are found to occur in animals that can do basic things like identify and remember the animal that they did a favour for, and also offer effective discipline if the favour is not returned. Matt Ridley has noticed that this sort of behaviour can properly be called a trust and has shown that trusting strategies can be expected to arise in evolution among social animals with adequate psychological and social abilities.[7] He goes on to show that even an attribute of character, like trustworthiness, might naturally come to be valued in an animal community with such trusting strategies. So, from a purely socio-biological standpoint, a moral connection is made. One key characteristic in this socio-biological development is the willingness to begin to explore other levels of description.

So, for example, in complex social animals it is necessary to have some general feel for what is going on in their minds. Animals have deep level motivations of various sorts. For years people have shied away from proper consideration of these for fear of the eugenics that can so easily follow discussions of 'instinct' and simplistic versions of the nature/nurture debate. More interesting commentators, such as Midgely and Hinde, have begun to explore ideas of motivation from the realization that there most certainly will be some patterning of our mental processes. We are not simply free to invent ourselves. Robert Hinde says:

> We must come to terms with an important aspect
> of the relation between genetic constitution and
> experience, namely the existence of predispositions in
> what an individual responds to and in what he or she
> learns, and constraints upon what he or she can learn
> that are not mere limitations of capacity.[8]

So human beings have both a givenness about their minds, which takes its roots from animal nature and deep level motivations, and an enormous creativity of expression that can arise from this givenness. Mary Midgely proposes that all animals, humans included, have within them a complex set of motivations and that the fundamental task of the brain is to explore the integration of these motivations so as to work for fruitful behaviour. In social animals, such integrative processes work outwards in formation of societies that are themselves integrative, continually looking for cooperative systems that make the best use of their potential. While, in the simplest animals, such integration might be solely oriented around the propagation of genes, giving socio-biology its *raison d'être*, in more complex animals there is an ability to develop all sorts of alternative and subsidiary goals. In human beings there also arises the possibility of a more systematic questioning of individual and collective purpose. These are the

'What is it all for?' questions implicit in much moral, political and religious thought.

This approach, then, suggests that human nature is best understood as in a continuum with animal nature, not as something that has wholly separable properties. This means that those aspects of ourselves that we share with animals are not necessarily things to be repressed, or overcome, but that the secret is rather to seek an integration of our lives. The complexity of this task and its ever changing environment demands that there is no one solution that can be found and imposed for all time and every circumstance, but that human society must and should continue to be diverse and exploring. The other reason for this necessary diversity is the uncertainty of our knowledge.

As soon as one accepts that we need to talk the language of human motivation in order to understand people and society, then one must also accept a high degree of uncertainty in our conclusions. To talk about motivation, be it animal or human, is to enter imaginatively into the mind of another and to construct what is essentially a narrative that purports to describe their purposes. Such narratives will be formed in response to the events, proceed by analogy with the motivations of the teller, and betray the teller's deepest commitments and beliefs. I would contend that all the humanities actually have to work with this sort of method when they talk about human purposes. Let me illustrate this process of multi-layered description.

The primatologist Frans de Waal sums up the most basic motivations of a primate by reference to strategies for genetic propagation. He notes how a social animal's motivations may have derived from a struggle between the perceived need to propagate their own genes and the commitment that this will be best achieved through cooperation with others. This tension is resolved by recourse to the power hierarchy. De Waal describes how animals higher in the power hierarchy have the greatest access to the necessities of life and therefore the greatest likelihood of propagation, yet the social order is of some advantage to all. He describes the conundrum as follows:

> The significance that monkeys and apes attach
> to dominance relationships and their jostling for
> positions and connections, mean that group life

> encompasses two conflicting strategies. The first is to probe the social order for weaknesses and look for openings to improve one's standing. In as much as this strategy subverts existing social structures and creates chaos, one might regard it as antisocial. Yet from the viewpoint of the parties knocking down the old walls, there is nothing antisocial about it; for them it is pure progress.
>
> The second strategy is a response to the first: conservation of the status quo. Although very much in the interest of the parties with the best positions, the resulting stability also benefits the young and weak, who are the first to suffer in the case of all-out war within a group. Hence the potential of a pact between top and bottom in which the lower echelons back the reigning powers, provided these guarantee their security.
>
> Society results from the equilibrium between these contradictory strategies . . .[9]

Here is politics from a socio-biological perspective. It is a powerful description working with deep level motivations towards status seeking, but aware that there are other countervailing dispositions such as a feeling for the social order as such. By allowing himself to describe primate behaviour and motivations in relation to this tension, de Waal is able to illustrate an extraordinary range of political strategies in primate colonies. Of course, in any particular case he may be wrong. That is the risk that one must take to follow this course, yet the explanatory pay-off is immense.

At the next level one might describe this tension in sociological and political terms by noticing that human societies generally work with systems of power of some sort and that the most fruitful are those that can somehow hold both ends of a closely related struggle namely

Upholding the social order ⬅━━━━━➤ **Allowing challenge**

Almost any period of human political history can be illuminated by consideration of this particular tension. At an individual level, there are always those who feel the importance of the social order particularly strongly at a deep level. There may be particular parties that form alliances of such people and they are likely to include those who are doing well by the present system. Likewise, there will be those who feel marginalized or unjustly treated and they will make their feelings known in forms of challenge. If a society can only uphold the social order and denies any challenge, it might be described as authoritarian. On the other hand, if challenge occurs to such a degree and in such a way that the social order disintegrates, then anarchy results and the fruits of cooperation are lost. Political orders can be plotted against their abilities to deal with this sort of struggle.

Narratives are important in explanation of social structures but they are also important in their justification, negotiation and change. For example, the Judaeo-Christian Scriptures can be understood as working within this sort of tension. Rex Mason has illustrated how different scriptural narratives set out either to justify the social and religious order or to subvert it.[10] So, for example, many of the priestly writings of the Old Testament implicitly strengthen and celebrate the social order, describe challenge in terms of rebellion against God and insist on a round of rituals and laws that draw the community together and implicitly alienate foreigners. On the other hand, there are also writings, most particularly from the prophetic tradition, that come from the margins of society, that speak up for those who feel alienated or unjustly treated and which call corrupt leadership to account. These voices from the edge also radically question the justifications put forward by those who support the status quo. The fascinating thing about biblical faith in this regard is that it holds these two processes together. Somehow the belief in God over all, the God who is the focus of all human striving, of all goodness, beauty and truth, means that the social order can be upheld in a creative way that allows challenge and change. It suggests that biblical faith might be an extraordinarily fruitful means of holding this most basic human tension. Such a faith might continually grow in understanding both of the nature of God and of what it means to be a good society.[11]

This biblical account also illustrates a general feature of societies, in that narrative of some sort is a frequent and useful means of negotiating political change. Stories of how slaves were treated were particularly important in the movement for abolition of slavery. Stories of children falling asleep in factories or being mangled in machinery were important in humanizing the Industrial Revolution. In today's global society, stories coming from the least 'developed' countries force us to consider the impact of the global market and become the cornerstone for political challenge in world trade talks.[12] The story, brought into the public arena, makes the 'other' real and prompts public discussion. The engagement of narratives, together with processes of reason and analysis that flow from them, make for an inclusive, integrating process in a good society.

These examples illustrate a general thesis about human nature, which has the following features:

- Human beings have within them a number of deep level motivations that give shape and pattern to their lives and the lives of their societies.

- Integration of these motivations is a basic task of each human being and each human society.

- A full understanding of human society requires an enquiry at a number of levels and must involve the use of narrative.

- Negotiation of the narratives that sustain and justify a society depends upon a process of engagement and public conversation.

- Faith in God can act as a focus for this narrative struggle, urging a society on to greater understanding of itself and of the God who is all goodness, truth and beauty.

The particular role of faith can be shown by reference to problems in this process. For example, at an individual level, some people develop addictive behaviour patterns. One way to understand addiction is as a failure of integrative engagement, as one particular deep level motivation in a person comes to dominate their psyche, be it through sex, drugs, money, power or whatever. Several of the character deficiencies mentioned in the Scriptures can be related to similar failures of integration, as one aspect of life becomes destructively dominant. So admiration turns to wilful envy, and want to obsessive greed. In this context the fall into addiction can be understood as the loss of an integrating personal story.[13] Faith can be important in this context in recovering a sense of identity and vision for life within a meaningful world, through a relationship to a personal God and a community of faith.

Similarly, many of the structures of a human society can be understood at one level as systems of trust. Derived from delayed tit for tat processes, all of our politics, commerce, law and moral understanding can be seen to involve processes of trust of some sort. This became all too clear recently as, with the terrorist attacks on America, there was a general loss of confidence. Not only did travel companies all suffer immediate loss of business, but stock markets threatened to dive, money moved to durables such as gold, new surveillance mechanisms were discussed and soothsayers warned that the prospects for global recession were considerably greater. Trust is a fragile but vital commodity for social cooperation. In the Judaeo-Christian story, the belief that the people were in a relationship, or covenant, with God would have specifically given value to virtues of character that promoted trustworthiness. This is reflected in understandings of God as faithful, together with the call to us to follow that example. It relates to core commandments that insist that forms of cheating such as lying and committing adultery are wrong. It results in a vision of God as one in authority that becomes a call to human leaders to demonstrate impartiality and sensitivity towards the weak and outcast.

Such a view of faith should ask hard questions of both society and the Church. What deep level motivations are present, but unacknowledged in the Church today? Why do more people go to church at the rich end of town than at the poor end? How does the way that we believe work out in our Churches' political structures? What happens when our leadership is challenged? Is so-called 'relational working' sometimes a cloak for dominant power relations?

One of the most important aspects of faith in these social and political terms is defined by the questions, 'Who knows God here?' and 'How well do people think they know God?' These questions can be reduced in secular terms to 'Who knows what

is good for us' and 'How certain are they of that knowledge?'
There are several biblical models available, from the dominant
politic of a 'Moses up the mountain' theology through to the
inclusiveness of Jeremiah's 'each shall know God from the least
of them to the greatest.'[14] If any community is to avoid being
dominated by its leadership, then there needs to be some sense
of all having knowledge of God or of good, not just the priests or
leaders. Also, it is necessary for there to be some humility about
how much we know and how certain we are about it. Too certain
theologies or ideologies are not open to the perspective and
challenge of others, fail to be genuinely participatory in their
outworking and lead to dangerous social relations. On the other
hand, without any common vision or search, a society is
in serious danger of losing social cohesion and disintegrating.

In conclusion, with regard to the image of God, I suggest that,
as Karl Barth and Emil Brunner suggested, human beings bear
the image of God in relational terms. I would contend that we
are made to search after a relational knowledge of God, and in
the quality of this relationship is to be measured our closeness to
the nature of God. The stories of the Scriptures reflect the struggles
of the community of faith to understand and discern the divine
nature. The stories of the Scriptures come to a unique focus in
Christ and together they constitute revelation. Yet they are at the
same time an example of the narrative process by which every
community negotiates its life. As such they appeal to all people,
that this faith truly makes sense of our human predicament.
Finally, the faith community needs to acknowledge in all humility
that 'now we see in a mirror dimly'. Only then shall we see face
to face.

Theological reflections on aspects of modern medical science – A point of view in favour

Mary J Seller

Introduction – infertility, an age-old problem

Infertility has long been recognized as a problem. It is recorded in the Old Testament that Sarai, wife of Abram, was barren, as also was Jacob's wife, Rachel. It is made clear that the males involved were fully fertile. Abram lay with Hagar and promptly produced Ishmael, while Jacob had a succession of children, two sons by Bilhah, another two by Zilphar and two more and a daughter by Leah. In the Bible it is always women who are infertile while the men are emphasized as being astonishingly fecund. Abraham as a centenarian produced six sons by his second wife and many more by concubines. Today, in many communities in Africa and Asia, infertility is not tolerated and the female partner is always blamed. If a couple does not produce children, the wife is divorced with no rights and often becomes an outcast of the community. Thus, by long tradition, infertility has been regarded solely as a female problem, and is often associated with stigmatization.

Yet the fact is, when couples fail to have children, in just under half the cases, the fault lies with the man. For more than 60 years, long before *in vitro* fertilization (IVF) was devised, doctors have been able to help couples with male infertility by donor insemination (DI), that is, obtaining sperm from an unrelated male donor and artificially inseminating the female partner. The child is not genetically related to the husband, but the couple is enabled to have a baby. Today, in the UK, more than 1,000 babies are born annually who have been conceived in this way. For so long, little could be done to alleviate female infertility, but then, in 1978, the first IVF baby was born. In this process eggs are surgically removed from the woman and sperm obtained from her husband. These are mixed together in a dish of culture fluid in the laboratory, and fertilization occurs in the warmth of an incubator. Two days later, the early embryos are placed in the uterus of the woman to undertake all of their usual prenatal growth and development over the next nine months. Unlike their infertile male counterparts employing DI, these women are genetically related to their children. Over 6,000 babies are now born each year by this means in the UK, and the demand for such infertility services far exceeds the supply.

Infertility is a pressing problem for many people: it is estimated that as many as one in seven couples experiences involuntary infertility. Yet that fact is often hidden from relatives and friends, and there is still an aura of disgrace in some people's minds. Also, some people are against infertility treatment in principle. They argue that infertility is not a disease and so should not take up scarce medical resources. Others say that the world is already over populated, so it is wrong to take active steps to bring yet more children into the world. Others still say that it must be God's will that a couple is infertile, otherwise they would have been given a child. Biblical stories such as that of Jacob, Rachel and Bilhah show that people have always sought ways around infertility. It certainly does not seem to be God's intention that couples are childless, for it goes against the biblical directive 'Be fruitful and multiply.' And, in those Bible stories, eventually both Sarai and Rachel did have their own children (sons of course).

There is no doubt that infertility can be a source of deep distress to the individuals concerned, engendering considerable dis-ease. The purpose of medicine is to alleviate disease. A daily insulin injection alleviates the symptoms of diabetes although it doesn't cure the disease. In like manner, IVF treatment alleviates infertility but does not cure it. Both treatments render appropriate remedies to circumvent a bodily malfunction and remove the dis-ease. Even in an overpopulated world, most civilized people consider that the needs of society should not take precedence over the needs of individuals. Each person is important and each one's needs should be met as far as possible. But is having a child of one's own a need, or is it simply a desire, a wish or a whim? It is universally recognized that having a child is one of the proper ends of marriage. It is considered a natural desire and it is the normal expectation of marriage. However, there are those who would argue that to have a child is actually a right, and that everyone, regardless, has an absolute right to have a child at all costs. But can this be correct? The child is another human being who has equal rights, parents are trustees for the child and have responsibility to serve the child's interests, and these should not be subordinated to those of anyone else, even those of a parent.

Modern medical science

Infertility is just one field in the burgeoning arena of modern medical science. Genetics is another, and is probably the one where advances are occurring most rapidly, and which people distrust most. Knowledge of the structure of DNA, the identification of genes, and the mapping of the complete human genome are beginning to make gene therapy and other forms of genetic manipulation possible. All this engenders concern and sometimes hostility in many people, provoking some to comment that scientists are 'playing God', or that scientists should not interfere with nature. So should scientists be acting in this way, and are they 'playing God'?

Are we interfering in nature?

The creation myths in Genesis convey our basic Christian belief that God is the creator of all things. They go on to place humans at the pinnacle of the created order, as they have been made 'in God's image'. There are various interpretations of this expression, but being made 'in God's image' often refers to our capacity for intellect, reason and emotions, and for exercising responsibility and relationships – relationships with the one who created us, and with others of our kind, and with the rest of creation. In Genesis there are also apparently divine instructions to us to have dominion over creation and to subdue it, possibly implying that godlike acts of intervention are permissible. However, as theology evolved, the interpretation has veered towards humans being called to have a stewardship role within creation, they are duty bound to care for it.

For a long time, it was believed that nature came as a fixed and complete package. It was assumed that the sun, moon, stars, the earth, animals, birds, insects and so on, all arrived as they were, and that they would all remain so for ever. It was just not understood that the whole of creation is a dynamic interacting system, and that it is for ever on the move and changing: it is evolving. Another aspect that was not readily appreciated for a long while is that humans themselves are extremely creative beings. From the invention of the wheel, right through to the multitude of contemporary examples, such as travelling to the moon and back, humans have shown themselves to be highly inventive, ingenious and original. Many Christians see this as being another facet of being made 'in the image of God' – humans reflect his creativity. Also, many consider that it is through people that God's process of creation continues in the world today. Since the times of primitive people who used fire for warmth and cooking, made knives out of flint, and smelted iron ore to extract the metal to forge tools, humans, in their creativity, have made use of natural things, often changing them in the process. So not only is change inherent in nature, and humans reflect God's creativity, but also humans have always taken natural things and changed them for their use. Thus, modern medical science that engineers nature so that infertile couples can have children, or inserts a gene into sick people with a genetic disease to make them well, would seem to be continuing to act in this manner. It is not interfering in nature, it is simply doing what people have always done in their Godlike image, being inventive and creative, and also doing what is already going on in nature: instituting change.

Are we 'playing God'?

In the New Testament, we see God in Christ in action in the world. He manifested God's love. He urged individuals on towards the perfection that God intended for them personally, and encouraged them as a community to help make God's kingdom come on earth. It is our belief that we are his eyes, his ears and his hands on earth now. We are the ones to carry out God's purposes, and we believe that we are called to cooperate with him in bringing both individuals and the world to good. So, in many respects, we should be acting as God – 'playing God'.

Further, an important aspect of Christ's ministry was healing, and he gave power and authority to his disciples to cure diseases, sending them out into the highways and byways to do so. Thus, healing is an expression of our discipleship, and is another way we are called upon to 'play God'. Christ always healed when he saw a need, and he flouted all convention to do so if compassion decreed: he healed on the Sabbath contrary to the law, he touched an outcast, a Samaritan leper. He often did astonishing things and overt and loud criticism did not stop him from making people whole. Today, many of the new assisted conception and genetic medicine techniques appear astonishing to the ordinary person in the street, but so did heart transplants when they first came in. All of these innovations have evoked disapproval. But, these new techniques are an aspect of the healing ministry we are all called upon to exercise at this juncture in our history and evolution. God's creativity through scientists is unbounded.

The supremacy of God and rules for Christian conduct

Knowledge is power, and all the knowledge that scientists now have obviously puts us in a very powerful position. However, although God has given us potent capacities for intellect and creativity, he reigns supreme, and we are always subordinate to him. This is the constraint that prevents us from abusing our powers. Implicit in being made 'in God's image' is humility and the need to be led by the Spirit, for we are always answerable to him. He gave us freedom but, although we are free to enquire and create, we do not have absolute freedom because we ourselves are created and sustained by him and, at our end, we will meet him face to face, and that encounter will go on for eternity. So, all that we do in this life must conform to the will of God. The will of God is most clearly discerned in the life of Christ. He loved everyone without exception, and he valued every single person whatever his or her state. So, when thinking of applying any of these new therapies to a patient, we should do so only if they enable us to act in love and care for that person, and also to respect his or her worth and dignity. These 'rules' should dictate the correct use of our knowledge and prevent its misuse or abuse. As an example, the application of gene therapy is proposed to treat serious genetic diseases for which there is no other cure. Gene therapy may involve some risk, but so do many modern forms of therapy such as cytotoxic drugs in cancer. Having responsibly weighed up the risk and found in favour of gene therapy, it can fairly be said that this offers hope for a cure where otherwise there is none. It thus enables us to care better for, and to show love to, the sufferers. If there is a cure, then it enhances people's dignity to be free from their disease. That is not to imply that sick people are lacking dignity but, without disease, they have more freedom to enjoy being human.

Uses and abuses of science

History is replete with examples of the abuse of our scientific knowledge, and it is this that heightens people's fear of contemporary science. The new reproductive technologies are already not completely innocent (although not all would agree). The use of these methods to allow women over 60 years of age to have a child would seem to be an abuse because it is not acting in love towards the child who is born. The child will be loved, for sure, but will be different from his or her peers, in the family setting, and in having an aged mother who might well die before she or he reaches maturity. Similarly, employing them in some surrogacy arrangements can be open to abuse and lead to problems for the child.

Cloning

Perhaps the clearest example of abuse of our new knowledge would be if the technology that produced Dolly the Sheep were applied to humans and a human being were cloned (reproductive cloning). Cloning means making a new individual with exactly the same genetic complement as an existing individual. Mistakenly, people assume this means that an identical copy of that person will be produced, and some have already expressed a wish to use this technique to replace a dearly loved dying child or other relative. The process involves taking a human egg, removing its nucleus and replacing it with the nucleus of a cell from the desired person, then stimulating this fabricated cell into division to produce an embryo that would be placed into the uterus of a woman for nurture to term. The prospect of cloning humans is abhorrent to most people. Nowhere does this adhere to the rules for Christian conduct. It is clearly not acting in love towards the children being made, for it is manipulating them as if they were objects. If a person is wanted as a replica of another, then the worth and dignity of the 'manufactured' individual are not being respected. Each person should be loved and respected for what she or he is. However, not only is cloning morally wrong, but also the concept that it will produce an identical person to the donor of the nucleus is basically flawed. It is well known that, while naturally occurring identical twins may well be very similar, they are two distinct individuals who may actually be very different people. Having the same genes does not guarantee the same person, for we are the product not only of our genes, but also of our environment. Influences enter from external sources both before birth, *in utero*, and throughout our postnatal life. We are definitely more than the sum of our genes. Christianity, too, is emphatically non reductionist in regarding the mystery of human identity as relational, intellectual, cultural and spiritual. By being made 'in the image of God' a uniqueness is conferred upon us through our personal relationship with God that is continuous throughout our lives.

A distinction between 'natural' and 'unnatural'

As time has passed, medical research, like everything else, has moved on, and assisted conception techniques have been further developed and extended. One advance is called ICSI, which enables infertile males to have children who are genetically their own. Most men are infertile because they cannot produce enough motile sperm. If even only one sperm can be obtained from them (and often it is aspirated direct from the testis) it can be injected directly into the wife's egg in the laboratory (IntraCytoplasmic Sperm Injection) so effecting fertilization and starting the process of embryonic development. The embryo is subsequently transferred to the mother's uterus as in IVF. This process enables us to act with caring love towards the infertile couple, and their baby so produced, and respect the worth and dignity of all three. Although ICSI may appear technically to be very similar to cloning, it is, in fact, very different. ICSI and all the other assisted conception methods simply involve, to a greater or a lesser extent, technical assistance, lending a hand where nature fails. Cloning, by contrast, involves completely unnatural steps, namely, the introduction into the egg of a mature, established nucleus, of a known and pre-selected genotype. This is totally removed from the situation in normal conception, and all the existing assisted conception techniques in which the embryo acquires its nucleus from the random and unselected fusion of a nucleus from its mother and one from its father. This ensures the arbitrary admixture of genes from one generation to the next, an essential biological mechanism, and creates a completely new and unique combination of genes that will never be repeated. The 'unnaturalness' of cloning is cited by some as another reason for judging cloning to be ethically unsound. However, the limits to this reasoning are difficult to define for, in IVF, conception occurs in an 'unnatural' place – in a dish in a laboratory. While a very small minority cite this as the reason for their being against IVF, most do not find this unnaturalness a stumbling block and, of course, much of medicine is 'unnatural'.

Healing, wholeness and being remade in the image of God

From the Gospel accounts, it would appear that Christ always healed whenever he encountered a person in need. He never ignored a deformed and twisted body or passed by a mentally disturbed person without treating them. Thus, God's will seems to be for healing of the body as well as the spirit. Unfortunately, medical science cannot yet restore every twisted body or all damaged minds to normality. But, step by step, progress is made, and the new genetics and the assisted conception techniques are among the new possibilities for particular diseases. As mentioned, since time immemorial, infertility has been a blight on the lives of some women, even if the fault actually lay with their husbands, and it has been yet another reason to oppress women. Today, at last, we are able to help them: the joy of such women after IVF treatment when they are finally able to hold their own baby in their arms is immeasurable. They are transformed as people, which is what is hoped for in any person who is cured of a disease. This property can certainly be construed in terms of being remade in the 'image of God'. For being made 'in the image of God' implies a wholeness. Being infertile does not mean that a woman is improperly or incompletely made in God's image. But, if a woman suffers stigmatization and oppression, some of that image is defaced because there is a breakdown of relationships. And, even if there is no oppression, as is usually the case in these islands today, infertile women often say that they feel less than whole, which suggests a breakdown of relationship within themselves so, again, the image has become disfigured. Assisted conception technology enables the image to be remade and restored. Similarly, having a severe genetic disease, or any illness, is costly in terms of energy and resolve. Our understanding is that being made 'in God's image' is not simply a one-off event. We, as people, like everything else in God's created order, are constantly on the move, and God through Christ is continually sustaining and recreating us. But the onus is on us, for we are required actively to participate in the remaking process in order for it to be fruitful. We have more reserves to fuel our attempts to do this if we are not preoccupied and having our reserves depleted by trying to overcome an illness. So, in this respect too, modern forms of genetic therapy can be considered to contribute to remaking people in God's image.

Consequentialist versus deontological reasoning

In ethical reasoning, there are two major approaches:
consequentialist and deontological. Most of this paper has been
consequentialist, that is, justifying actions by examining the ends
or the consequences. It is good for an infertile couple to have a
child, so IVF is justified. Gene therapy is a good thing because
it cures genetic disease and relieves pain and suffering. This
system takes account of harmful consequences, but a particular
technique or way of acting is regarded as morally acceptable
if its consequences are beneficial and outweigh any harmful
consequences that might arise. This is, basically, how medicine
and medical science always operate.

Deontological theory is governed by absolute imperatives and
inherent rules for living. It says that there are powers reserved to
the individual just by being, such that they may not be interfered
with or taken away. They have rights, and these are correlated
with duties, an acknowledgement of what ought to be done and
of what we are bound to do. It says that people have an intrinsic
moral worth that prevents them from being used merely as means
to an end. In this paper, that type of reasoning has been invoked
solely in the case of human reproductive cloning.

Consequentialists continually ask questions to test possibilities –
what is likely to happen? Can human ingenuity devise ways of
preventing disease without undesirable consequences? What
will be the extent of the risk and the good be? The relative risks
and benefits are weighed up and a balance sheet produced.
That is the way medical scientists work. Deontologists are just
not open to such ways of working or of following lines of enquiry.
They never base their case on probabilities or even certainties.
Consequences of actions are not for them, they are concerned
solely with the action itself. Is it intrinsically good? In most of the
new genetic and reproductive technologies, they believe that the
action is wrong, and that it is intrinsically flawed because it is
contrary to the essential nature of the persons involved. There
is no weighing things up, they know it is inherently wrong.

There is an aspect of IVF that so far has not been mentioned, but
which some would consider should be included. It resides firmly
within the deontological perspective. In order to develop IVF, and
also in most treatment programmes, many embryos have been,

and are, created which are subsequently not used and so discarded and allowed to die. Whether this is an issue, and how important it is, depends on one's view of the status of the early human embryo. The critical question is: when is personhood acquired? Is the embryo a human being immediately, from conception, or does it become one at some time later in its development? If the former, then the embryo, simply by existing, has the right to life. If it is killed, the act is of the same gravity as killing a baby or an adult person. On this view, IVF should never have been developed, and it should not be performed. If, on the other hand, personhood is acquired sometime later on, during development, then killing an embryo is not equivalent to killing a person. IVF is thus probably permissible. The notion that personhood is not immediately endowed but acquired later on is consistent with the concept that 'the image of God' relates to such aspects as rationality, emotions and relationships. For these capacities are founded upon certain bodily structures, notably the central nervous system. An early embryo does not have these, for a certain degree of development has to have taken place for even a rudimentary central nervous system to exist. However, with respect to this view, there always remains the unanswered and unanswerable question, which is: exactly when is it in prenatal development that personhood is achieved?

Conclusion

This paper has been written from a particular perspective, that of one who welcomes advances in medicine and science. Someone else might write in a completely different and opposite vein. For myself, I take great delight in the natural world, and I feel so privileged to be a scientist, because I believe this enables me to discover a few of the mysteries already known by God, and to obtain unique glimpses into the majesty and might of God the creator.

Human individuality and inclusive community: Concepts of self, vocation and imago Dei

Donald Macaskill

Over the last few decades there has been much talk about the importance of the human individual over and against society. From the moment Margaret Thatcher uttered the words that 'there is no such thing as society' in her Sermon on the Mound to the New Labour obsession with all things 'community', the concepts of self, identity, individuality, relationship and community have been much debated.

To be created in the image of God is somehow to be made a unique individual, specially and specifically created, and yet, according to traditional theology, to be created for community and for relationship to others. How is this tension held in place? Indeed, is there a tension?

A number of papers in this collection have also served to highlight the way in which people who have been 'different', whether through physical disability, intellectual disability, gender or sexuality, have at points in history been excluded from being treated as made in God's image. This paper will argue that it is intrinsic to the human self made in God's image that we are related to those who are different from us and that inclusive community, far from being an optional extra, is an imperative for humanness, that such community is within our vocation to be human made in God's image.

We begin, however, by examining the way in which the concepts of self relate to human identity and individuality.

The human self

Phrases such as self-actualization, self-fulfilment, self-realization and self-denial are often used within the modern context, both positively and negatively. Their use, often interchangeably, hides the considerable variance among psychological and theological thinkers as to the precise nature of the self and what it consists of. Yet, for any theology of *imago Dei*, understanding what the self is and how it relates to personhood and identity is extremely important.

What makes me who I am? What is it that gives me my personal identity?

There are many approaches to understanding the human self, among them biological, cognitive experimentalist, experiential, social constructionist and psychodynamic perspectives. Undoubtedly, however, the field has been dominated by the work of developmental psychologists.

For many writers within a theological context, the most appropriate definition and working understanding of the self as it relates to identity remains that found substantially within the work of Gustav Jung. As with all major depth psychologists, Jung suggests that we all exist in two worlds: the outer world of function and doing and an inner existence of being. Life, particularly in its earlier stages, is an attempt to reconcile one to the other. Intrinsic to that process is the establishing of a sense of identity in relation both to the inner self and the outer world.

For Jung the self was very important, although there seems to be an inconsistency in his use of the word in his work. He uses it on the one hand to mean the whole personality, the unconscious as well as the conscious, but on the other hand he also uses it to denote that inner centre of the personality. In our dealings in the outer world, Jung argues that we all possess a persona, the 'mask', which is usually worn when carrying out different roles and their attendant functions in our outer world. Another key Jungian concept for human identity is that of individuation, the process that moves us towards becoming a whole person.

In addition to Jung there are numerous other writers who have developed their own models and emphases on the self and of the human person. More recently, however, while not completely rejecting the insights of developmentalists, there has arisen a general critique of developmental psychology both from a theological and psychological perspective. Two main features of this have been an increased awareness of narcissism[1] and the emergence of what has been described as the 'postmodern' self.

'The Threatened Swan' (Jan Asselijn, Rijksmuseum, Amsterdam –
Symbolizing the wild bird and the Holy Spirit)

'Il Volto Santo' (unknown eleventh-century artist, Lucca Cathedral, Italy –
Between suffering and hope)

Postmodern self

The term 'postmodern self' is used to describe the predicament of
the human self in relation to the suspicions of postmodernism. While
there is a continuing debate about the nature of modernity and,
indeed, postmodernity, there is evidence that the rational optimism,
security and relative constancy of the modern era has passed and
it is argued that the optimism of much of psychoanalytic theory
and developmental models of the self are no longer wholly valid.

There is, in addition, an increased awareness that much of
humanistic psychology has been essentially individualist in nature,
ignoring the insights of collective cultures. Alongside this the
modern emphasis on the self almost to the point of narcissism,
and an overtly optimistic view of the self, have been sharply
criticized, particularly from a religious perspective. A hermeneutic
of suspicion has thus replaced the basic optimism of the modern
self. The self, it is argued, is depleted, fragmented and marginalized;
it has variously been described as 'empty' and 'saturated'. Kenneth
Gergen has argued that the self has become saturated, resulting
in the demise of personal definition, the sense of authenticity,
sincerity, belief in leadership, depth of feeling, and faith in
progress.[2] An open slate now exists for people to write and
scribe their identities on.

Gergen and others, in response to such a context, argue for a
greater sense of the relational. He suggests that, while culture may
be becoming postmodern, the individual still lives his or her life as
essentially an individual, a modern, romantic and optimistic self,
unrelated to others for their sense of being and identity. In this he
and others are accepting and linking with the insights of social
psychologists who have argued that the self has to be perceived
of in relational terms as is evident in many non-Western cultures.

Without wishing to ignore or dismiss the insights of developmental
psychology or to accept wholly the critique of postmodernism,
this present paper would suggest that there is a potentially creative
relationship between Christian theology and a postmodern
understanding of the self. In particular the emphasis on the
relational, the insights of dialectical psychology and the growth
of a rigorous suspicion may prove profitable in understanding the
crisis facing human identity, especially in relation to *imago Dei*.
Arguably much theological writing in relation to the *imago* has been
based on a traditionalist psychological and philosophical debate.

Two recent writers who have begun to develop work on the human self and personal identity in this regard are Moseley and Thiselton.

Moseley has sought to move away from too strong a dependence on developmental psychological models of the self and to utilize the insights of dialectical psychology and a theology of kenosis to understand the human self. Arguing against James Fowler in particular, but also many of the other major developmental approaches, he suggests that they are essentially optimistic and lacking in what he terms 'paradox'.[3] He believes that multidimensionality and plurality of reality are intrinsic to an understanding of the self in the present context. The transformation of the self is a response to multiple arenas of conflict and ambiguity. Dialectical psychology advocates a continuing dialogue with the world – a questioning and reinterpreting of the multidimensionality of reality. It is concerned with social dialectics – the changing relationship between a changing self and a changing world. Dialectical psychology may be considered as a hermeneutic of suspicion in questioning the perceptions of tranquillity and balance in human development.

He suggests that 'dialectical psychology, operating out of an appreciation of the elusive, contrary, and paradoxical contours of human existence, complements metaphorical theology in interpreting the changing relationship between a changing self and a changing world.'

Adopting a broadly ecological, interdisciplinary lifespan approach to human development, dialectical psychologists seek to expand the concept of development 'beyond its strictly biological (organismic) roots as a process of adaptation to the environment, and to emphasize constant change over adaptation'. There is no sense of linear continuousness in this development, which is open-ended and unstructured.

Moseley warns against too simplistic an understanding of individuation and integration evident in many human developmental models, and in some writing on the development of the self. Essentially for Moseley the process of becoming a self, of becoming a person, is achieved through the mutual exchange of self with an other in a conflicting set of contexts. He writes: 'becoming a self before God means becoming free to love God

and to help others and ourselves love God as neighbour. For
the Christian this means living contemporaneously with Christ.'

Anthony Thiselton has also attempted to relate and compare
modern and postmodern understandings of the self to
Christian theology.

Thiselton argues for a deeper understanding of the self and its
destiny. He draws on a Trinitarian theology of promise to trace
how 'love without strings' can replace manipulation and
reconstitute the self. In many regards his approach is similar
to that of Moseley, emphasizing that personhood arises from
a dialectic of self-identity and in relation to the 'other'. Yet he
is critical of the de-centred nature of the postmodern self:

> It no longer regards itself as active agent carving
> out any possibility with the aid of natural or social
> sciences, but as an opaque product of variable roles
> and performances which have been imposed upon it
> by the constraints of society and by its own inner
> drives or conflicts.[4]

The stress on the fulfilment of roles as a mark of identity is
criticized by Thiselton for, whilst he recognizes that roles are
intrinsic to identity, they do not wholly constitute that identity.
Response to external agencies must not solely create identity.
What has resulted in the postmodern context is despair, conflict
and manipulation because roles have altered so dramatically
and have become marginal to life.

The autonomous self of modernity and the de-centred, self-
interpretation of postmodernity both offer an inadequate
understanding of human personhood.[5] There is a need for a
theology of hope or promise for the postmodern self, a theology
that Thiselton bases on an essentially social trinitarian model
of God and human personhood. He argues for the need of a
hermeneutic of selfhood that locates self-identity within the larger
story of God's dealings with the world but which recognizes that
that story is constantly and continually changing.

A renewed understanding of the social Trinity lies at the heart of
Thiselton's hermeneutic of the postmodern self. The self, as for
Moltmann, Gunton, Zizioulas and Boff, and personhood are

profoundly relational: personhood, unlike mere individuality, is 'true personhood' not in solitariness but only in relation to other persons. 'This is instantiated not only in the personhood of God as Trinity, but also in the need for mutual respect, each for the other as other in society.'[6]

This paper seeks to advance and adopt Thiselton's conception of a relational postmodern self as being the most appropriate practical and theological model of the self in relation to the *imago Dei*. Such an articulation of the self is reflected throughout much recent theology and philosophy, most notably in the work of Alistair McFadyen.[7]

In his work, McFadyen seeks to reject both individualism and collectivism and emphasizes the person as 'dialogical' (formed through social interaction, through address and response) and dialectical (never coming to rest in a final unity). Yet he is also wary of too simplistic an understanding of the nature of the self in relation:

> In dialogue the partners are simultaneously
> independent (otherwise the listening and speaking
> of both would be unnecessary) and inseparably
> bound together in the search for a mutuality
> of understanding. The basis of a dialogical
> understanding of personhood is that we are
> what we are in ourselves only through relation to
> others . . . So they are centered beings but they are
> so only through their intrinsic relation to others.[8]

Human relations at a personal level take their form from the relations in the Trinity. Persons are 'ex-centric', they acquire their own identity through becoming centred outside themselves and on others.[9] McFadyen underlines the importance of personal identity being formed in relation.

Humanity is formed by the nature of its response to God's call. Dialogue is essential to relationship based upon the mutual recognition of the partners' unique identities. McFadyen's work, therefore, provides a further grounding for the postmodern self in relation to others. It is not alone in centring personhood in an understanding of the social relations of the Trinity[10] and in social relations in general.[11] The nature of both these relationships is therefore important. Personhood is something both given and formed. It is expressive of the potential in each human being, in each self.[12]

Relationship

Relationship is, therefore, intrinsic to what it means to be a person, to the nature of self, and to individual identity. While the postmodern reality is that the self has become essentially privatized and individualized, the real self emerges only in relation, in particular, in relation to God. To be a person is to be in relationship in totality. Such an emphasis on relationship is potentially very helpful in affirming the value of each individual and in celebrating difference. It offers an essentially cooperative model of the self,[13] yet a relationship emphasizing the partiality of what is related and the need for even greater involvement with another to enable a deepening of individual humanness.

It is through relationships that we learn that we need one another in order to be ourselves. The Christian community is a community of persons actively committed to being related one to the other. There is nothing new in such an analysis. Macmurray called for an end to traditional philosophical individualism and suggested that the 'pure individual self was a fiction' because the self is irreducibly relational.[14] It cannot be conceived as self-contained because of the relational dynamic of Christian vocation and divine creation. Humanity is created inescapably personal, and is enabled in this by a dynamic of love and *koinonia.*

It is perhaps a truism to state that knowledge of self is inextricably bound up with knowledge of God and relationship to others in community. This paper would argue that self-denial and self-affirmation are not opposites but are necessary partners in tension in a relationship within the self. The Christian self is called into being not by denial or narcissism but by being related to others.

Salvation cannot be equated with self-actualization or self-expression. Being true to oneself, in Christian perspective, means to be true to the self one is called to be. Our appeal is not that people be reconciled to themselves, rather, 'We beseech you on behalf of Christ, be reconciled to God.'[15]

One has to be conformed to Christ, a transformation that both grants and safeguards the unique identity of each human person. There is no means by which a person can avoid communication and relationship to another.[16] Identity, in the theological sense, is both individual and corporate.[17]

In an essay that considers how the Christian body can be identified and which appeals for a re-evaluation of the image 'the body of Christ' in a less metaphorical way, Oppenheimer writes of the notion of embodiment and the importance of the concept of 'incorporation'. She wants the Church to leave behind Descartes' notion that a spirit is tacked on to a body, suggesting that Gilbert Ryle, Macmurray and Strawson have restored the notion of corporeal agency. She both emphasizes the particularity of the individual in light of the incarnational presence of God and the corporateness of Christian personality and identity:

> One human being has a unique consecration to carry the presence of God. The concept of incarnation is at the centre of sacramental understanding . . . The upshot is that God's people are identifiable, not by their pronouncements but by their corporateness. Their identity is theological not political . . . they have the greater but hopeful responsibility of being the presence, the findability, of God upon earth . . . It is their belonging to him that makes them Christians and gives them identity.[18]

Such relational identity is closely linked to what we have noted above about the relational dimensions of the Trinity. It provides a concept of being in relation that accepts that identity comes from the other but also recognizes that a relationship is not just the sum of two people coming together. Mature identity enables us to develop an open relational style; it is a process of self-in-communion, which is reflective of the divine nature, where Three Persons relate to one another.

Vocation and *imago Dei*

Human vocation is rooted in the call of God. Vocation is firstly addressed to humanity. We become who we are in response to the call of God to personhood. This is our primary vocation. It is a call to being rather than doing. It is a call to self rather than role. Throughout life we become who we are in response to others, in community with others.[19] We thus grow into a state of becoming the *imago Dei*. Nichol highlights the dynamic relationship that exists between the vocation of God and the human vocation thus:

God's call, then, as the call to freedom mediated
through Christ, is that which establishes us in our
vocation to be human and in our adventure toward
humanness. It is a call to become who we are, to lay
hold of our identity not by excluding others or at the
expense of others, but in the mutual recognition and
acceptance of them in a community in which one is
set free from oneself to be with and for others both
with respect to their otherness and . . . in the things
which we share in common.[20]

There is tremendous importance in acquiring a healthy sense
of vocation because vocation is intrinsic to personal and faith
identity. In this regard James Fowler has been influential in linking
vocation to a model of human identity. He defines vocation as 'the
response a person makes with his or her total self to the address
of God and to the calling to partnership'.[21] Arguing that this means
the 'orchestration' of the whole of our life to God, Fowler suggests
that the term vocation is more healthy than either the concepts
of 'destiny' or 'self-actualization'.[22] It is a vocation that calls an
individual to personhood in relationship.[23]

The stress on the individual particularity of God's vocation to each
individual therefore places tremendous emphasis on each person.
It is in itself a celebration of difference and anything that limits
that celebration and acceptance is a denial of the call of God.
The individual's response to the vocation of God is unique and
irreplaceable. There is an intimate relationship between fulfilling
one's vocation and acquiring identity. This is not solely by
performing roles but by being in relationship with others:[24]

Vocation is a calling to the discovery of identity in
community . . . One's Christian calling is therefore
essentially an ek-klesis, a calling away or a calling
out of our isolated individualism and unrelatedness
into the common solidarity of 'having nothing' yet
'possessing everything' in the rediscovery and
acceptance of each other.[25]

This is not a matter of self-justification, however. Identity is not
discovered through being called into a closed community, but
rather through participating in *koinonia*, a community that values

difference and diversity, a society where such differences are celebrated and affirmed, where all are included. It is a maturing Christian vocation. The Spirit moves us towards wholeness and completion; a process which is enabled by its opening the horizons of the individual so that those who count as neighbour 'include the whole commonwealth of being, where concern for others is not limited by their mutual concern for us'.[26] There is a recognition that vocation takes place within a fallen dimension and needs to be understood as a move from a theology of creation to a theology of grace and redemption. It is an active dynamic, particular of time and place yet demanding considerable interpretation, it is about discovering the nature of personal identity and combines both being and response.

Therefore, vocation is more than the delegation of particular roles and functions to individuals, it is inextricably linked with the dynamic of call and response that is at the heart of becoming Christian and becoming human. Vocation is intrinsic to *imago Dei*. Nevertheless, such vocation 'is always a call to action' broadly understood. All activity therefore is spent in engaging in this work of God:[27]

> that men and women have a vocation to share in the
> *opus Dei*, to mirror the work of the Creator in their
> own work by establishing human relationships and
> in creating human community in response to God's
> affirmation of human life. It is within the framework
> of this common calling that our daily occupation is
> set, so that whatever our occupational situation may
> be, it can never constitute a neutral sphere from which
> God's call is excluded.[28]

To conclude, this paper has argued for a more relational and dialectical understanding of the human self rooted in a theology of vocation. In so doing it unashamedly has advanced a Trinitarian conception of the divine. It is only when people see themselves as unrelated, constricted individuals that the apartheid systems of our world take root. It is only when women and men celebrate and recognize their inter-connectedness and inter-being that inclusion really happens. In that sense there is the need to rediscover a truly inclusive human community as the basis for the Christian witness to *imago Dei* today.

Section Six –
The Church 'Between Suffering and Hope'

Created in the image – The suffering, broken Body of Christ, the Church

Mary Grey

There is a famous image of the crucified Christ from Italy known as *Il Volto Santo* (from Lucca Cathedral, and exhibited as part of the exhibition *Seeing Salvation*, the National Gallery), an image influential in the development of other images of Christ. Christ is clearly suffering, yet not crushed. He has willingly embraced world sorrow, human sorrow and the pain of creation and yet all hope is not banished. Resurrection has not been ruled out. *Between suffering and hope* – this sums up one of the ways the Church's life is lived out as the suffering, broken Body of Christ, the social and corporeal expression of *imago Dei.*

Let me retrace my steps to our founding belief that human beings, women and men, are created in the image of God – body, mind, heart and spirit. Did we lose the image through sin and the Fall? asked Western theology, replying in the affirmative. Or did we, as the Orthodox Church believes, retain the image with the invitation to become the *likeness* of God through virtue, through Christian sacramental life and practice? I hold these tensions together as I develop my narrative.

Let us go a stage further. Created in the image of which God? 'We will create humankind in our own image', says the biblical text (Genesis 1.26-7). A plural God, *elohim*, creates the human being – plurality at the heart of the Godhead. Thus does a relational God call forth a human being in relationship. The fundamental insight here is of a creator God who creates out of a yearning for relation, the God whose fundamental creative energy is not primarily the speaking word but the relation from which this Word is bodied forth:[1]

> For in the beginning is the relation, and in the relation is the power which creates the world, through us, and with us, and by us, you and I, you and we, and none of us alone.[2]

Martin Buber, in his inspirational 'In the beginning is the relation', meant to restore mutuality to the spoken word, the communication situation, and not to diminish the creative significance of the spoken word or *logos*.[3] God's yearning for relation cannot be separated from God's passion for right relation nor from God's passion for justice. Justice is the very heartbeat of God. This creating, relational God is the Trinitarian God of faith, a God of communion, movement, dynamism. In both Eastern and Western traditions, the dynamic movement of the Trinitarian God is the prototype of human relationality *and also, at the same time,* of distinctiveness, differentiation and diversity.

Thus, created as *imago Dei*, the anthropology of the human person is based on this iconicity of the divine, and increasingly we begin to understand the person in relationship as being an ecological self, in relationship with the environment and with the earth as filled with divine presence.[4] Not only that, but the Trinity has become understood in relation to society. *God is our social programme,* as the Russian theologian Fedorov cried.[5] The inspiration of Trinity as inspiring politics and social justice has become increasingly significant for liberation theologians like Leonardo Boff, and the Brazilian ecofeminist, Ivone Gebara.[6]

So this passionate God-in-movement and relationship became flesh in Jesus of Nazareth. I suggest that we move away from any lurking shred of Platonic theory of image here. Yes, Jesus is the image of the living God; no pale shadow (as in Plato's cave), but, as flesh-and-blood embodiment of a relational God, the pattern and practices of his relating are significant for messianic community.

Christ, therefore, as embodiment of this divine *relational* power that drives to justice, is both *relational* Christ and *ecological* Christ, the lived embodiment of the pattern that connects all webs of interdependencies throughout creation. As the historical Jesus of Nazareth he lived as the embodiment of the making of just relationship in community. He lived out the Christic pattern, which is also a divine pattern – in such a way as to make it possible for prophetic, messianic communities who follow him right through the ages also to embody this pattern – and flesh it out in new ways. (I want to use *patterning* as a more dynamic word than *imaging*, which has a certain static sense). The Christic pattern can be embodied by women and men alike – by children too – and can extend to all creation in a cosmic dimension. In this sense I want to move on from an oversimplistic gendering of *imago Christi*, especially as it rumbles on in the ordination controversy in some of our Churches. I do not address here the issues of tradition and discipline, integral to the way that certain decisions have been taken, but consider that the representation question has been wrongly narrowed down to the gender question, instead of to the quality of relational representation and faithfulness of the whole community responsibility of becoming image-of-the-image.

The significance of Jesus of Nazareth as *imago Dei* in his earthly history was embodied in the proclamation and preaching of the kingdom, the call to discipleship, the radicality of his eating practices – with prostitutes and sinners – and his healing of broken and fragmented people. (Healing is used in the sense of spiritual and psychological maturity – as it was used in the discussions of this Colloquium.) This is the core of Christic patterning. So, if *Die Sache Jesu geht weiter*[7] (the Christic project moves on), this is how the relational pattern continues to be historicized. This is the heart of seeing the following of Jesus as the corporate Body of Christ. Wherever there is following of Jesus – bodily, communitarian, practices of healing, compassionate love of neighbour, the patterning (= imaging) of the Christic Body moves through history in new contexts, facing new challenges.

Thus, Christ as *imago Dei* is also *living dynamic presence –* in surprising ways: in the *passion for justice and right relation* discovered in marginal communities of women and men, in movements for peace and justice – even beyond Christianity; the Christic Body is dynamically present, too, in the search for and embodiment of wisdom, the way the Christic pattern inspires, encourages, empowers us to burst out of tired structures that paralyse our institutions. Seeking the Trinitarian trace, Christ is also Spirit-Sophia/Wisdom in the new embodied and passionate knowing that calls ceaselessly to form and re-form relations and make new and healing connections. Thus the energy and courage of Christo-praxis is the new ethical basis created for numerous liberation communities that privilege the poor and the most vulnerable. Thus Christ does not function as the Lord of history in a dominating sense: rather, the cosmic Christ is the divine energy and vitality to make just relation, a unique patterning and embodying of Trinitarian creativity.

This sounds ideal and needs to be earthed in a more practical way in the context of how we understand Church as the drawing together of each of us, in all our diversity, created in the image, within a social vision of *imago Dei*. But there is a prior theological obstacle. I have related the human being as *imago Dei* to Christ as image of the Trinitarian divine image. It is not clear how the Holy Spirit fits into such a Christological patterning. As you are all aware, in the West we are not proud of our neglect of the Holy Spirit and largely Christocentric focus, which has acquired ideological dimensions. (Of course there have been charismatic and prophetic movements of the Spirit on the edges of mainstream developments.) But many well-meaning attempts to restore a full-blown understanding of the Spirit are deficient either in Trinitarian understanding or because they reduce the Spirit to a function of Christ, as *the bridge*, the mediator, between God and the world.[8] As Rowan Williams argues, to do so is to miss the point of the intimate connection of spirit and the authentic spirituality of the gathered people.[9] The grammar of the spirit is the grammar of spirituality in the fullest sense of the word. I now briefly explore the meaning of spirit in this sense.

Excursus: The Holy Spirit, breath of the Body

I use *spirit* in the widened sense, in the way Moltmann does, as 'the power of life and space for living', and as splicing a way through the false dichotomies, *God – or freedom? God – or world?*[10] Spirit is understood as vitality, as energy, as the great awakener of the Body to widened visions of truth. (See the theologians of the Chartres School.) I wrote earlier of the Spirit's power to discover cracks in culture to give birth to alternative cultural expressions, as appealing to the disenchanted, as well as to the disenfranchised.[11] If the Spirit is associated with bringing to birth ('Fill the earth, bring it to birth', as the old hymn put it), then the imagery of the cosmic egg is timely. The Spirit is watchful for the moment where the cracks in the discourses of violence appear, where humanity at last admits vulnerability in having no answers, and commits itself at last *to a different kind of listening*. The very cracks that postmodernism creates admit a new vulnerability to the Spirit's power.

The basic biblical concept is of the Spirit, the breath of Life, the Spirit of creativity since the dawn of creation. From those few words at the beginning of the Bible:

A mighty wind that swept over the surface of the
waters (Genesis 1.2 NEB)

we are given the sense of elemental, creative, formless energy, the
energy of connection breathing life into all creatures, emerging
from chaos, from formless void. The sense that the Spirit is the
energy of connection, communion, links God's spirit/human spirit
in a rich way, a way important for our understanding of spirit as
breath of the social body we call Church. But the breath of the
Body is not something *separate* from Christic presence, from
Trinitarian presence. The late John V. Taylor saw the Spirit as the
spirit of mutuality (in my terms, relation and connection), the life
force drawing people together.[12] Taylor calls these experiences
annunciations. I call them *epiphanies* of the Spirit whose field
force, the field force of mutuality, is wider than all established
religions.

The Spirit as mutuality, drawing us into relationships of just
relation, is a key directional impulse today, where our problems
cluster around broken relation, trivial relation, the cheapening
of sexual relation by the absence of commitment. Feminist
theologian, Nancy M. Victorin Vangerud, in her book *The Raging
Hearth*, has developed a theology of spirit as 'mutual recognition,
transforming political, church and household monotheism'.[13] The
key to this mutuality, mutual recognition, is no cosy 'I–Thou' of
commercial romanticism, but *a qualitatively different patterning
of social relations.*

This links with the ancient meaning of the Spirit as the *depth
dimension of God.* The Spirit as depth challenges a culture that
lives to superficiality, to boundless consumerism, to virtual reality
instead of embodied relationships. When the WTO protesters – at
Genoa, Davos, Seattle, know they want an alternative world, but
as yet cannot articulate its content, it is the Spirit who keeps open
the questioning and searching, pushing towards a new social
shape and inviting Christian discipleship to embody authentic
Christic patterning in society. As Rowan Williams wrote:

The world we inhabit is the potential scope of
the community that is created in relation to Jesus.[14]

The Spirit is also active in the waiting, the openness, the
attentiveness, the *waiting-on-God* stance of prophetic people

who stand in direct relation to the social body – like Simone Weil;[15] even in the mystical 'I said to my soul, be still, wait without hope' stance of the poet T. S. Eliot,[16] linked with what the Buddhists call *sunyata* – emptiness, or no-thing, paying attention requires listening, hearing into speech, reaching out across the silences, spanning the gulf between suffering and hope with courage, perseverance, refusal to give way to despair.

This in turn links with the Spirit as leading us into the unknown. Rooted in Jewish and Christian history, the urging of the prophetic Spirit of hope has created and is creating the force field of witness, of solidarity, of prophetic community. The Spirit of truth cracks open not only new possibilities but also the false assumptions, the notions of personhood that sell humanity short, that cheapen and devalue relationships.

Through this movement into uncharted territory, the Spirit urges the formation of the social body across boundaries. The Spirit is a great *boundary-crosser* – as became clear, for example, with the Jubilee 2000 campaign, the many coalitions of the Kairos movement, the global networking against trafficking in women. Many of these themes come together in another ancient meaning for the Spirit as *vinculum amoris, vinculum caritatis.* The Spirit as bond of charity and love enfleshed in myriads of ways is as much an inspiration for the recovering heart of public life as for encouraging a new body/soul/mind/heart *integration.* Resisting the splits and dualisms of history that set men over against women, mind as superior to body, human beings as superior to animals and so on, the Spirit prompts an integration promoting the flourishing of all life forms.

Since the context in which the social body lives and struggles for breath is that of globalization, an all-encompassing network of corporate power systems, the Spirit operates counterculturally, energizing the body, not with the power of coercion and dominance, but with power as empowerment; the power of compassion, love, empathy, insight, integration, wisdom; with relational power – fragile though it may be – the empowerment and energy that arises when we get structures of relationships and institutions functioning for the good. The two Dutch words 'macht' and 'kracht' give a clear picture. 'Macht' is *macho power*, the power of might and armies. 'Kracht' is energy, the power of being vitalized and empowered and can have a relational meaning.

The final dimension, a special one for our times, is the symbol of the Spirit as 'The Wild Bird who heals'.[17] The Spirit in a new and urgent emphasis to extend the parameters of the social body is calling us to protect the wildernesses and the creatures who live there. The Spirit as the green face of Trinity, the 'Wild Bird who heals' emerges, signalling the end of theologies of stewardships of creation, to ignite full-blown biocentric theology and practice. As Mark Wallace says:

> If we allow the Spirit's biophilic insurgency to redefine us as pilgrims and sojourners rather than wardens and stewards, our legacy to posterity might well be healing and life-giving, and not destructive of the hopes of future generations.[18]

The image of the wild bird is owed to Mark Wallace, although the themes of wildness, chaotic creativity and embodiment, at home with ecofeminism and ecological theology alike, are integral to the material struggles of the social body. He discovered in the *Rothschild Canticles* of the Middle Ages the image of the Spirit as

> giant encircling dove, whose wings enfold Father and Son and whose large talons and tail provide points of intersection for all those figures. In the Canticles the Spirit is represented less like the domesticated birds or pigeons of traditional Church art and more like the mountain raptors of the mountain wildernesses. The Spirit-Bird in the Canticles spins and twirls the other two members of the Godhead into amorous and novel combinations and permutations. As the Canticles progress, each life-form within the Trinity loses its separate identity in a blur of erotic passion and movement and colour.[19]

Thus, the Wild Bird, not as feeble addition to the vertical Father/Son relation, but as the dynamic symbolic – and passionate – unity of all life forms. In this biophilic revelation of Spirit, the density of much of former theological inspiration moves forward. The prophetic Spirit as green face of God speaks forth (the meaning of *pro-phetes*) a language linking human and non-human, revealing the false logic on which this split is built. This ecological model of the Spirit, evoking multiple biotic interdependencies, is a model for other levels of liberating mutuality. As Spirit of truth, the Wild Bird leads us into a truth that builds just practices, enabling flourishing for all life forms.

In our fragmentation we look to the Spirit as *Wild Bird who heals* for a re-enchantment of this broken world, not for Magic Kingdoms but for embodied kinships of women, men, children and earth creatures in a reimagined and transformed world of sustainable earth communities of healing and hope. As Hildegarde of Bingen put it:

> The Spirit is life, movement, colour, radiance, restorative stillness in the din. She pours the juice of contrition into hardened hearts. Her power makes dry twigs and withered souls green again with the juice of life. She purifies, absolves, strengthens, heals, gathers the perplexed, seeks the lost. She plays the music in the soul, being herself the melody of praise and joy. She awakens mighty hope, blowing everywhere the winds of renewal in creation.[20]

Ecclesia – The social shape of the Body

I began with the passion of the relational God irrupting in history with creativity and love. Not in the old interventionist language of penetrating from the outside: attentiveness to the passion of God is listening to that power and passion from within creation, from within the Spirit's vitality and energizing activity, with faith in the power of healing connections.

Secondly, the social body of the Christian Church operates from within the space offered by the image I began with, between suffering and hope of the *Il Volto Santo* image, the gap spanned by the work of the Spirit. Being *imago Dei* in his earthly history brought Jesus into conflict with what Walter Wink called the powers,[21] the systems of dominance, the intertwined oppressions of economic poverty, racism, colonial conquest, the vulnerability and non-personhood of women and children. The messianic community, those called to be *ecclesia* (I realize that the word came later) or *ecclesians* (called-out),[22] were called into qualitatively different, expanding networks of relationships. As *lumen gentium* the social body was called *out* of tribalism, not back into exclusive patterns of superiority, or irrelevant huddles.

So, thirdly, the Christic patterning or imaging, distinctive from any other pattern offered by world faiths – even though of course there are commonalities – needs practices to make the Body a vibrant reality and not mystification or even parody. And even the practices have become parodies in some contexts. And glaring at us from the wounds of history is the fact that the social body has not mirrored the twofold creation-in-the-image, women and men. As social body the Church has enabled – until recently – the leadership of men, authority of men, and the invisibility of women, in document, structures and reflected experience. Even Liberation Theology, with its option for the poor of Medellín and Puebla, displayed a glaring insensitivity to both women and the environment, as the work of Maria Pilar Aquino, together with many theologians of the Ecumenical Association of Third World Theologians (EATWOT) women's commission has shown. As the contributors to the previous consultation also argued, this shrunken form of *imago Dei* left no space for the black community, for groups marginalized through disability, race, through sexuality, age and economic poverty. Together with these exclusions has come an absolutizing of structures that makes the listening and paying attention to many neglected limbs of the social body impossible. As a child I was taught that the three dimensions of the Church as Body of Christ were Church militant, suffering and triumphant – and I do not think that anyone here would disagree that at this moment we are experiencing the Church suffering – in so many ways, because of the sickness of the social body.

But, rather than highlighting all that is wrong, I want to return to the Trinitarian focus of this paper, asking how the social body of Christ can be *imago Trinitatis*. I take inspiration from Thomas Berry's intuition that, in its very cellular structure, the universe mirrors the Trinitarian God[23] – the structures of autonomy or freedom, of communion and of diversity. In paying attention to the interwovenness of these three dimensions, can we discover the patterning of becoming, moving towards being *imago Trinitatis*? I suggest that, in the Ecumenical Movement, we have leant too far in imposing the 'communion' dimension – witness the recent Synod of the Roman Catholic bishops – while ignoring the dimensions of 'freedom/autonomy' and 'diversity'.

Is it not crucial that, for the body to be healthy, its constituent organs need freedom to breathe and move, psychologically, physically and spiritually? Our rootedness in the Christ Body harks back to Christ's promise that, in feeding and caring for the most vulnerable, the cup of cold water to the least of the little ones, we would experience his presence and would embody the Christic patterning. Fidelity to this is the space I have been calling *being between suffering and hope*. Witnesses to this – women and men – from early Christianity onwards have believed that their sufferings were integral with suffering of the Christic Body. The story of Perpetua and Felicity in Carthage is striking: about to be thrown to the wild beasts in the arena for persevering in Christian faith, Felicity, a slave, gave birth to a baby in prison. When her gaoler taunted her:

> If you're complaining now, what will you do when you're thrown to the wild beasts?

Felicitas replied:

> Now it is I who suffer, but then another shall be in me, since I am now suffering for him.[24]

The members of the body suffer individually when their freedom, their possibility of surviving with dignity, is threatened. And this suffering cannot always be called redemptive suffering on behalf of the Body. Suffering is only redemptive when engaged in freely for what makes the body distinctive vis-à-vis the world – the healing of brokenness, the enlarging of the capacities for making social justice and the commitment to offering the vision of a society where these values are embodied. So when the third Trinitarian dimension of distinction and otherness is taken seriously as a dimension of the body's proper activity, we can see how the perichoretic movement enlarges the body's capacity for healing. The movement is outward while drawing on inner strength. It means that the outer skin of the body – forgive what appears to be literalism, but is really inherent in the idea of the Body as ecological organism – is porous, capable of letting in the world. The Truth and Reconciliation Commission (TRC) in South Africa is an example of listening and hearing the other while creating spaces where such hearing is possible. The Body is a re-membering body – and the Recovery of Historical Memory (REMH) project in Guatemala is another example of hearing stories of violence to enable the healing of memories of trauma.

Recovering the embodied nature of the practices of the social body (what I have called *Christic patterning*), within the process of becoming *imago Trinitatis*, is a corrective to the imposed priorities of unity and reconciliation. Commitment to reconciliation means a long process where historically remembering, learning to respect difference, and commitment to the freedom of the other are integral. Dare I say it? – feeding the Afghan people and the people of Iraq, instead of dropping bombs! The costly process of confessing historical wrongs and commitment to new beginnings. As the South African poet Antjie Krog wrote so movingly in the midst of the TRC process in South Africa, a process which, as a journalist, she was covering:

Poem of Antjie Krog, from *Country of My Skull.*

Because of you
this country no longer lies
between us but within …
in the cradle of my skull
it sings, it ignites
my tongue, my inner ear, the cavity of heart
shudders towards the outline
new in soft intimate clicks and gutturals
of my soul the retina learns to expand
daily because of a thousand stories
I was scorched.
A new skin.
I am changed forever. I want to say:
forgive me
forgive me
forgive
You whom I have wronged, please
take me
with you.[25]

It may mean learning new patterns and unlearning patterns of functioning that have stifled the Body's life – routinized sacramental practices that block off the earth, automatic forgiveness, locking the social body into ecclesiastical compartments, starving vital parts of the body of anything life-giving and failing to implement in the Body's own life the very principles of truth, openness and justice flaunted to the world as being Christian.

Becoming *imago Trinitatis* as the social body of the Church is a call to begin to nurture and empower the rejected and neglected parts of the suffering Body; to build communion on authentic mutuality; to enable processes of encountering otherness with a spirit of conversion; and to follow the energizing spirit across boundaries into as yet uncharted territories.

Just as Trinitarian love is kenotic in God's generous self-emptying of omnipotence, could we begin to discover our true vocation as *kenotic* Church? And thus the old divisions, institution versus charismatic, cleric or lay, sacred/profane, will simply fall away, because the true identity is experienced in shedding not distinctions or diversity but *divisions*?

As Thomas Merton so prophetically wrote – of a divine *kenosis* we have not even begun to image:

> The shadows fall. The stars appear, the birds begin to sleep. Night embraces the silent half of the earth. A vagrant, a destitute wanderer with dusty feet, finds his [her] way down a new road. A homeless God, lost in the night, without papers, without identification, without even a number, a frail expendable exile lies down in desolation under the sweet stars of the world and entrusts herself to sleep.[26]

Notes

Contributors

1 Zoë Bennett Moore, *Introducing Feminist Perspectives on Pastoral Theology*, Continuum International Publishing Group, 2002.
2 Lisa M. Clark and Donald Macaskill, *Rediscovering Faith: Explorations in Christian Belief*, Parish Education Publications, 2000.
3 Anne Primavesi, *Gaia's Gift: Earth, Ourselves and God after Copernicus*, Routledge, July 2003.

Introduction

1 Darwin's *Origin of the Species* was first published (privately) in 1859.
2 J. Hick, *Evil and the God of Love*, The Fontana Library Theology and Philosophy, now Palgrave Macmillan, 1966, p. 181.
3 This phrase has been used by theologians to sum up Irenaeus' thought and ideas (see Hick, 1966).
4 Pierre Teilhard de Chardin wrote a number of books during his lifetime. *The Phenomenon of Man* was published by Collins, London, in 1959.
5 From The Collect for the First Sunday of Christmas, *Common Worship; Services and Prayers for the Church of England*, Church House Publishing, 2000.
6 From a translation of the Liturgy of St James by C. W. Humphreys.

Section One – Reflections on the Biblical Background

Made in the image and likeness of God – John W. Rogerson

1 Theo Kobusch, *Die Entdeckung der Person: Metaphysik der Freiheit und modernes Menschenbild,* Darmstadt, 1997, p. 11.
2 Wolfhart Pannenberg, *Systematic Theology* (trans. Geoffrey Bromiley), Continuum International, 1991.
3 G. A. Jónsson, 'The Image of God: Genesis 1.26-28' in *A Century of Old Testament Research*, Stockholm, Almqvist and Wiksell, 1988.
4 Charles Taylor, *Sources of the Self: The Making of Modern Identity*, Cambridge University Press, 1989.
5 Seyla Benhabib, *Situating the Self: Gender, Community and Post-Modernism in Contemporary Ethics*, Polity Press, 1992.
6 Anthony Giddens, *Modernity and Self-identity: Self and Society in the Late Modern Age*, Polity Press, 1991.
7 Theodor Adorno (trans. E. B. Ashton), *Negative Dialectics*, Thomson Publishing Services, 1973.
8 Benhabib, 1992.

The phrase 'image of God' in the New Testament – Stephen I. Wright

1 I am grateful to Arthur Rowe for his comments on an earlier draft of this chapter.

2 The main Greek words in question are *eikōn* (image) and *homoiōsis* (likeness). These are also the words found in the Greek (LXX) translation of Genesis 1.26f. In 1 Corinthians 11.7, discussed below, the word *doxa* (glory) also appears. We shall also mention the phrase in Hebrews 1.3: *hapaugasma tēs doxēs kai charaktēr tēs hupostaseōs* (reflection of his glory and impress of his being).

3 Philippians 2.6 uses the similar, much-disputed phrase *morphē Theou* (form of God).

4 S. B. Ferguson, 'Image of God' in Sinclair B. Ferguson and David F. Wright (eds), *New Dictionary of Theology*, IVP, 1988, pp. 328f.

5 Hans Walter Wolff, *Anthropology of the Old Testament* (trans. Margaret Kohl), SCM Press, 1974, p. 160.

6 For a very good account of this situation, see J. Richard Middleton, and Brian Walsh, *Truth is Stranger than it Used to Be: Biblical Faith in a Postmodern Age*, SPCK, 1995, pp. 108–25.

7 Ferguson, 1988.

8 Wolff, 1974, p. 163f.

9 Anthony Thiselton, following A. Feuillet, rejects the translation 'reflection' for *doxa* here, preferring the more literal 'glory' in the sense of 'a sign of honour'. 'Because of woman, man is all the more man, just as because of man woman is all the more woman, and as humankind woman and man manifest the divine attributes . . . as expressions of God's creative being': *The First Epistle to the Corinthians*, NIGTC, Eerdmans/Paternoster, 2000, p. 835.

10 On this see further Wansbrough's paper.

11 A passage with a very similar thrust to Colossians 3.9-11 is Ephesians 4.20-24. The Ephesians have been taught to 'clothe' themselves 'with the new self, created according to the likeness of God in true righteousness and holiness'. The word 'likeness' is not found in the Greek which simply says 'according to God'. God himself is the pattern of this new humanity.

Made and remade in the image of God – The New Testament evidence – Henry Wansbrough OSB

1 Quotations from the New Testament are the author's own translation.

2 John Robinson, *The Body*, SCM Press, 1966, p. 65.

Section Two – Insights from Orthodox Christians

In the image and likeness of God – David Melling

1 *On the Making of Man* (16:16ff). The translation is that of the Nicene and Post-Nicene Fathers, Series II, vol. V. Available at http://ccel.wheafon.edu/fathers/.

2 *On the Making of Man* (4).

3 Ernest G. Clarke (ed. and trans.), *The Selected Questions of Isho bar Nun on the Pentateuch*, E. J. Brill, 1962.

4 Gregory Nazianzus, *Oration 38:13* NPNF.

5 Clarke, 1962, p. 95.

6 David Melling translated *Logos Asketikos*, chapter 5 from Pholikalia.

7 Melling, chapter 89.

The image of God in humankind – A bridge between the Eastern and Wesleyan theological traditions – David Carter

1 The best modern studies of the Wesleyan theological tradition, both of which show clearly the influence of the Eastern Christian tradition upon the Wesleys, are R. Maddox, *Responsible Grace*, Kingswood Books, 1994, and T. Runyon, *The New Creation*, Abingdon Press, 1998.

2 Runyon, 1998, pp. 13–14.

3 Runyon, 1998, pp. 14, 18.

4 O. Clément, *Questions sur l'homme*, Editions Anne Sigier, 1986, especially pp. 29, 44, 55.

5 Clément, 1986, p. 55.

6 *Hymns and Psalms: A Methodist and Ecumenical Hymn Book* (the current official hymnal of British Methodism), Methodist Publishing House, 1983, no. 753.

7 *Hymns and Psalms* 300.

8 B. Gregory, *The Holy Catholic Church*, Wesleyan Conference Centre, 1873, pp. 1–2.

9 Clément, 1986, p. 31.

10 For relevant Methodist hymns see, for example, *Hymns and Psalms*, 4, 35, 46, 47, 101, 109, 300; also the collected Eucharistic hymns of the Wesleys in E. Rattenbury, *The Eucharistic Hymns of John and Charles Wesley*, Epworth Press, 1948.

11 St Ephraim cited in Kallistos Ware, *The Orthodox Way*, St Vladimir's Seminary Press, 1980, pp. 114–15.

12 *Hymns and Psalms* 101.

13 D. F. Hardy and D. W. Ford, *Jubilate, Theology in Praise*, SPCK, 1984.

14 Hardy and Ford, 1984, pp. 6–11.

15 From *The Book of Common Prayer*.

16 *Hymns and Psalms* 664.

17 1820–1903. His chief work is W. B. Pope, *A Compendium of Christian Theology* (3 vols), Wesleyan Conference Office, 1880.

18 Runyon, 1998, p. 14.
19 Runyon, 1998, p. 17.
20 Runyon, 1998, p. 17.
21 *Hymns and Psalms* 504.
22 Runyon, 1998, p. 18.
23 *Hymns and Psalms* 649.
24 A. Schmemann, *Of Water and the Spirit*, New York, St Vladimir's Seminary Press, 1974.
25 Paul Evdokimov, *L'Orthodoxie*, Desclée de Bouwer, 1979, p. 83.
26 *Hymns and Psalms* 267.
27 *Hymns and Psalms* 756.
28 *Hymns and Psalms* 563.
29 J. H. Rigg, *A Comparative View of Church Organisation: Primitive and Protestant*, T. Woolmer, 1887, p. 208.
30 Cited in John Fletcher, *The Last Check to Antimonianism: A Polemical Essay against the Twin Doctrines of Christian Imperfection and a Death Purgatory*, London, 1775, pp. 311–12 (printed by R. Hawes and sold by J. Buckland).
31 See his essay in A. J. Philippou (ed.), *Orthodoxy, Life and Freedom*, Studion Publications, 1973, pp. 31–47.
32 Cited in H. Meyer and L. Vischer (eds), *Growth in Agreement*, World Council of Churches, 1984, p. 46.
33 *Hymns and Psalms* 109.
34 Brian Frost, *Living in Tension Between East and West*, New World, 1984, pp. 38–43.
35 *Hymns and Psalms* 690.
36 *Hymns and Psalms* 101.
37 1 John 4.8.
38 *Hymns and Psalms* 216.
39 Clément, 1986.
40 *Methodist Hymn Book*, London, 1933, no. 876.
41 *Ut Unum Sint*, Rome, 1995, para 29, quoting decree 'Gaudium et Spes' of Vatican II.
42 *Methodist Hymn Book*, London, 1877 edition, no. 537.
43 John D. Zizioulas, *Being as Communion*, Darton, Longman and Todd, 1985, is the fullest treatment.
44 *Hymns and Psalms* 622.
45 Pope, 1880, vol. 1, pp. 423–4.
46 Cited in Lars Thunberg, *Man and the Cosmos*, New York, St Vladimir's Seminary Press, 1985, p. 75.
47 Pope, 1880, vol. 3, p. 4.
48 Romans 11.33.
49 Runyon, 1998, pp. 33–42 for Wesley's insistence on the universality of the offer of grace and salvation.

50 Isaac of Syria, *The Heart of Compassion* (trans. S. Brock), Darton, Longman and Todd, 1989, p. 9.

51 B. Gregory, *Handbook of Scriptural Church Principles*, Wesleyan Methodist Bookroom, 1888, vol. 2, p. 25.

52 T. Jennings, *Good News to the Poor*, Abingdon Press, 1990, p. 109.

53 W. J. Shrewsbury, *An Essay on the Scriptural Character of the Wesleyan Methodist Economy*, London, J. Mason, 1839, pp. 288–91.

54 *Hymns and Psalms* 520.

55 Shrewsbury, 1839, p. 291.

56 Jennings, 1990, p. 112.

57 Rigg, 1887, p. 207.

58 1 John 2.20.

59 1 Peter 5.

60 Gregory, 1888, pp. 54, 152; Shrewsbury, 1839, p. 54.

61 Developed in his Cambridge sermon, reported in *The Tablet*, 24 January 1970.

62 Ephesians 5.27.

63 *Hymns and Psalms* 753.

Section Three – Not Fully Made in God's Image?
Black people made in the image of God – Arlington Trotman

1   M. Washington (ed.), *A Testament of Hope, The Essential Writings and Speeches of Martin Luther King Jr.*, San Francisco, Harper, 1991, p. 10.

2   This tradition is carried on in and through the *Holiness Pentecostal and Sabbatarian Churches*: Church of God of Prophecy, New Testament Church of God, Wesleyan Holiness, New Testament Assembly, United Church of Jesus Christ, Seventh Day Adventists, other independent groups; *African Independent Churches*: Kingsway International Christian Centre, Cherubim and Seraphim, the Celestial Church, and other African independents.

3   Division of the race can be seen in the Nazi concept of a higher race based on the Nietzschean philosophy of 'will to power' and its Fascist manifestation in Europe. These features of the modem period, far from being the domain of religion, had an enduring cultural impact on the history of the modern racially divided world.

4   H. Richard Niebuhr, *Christ and Culture*, London, HarperCollins Publishers USA, 1975.

5   Niebuhr, 1975, p. 46. Here he includes language, habits, ideas, beliefs, customs, social organization, inherited artefacts, and things such as technical processes and values.

6   Niebuhr, 1975, p. 47. Speech, education, myth, science, art, philosophy, government, law, rite, beliefs.

7   Niebuhr, 1975, p. 48. Inventions and technologies all demand effort on the part of the recipient, and constitute culture.

8   Niebuhr, 1975, pp. 51–2. Given the nature of modern categories (peace and prosperity, justice and order, freedom and welfare, truth with beauty, scientific truth with moral good, technological proficiency with practical wisdom, holiness with life), this is a most insightful observation. Divine truth becomes one among many in the cultural complex. It describes the modern interpretation of human life, and
    yet, in all of its dimensions, culture is an obviously inescapable reality.

9   Washington, 1991, p. 6.

10 Washington, 1991, p. 7.

11 Paul Tillich, *Systematic Theology* (Combined Volume), James Nesbet & Co. Ltd., 1968, pp. 42, 84–7.

12 Darwin wondered why the 'creative power' was more active in one place than another if beings were individually created as Christian theology maintained. The crux of his position was that all beings are similar and had not, therefore, been individually created, but 'evolved' from more primitive species – in effect the species change with the passage of time. Further, according to Darwin's theory of natural selection, there are small random variations in individuals of each generation, and species are well adapted because of the struggle to survive and effect a more perfect adaptation, which gives rise to the evolution of life, ending in complex forms of life as *homo Sapiens*. John Hick, *Philosophy of Religion*, Prentice Hall Press, 1963, p. 25.

13 Paul Edwards (ed.), *The Encyclopaedia of Philosophy*, vol. 2, Macmillan, 1967, pp. 297–9. See also *The Encyclopaedia Americana* (International edition), Franklin Watts, 1981, vol. 8, p. 510.

14 What is 'given' in Torrance's view is the self-presentation of divine reality which becomes scientific when theology comes to rest on it: this includes not only the physical sciences, but also natural science which thinks in accordance with given contingent reality. See David Ford (ed.), *The Modern Theologians, Vol. 1: An Introduction to Christian Theology in the Twentieth Century*, Blackwell, 1989, p. 71.

15 Ford, 1989, p. 74. Tillich and Torrance unite in their claim that the coexistence of science and theology undercuts the autonomous grasping for truth in the fashion of modern culture.

16 Ford, 1989.

17 David Hume, 'Essay on National Characters', *Essays Moral, Political and Literary*, 1776, Oxford University Press, The World's Classics, vol.XXXIII, footnote p. 213.

18 Hume, 1776.

19 Hence religion, or more particularly, Christianity as a reasoned moral call to humanity, is thought 'private' and therefore relative to one's personal deterministic standards of the good. Truth is regarded, therefore, as personal, and lacks universal application. Hence chaos is likely to, and in modern culture actually does, prevail. The purpose of human existence and destiny is continually subjected to non-objective criteria, which leaves modern man detached and rooted in estrangement.

20 Tillich, 1968, vol. 3, p. 51.

21 Tillich (1968) avoids a definition of love since there is no higher principle by which it could be defined, except that it is *agape*, 'realising itself from *kairos* to *kairos* [and] creates an ethics which is beyond the alternative of absolute and relative ethics'. For an ontological description of love, cf. Paul Tillich, *Love Power and Justice*, Galaxy, 1992, pp. 24–34.

22 Both philosophy and some theologies have contributed to the destruction of inclusive world views, as Nietzsche's philosophy of life, Freud's philosophy of the unconscious, the rediscovery of Kierkegaard's theosophical movements, and the failure of the historical theologies of synthesis. And, as Tillich said: 'These are more powerful just because they are not world views.' There is a perceptible fatalism present in modern culture that appears to have its foundations in the historical despair characteristic of a culture loosened from its Christological foundation. It appears that the Enlightenment attitude of progress and the fulfilment of 'superior man's' temporal desires are yet to be superseded. It is clear that intellectualism was made almost unjustifiably inevitable by the Protestant protest against the divine. But the 'Gestalt of grace' in the heart of the divine Word which involves his being, deeds and suffering, is the reality that protects theology from intellectualism, and the weakest from dehumanization. Modern humanity, in this framework, is the heart of 'cultural disintegration', on which racism and exclusion feed.

23 During the plantation period in American slave history, while some slaves were missionized by European missionary societies, a vibrant 'church' was also evolving almost unnoticed by slave masters. These people found in themselves the resources to expect that God would one day release them from oppression. Led by free blacks, this movement was regarded as the 'invisible institution', which led ultimately to the establishment of large black congregations such as Baptists, Episcopalians, Congregationalists, African Methodist Episcopal and Zion Churches in the USA today.

24 It is legitimate to ask whether this is not the consequence of unclear or distorted fundamental presuppositions having been abandoned since the Enlightenment. Celebration of the sacraments, for example, and the concept of the sacramental embodiment of the Spiritual reality in male clerics alone, has to all intents and purposes prejudiced the female cleric.

25 See *Out of the Shadows, An Audio Visual History of the Black Presence in Britain, 1500-1950*, The Catholic Association for Racial Justice, 1988.

26 Washington, 1991, p. 10.

'One ladies' one normal': Made in the image of God – Issues for women – Zoë Bennett Moore

1 A. Sen, 'More than 100 Million Women are Missing' quoted in J. M. Soskice, 'Women's Problems', *Priest and People* 6, pp. 301–6, p. 306.

2 Containing research from the Ecumenical Decade of Churches in Solidarity with Women 1988–1998, p. 48.

3 WCC, *Ministerial Formation*, issue 93, 2001, p. 51.

4 Catherine MacKinnon, *Towards a Feminist Theory of the State*, Harvard University Press, 1989, p. 219.

5   Zoë Bennett Moore, see further *Introducing Feminist Perspectives on Pastoral Theology*, Sheffield Academic Press, 2002.

6   Kari Elisabeth Børresen (ed.), *The Image of God: Gender Models in Judaeo-Christian Tradition*, Solum Forlag, 1991.

7   Jacquelyn Grant, *White Women's Christ and Black Women's Jesus: Feminist Christology and Womanist Response*, The American Academy of Religion, 1989.

8   Mary Daly, *Beyond God the Father: Towards a Philosophy of Women's Liberation*, The Women's Press, 1986, p. 19.

9   See for example the work of Rosemary Radford Ruether or Mary Grey.

10 Jo Ind, *Fat is a Spiritual Issue: My Journey*, Mowbray, 1993.

11 Ind, 1993, p. 41.

12 *The Christ We Share*, CMS/USPG/Methodist Church, 1999.

13 Riet Bons-Storm, *The Incredible Woman*, Abingdon Press, 1996.

14 Bons-Storm, 1996, p. 115.

15 See further Zoë Bennett Moore, 'Women and the Cost of Loving: Towards Transformative Christian Practice', *Contact*, 1998, 127:11–16.

Made in the image of God: A womanist perspective – Lorraine Dixon

1   Alice Walker, *In Search of Our Mothers' Gardens*, The Women's Press, 1984, p. xi.

2   Walker, 1984, p. xii.

3   Walker, 1984, p. xi.

4   Some early African American womanist theology from the 1970s through to the early 1990s can be found in James Cone and Gayraud Wilmore (eds), *Black Theology: A Documentary History, Volumes 1 and 2*, Orbis, 1993.

5   Jacquelyn Grant, *White Women's Christ and Black Women's Jesus*, The American Academy of Religion, 1989, pp. 1–2.

6   For example, James Cone in the twentieth anniversary edition of his book *A Black Theology of Liberation* (Orbis, 1990) includes an essay by Delores Williams. She affirms the black liberation perspective that Cone offers, but calls him to account for his silence on the plight of black women living at the intersection of both white and black communities.

7   Kelly Delaine Brown Douglas, 'Womanist Theology: What is its Relationship to Black Theology' in Cone and Wilmore (eds), *Black Theology: A Documentary History vol. 2*: 1980–1992, p. 292.

8   Grant, 1989, p. 205.

9   Paul Grant and Raj Patel (eds), *A Time to Speak*, Racial Justice and the Black Theology Working Group, 1990, and *A Time to Act: Kairos 1992*, Evangelical Christians for Racial Justice, 1992.

10 Sybil Phoenix, *Willing Hands*, Bible Reading Fellowship, 1984.

11 *Black Theology in Britain: A Journal of Contextual Praxis*, Sheffield Academic Press, 1998 to present day.

12 Cone, *Black Theology and Black Power*, Seabury Press, 1969.

13 J. Cone, *A Black Theology of Liberation*, Orbis, 1990.

14 Cone, 1990, p. xiii.

15 Statement by the National Committee of Black Churchmen, June 13, 1969, 'Black Theology' in Cone and Wilmore (eds), *Black Theology: A Documentary History, volume one 1966–79*, p. 101.

16 Katie Stewart, *When Our Ship Comes In*, Yorkshire Art Circus, 1992, p. 36.

17 Kelly Delaine Brown Douglas, *The Black Christ*, Orbis, 1994, pp. 116–17.

18 Carlyle Fielding Stewart III, *Soul Survivors: An African American Spirituality*, Westminster John Knox, 1991, p. 23.

19 Grant, 1989.

20 Renita Weems, 'Reading Her Way through the Struggle' in Cone, 1990, p. 77

21 Suggested further reading: Karen Baker-Fletcher, 'Immanuel' in Karen and Garth Baker-Fletcher, *My Sister, My Brother: Womanist and Xodus God-Talk*, Orbis, 1997; B. Bryan, S. Dadzie and S. Scafe, *The Heart of the Race: Black Women's Lives in Britain*, Virago Press, 1985; Mark Chapman, *Christianity on Trial: African-American Religious Thought before and after Black Power*, Orbis, 1996; Lorraine Dixon, '"Teach it Sister!": Mahalia Jackson as Theologian in Song' in *Black Theology in Britain: A Journal of Contextual Praxis 2*, 1999, pp. 72–89.

Disabled and made in the image of God – Elisabeth Davies-John

1 1980, directed by David Lynch, produced by Brooks Films/Paramount.

Gay and lesbian and in God's image – Martin Hogg

1 See Elizabeth Stuart, *Just Good Friends: Towards a Lesbian and Gay Theology of Relationships*, Continuum International Publishing Group/Mowbray, 1995.

What do I want to say to the Churches about my God-given sexuality? – Colin Coward

1 John Robinson, *Honest to God*, SCM Press, 1963.

2 Church of England General Synod and House of Bishops, *Issues in Human Sexuality*, Church House Publishing, 1991.

Section Four – Back to the Bible

Gone fishing *or* Saussure or not so sure: Why we need a methodology to read the Bible – Alastair Hunter

1 This is as true of ecumenical ecclesiastics as it is of seemingly more authoritarian individual denominations. The implicit authority of the liberal ecumenical zeitgeist is as pervasive in its own way as is that of the Curia or the General Assembly of the Church of Scotland.

2 William Wimsatt and Monroe Beardsley, *The Verbal Icon*, University of Kentucky Press, 1954.

3 Joseph Childers and G. Hentzi (eds), *The Columbia Dictionary of Modern Literary and Cultural Criticism*, Columbia University Press, 1995, p. 157.

4 Stanley Fish, *Is There a Text in This Class?*, Harvard University Press, 1980.

5 Fish, 1980, pp. 2ff.

6 Fish, 1980, pp. 4ff.

7 Fish, 1980, p. 6.

8 Fish, 1980, p. 14.

9 This one is particularly interesting since the underlying Hebrew is unclear; many modern versions of Deuteronomy 33.27 do not use this phrase.

10 Saussure famously rejected the traditions of historical etymology, preferring a synchronous approach to the description of language and the definition of 'words'. The kind of quest for historic meaning beloved of certain kinds of biblical scholar, in which the meaning of a word is the accumulation of its use through time, is not permissible in structuralist discourse.

11 My version of this story is taken from M. Wadsworth (ed.), *Ways of Reading the Bible*, Harvester Press, 1981, p. 402.

12 I suppose that the archaeological model is best represented by Griemas and the Russian Formalists.

13 See 'The Structural Activity' in Roland Barthes, *Critical Essays* (trans. Richard Howard), Northwest University Press, 1972.

Homosexuality and Scripture – David Hilborn

1 For an exposition of this teaching tradition see Thomas E. Schmidt, *Straight and Narrow? Compassion and Clarity on the Homosexuality Debate*, IVP, 1995, pp. 39–63.

2 For a summary of this critique see Michael Vasey, *Strangers and Friends*, Hodder and Stoughton, 1995, pp. 49ff.

3 Rowan Williams, 'The Body's Grace' in Eugene F. Rogers (ed.), *Theology and Sexuality: Classic and Contemporary Readings*, Blackwell, 2002, p. 320.

4 For an elaboration of this argument see my own essay, 'For the Procreation of Children', in Susan Durber (ed.), *As Man and Woman Made: Theological Reflections on Marriage*, The United Reformed Church, 1994, pp. 22–32.

5 Cf. Vasey, 1995, pp. 115–18.

6 1 Samuel 18.1-2; 2 Samuel 1.26. Cf. Vasey, 1995, pp. 120–21, and D. Halperin, *One Hundred Years of Homosexuality*, Routledge, 1990, chapter 4. But even David Greenberg, who is usually more even-handed on such matters, resorts to speculating and arguing from silence on this point. He begins by admitting, 'In neither case does the text mention a sexual aspect to the relationship.' Yet then he goes on to surmise that 'an explicit homosexual relationship could easily have been

deleted by priestly editors . . .' So, for that matter, could much else which we should like to be in Scripture, but which does not appear there! David F. Greenberg, *The construction of Homosexuality*, University of Chicago Press, 1988, pp. 113-14.

7   Derrick Sherwin Bailey, *Homosexuality and the Western Christian Tradition*, Longman, 1955, pp. 3–4; John Boswell, *Christianity, Social Tolerance and Homosexuality*, University of Chicago Press, 1980, pp. 9–94; John J. McNeill, *The Church and the Homosexual*, Sheed, Andrews and McMeel, 1976, pp. 54–5.

8   For more detail on all this see Robert A. J.Gagnon, *The Bible and Homosexual Practice: Text and Hermeneutics*, Abingdon Press, 2001, pp. 71–8.

9   Robert A. J. Gagnon, *The Bible and Homosexual Practice: Text and Hermeneutics*, Abingdon Press, 2001, p. 88.

10 These points are based on David F. Wright, 'Homosexuals or Prostitutes? The Meaning of *arsenokoitai* (1 Corinthians 6.9; 1 Timothy 1.10)', *Vigiliae Christianae* 38 (1984), pp. 125–53; Gordon Wenham, 'Homosexuality in the Bible', in Tony Higton (ed.), *Sexuality and the Church*, ABWON, 1987; and Richard B. Hays, *The Moral Vision of the New Testament*, T&T Clark, 1997, pp. 382–3.

11 Michael L. Saltlow, *Tasting the Dish: Rabbinic Rhetorics of Sexuality*, Scholars Press, 1995. Brown Judaic Studies, no. 303.

12 K. W. Huggins, 'An Investigation into the Jewish Theology of Sexuality Influencing the References to Homosexuality in Romans 1.18-32', PhD. dissertation, Southwestern Baptist Theological Seminary, 1986.

13 There are very marginal readings that deny that Paul is referring to lesbian activity. These are discussed below. For contemporary Graeco-Roman references to lesbianism see B. Brooten, 'Patristic Interpretations of Romans 1.26', paper delivered at the Ninth International Conference on Patristic Studies, Oxford, England.

14 See, for example, G. A. Edwards, *Gay/Lesbian Liberation: A Biblical Perspective*, Pilgrim, 1984, pp. 85–102; L. William Countryman, *Dirt, Greed and Sex*, Fortress and SCM Press, 1988, pp. 98–123.

15 T. E. Schmidt, *Straight and Narrow*, IVP, p. 66.

16 John Boswell, *Christianity, Social Tolerance and Homosexuality*, University of Chicago Press, 1980, p. 110. This is the main pretext on which Boswell argues that Paul is only condemning certain forms of same-sex sexual activity, rather than working from universal or 'natural' principles to condemn it all. Specifically, he concludes that 'Paul did not discuss gay *persons*, but only homosexual acts committed by heterosexual persons' (p. 109).

17 E. F. Harrison, *Expositor's Bible Commentary: Romans*, Zondervan, 1976, p. 25.

18 Hays, 1997, p. 386.

19 V. P. Furnish, 'The Bible and Homosexuality: Reading the Texts in Context' in J. Siker, (ed.), *Homosexuality in the Church*, Westminster John Knox, 1994, p. 30; Vasey, 1995, pp. 131–2.

20 For pertinent references see James D. G. Dunn, *Romans 1-8*, Word, p. 65.

21 Mark Bonnington and Bob Fyall, *Homosexuality and the Bible*, Grove Books, 1996, p. 20; Hays, 1997, p. 386.

22 Derrick Sherwin Bailey, *Homosexuality and the Western Christian Tradition*, Longman, 1955, p. 40; Vern Bullough, *Sexual Variance in Society and History*, Wiley, p. 180.

23 A point made by C. E. B. Cranfield, *Romans I – VIII*, T&T Clark, 1975, p. 125; and Leon Morris, *The Epistle to the Romans*, Eerdmans, 1995, p. 92.

24 V. P. Furnish, 'The Bible and Homosexuality: Reading the Texts in Context', in J. Siker (ed.), *Homosexuality in the Church*, Westminster John Knox, 1994.

25 C. C. Caragounis, 'The Biblical Attitude to Homosexuality Against its Ancient Background', *Vox Evangelica*, XXVII, 1997, p. 38.

26 Boswell, 1980, p. 108.

27 Caragounis, 1997, p. 35.

28 K. J. Dover, *Greek Homosexuality*, Harvard University Press, 1978.

29 Church House Publishing, 1991, p. 12.

30 J. N. D. Kelly, *The Pastoral Epistles*, A. & C. Black, pp. 44–5.

31 Similar 'vice lists' appear at Romans 1.29-31; 13.13; 1 Corinthians 10, 11; 6.9-10; 2 Corinthians 12.20-1; Galatians 5.19-21; Ephesians 4.31; 5.3-5; Colossians 3.5-8; 2 Timothy 3.2-5; Titus 3.3.

32 G. W. Knight III, *The Pastoral Epistles*, Paternoster, 1992, p. 85.

33 Knight, 1992, pp. 85–6.

34 Vasey, 1995, pp. 135–7. See also Boswell, 1980, pp. 107–9.

35 Typical, for example, is Josephus (*Against Apion* 2:24; 199): 'The law recognises no sexual connections, except the natural union of man and wife . . . Sodomy it abhors, and punishes any guilt of such assault with death.'

Interpreting the biblical texts on homosexuality – Michael Williams

1 Bruce Birch and Larry Rasmussen, *Bible and Ethics in the Christian Life*, Augsburg, 1989.

2 Michael Vasey, *Strangers and Friends*, Hodder and Stoughton, 1995.

3 Wolfgang Schrage, *The Ethics of the New Testament*, Fortress Press, 1988.

4 Thomas W. Ogletree, *The Use of the Bible in Christian Ethics*, Blackwell, 1984.

5 The human is 'adam'. In Genesis there is a pun on *adam* = human being, *adamah* = earth or dust, and *dam* = blood.

6 *Zakar* comes from a root meaning remember or name and means male person, phallus, male animal, ram. *Neqebah* comes from a root meaning to bore through, but, being passive, means to be bored through, a hole, a woman, a sexual being.

7 Emmanuel Levinas, *Nine Talmudic Readings*, Indiana University Press, 1990, and *Ethics and Infinity*, Duquesne University Press, 1985.

8   See Jacques Derrida, *The Gift of Death* (trans. David Wills), University of Chicago Press, 1995.

9   *Ish* means man in relation to *Ishah*, which means wife. *Enosh* is also used in Hebrew to mean man as mortal, as human.

10 *Bazar* means flesh in a similar way to the New Testament *sarx* meaning the whole human being considered from the point of view of being physical, enfleshed.

11 The social meaning of the text comes first but the sociality of being is enfleshed in sexual penetration. The Hebrew mind sees sociality not as an abstract concept but as a physical reality. You can't have sociality without it being physically real. But could it not be physically real in a gay relationship?

12 To say this may not be sophisticated enough in terms of biblical scholarship. The question may hinge on when the text of Genesis was written. It may have been written during the time of Ezra, in which case there may be an appeal here to monogamy so as to prevent the returning exiles having more than one wife thus risking taking a wife outside of the pure remnant.

13 The word translated rib (*tsala*) in Genesis 2.21 would be better translated 'side'. This is its meaning in other biblical texts. To say that God made the woman out of the side of a man means that woman is not created out of the substance of a man but is a separate substance created in relation to man. This would tend towards an equality of the sexes from creation.

14 Aelred of Rievaulx, *On Spiritual Friendship*, Cistercian Publications, 1974.

15 In the mid-twentieth century, biblical scholarship tended to suggest that there were practical reasons for the food laws. For example, the ban on eating shellfish could have been that, in a hot climate, to eat such things was to run the risk of food poisoning. More recent scholarship, including Countryman (Fortress and SCM Press, 1988), suggests a different way of reading the text. Following the work of Mary Douglas, these texts are about the separation or purity of the people of God. As all peoples need symbols of their separateness, especially when they are threatened with extinction, so the returning Hebrews after the Exile needed very strong social boundaries. These rules were the way in which they set themselves apart. If this is nearer to the truth of these texts then they cannot be separated out into ceremonial texts (transcended by Christ) and moral texts (to be retained). I am indebted to the Revd Chris Sterry, Vicar of Whalley, for these and other comments on the Hebrew Text.

16 Nakedness is also a theme in other Hebrew texts. To see your father naked, or another man's wife naked, was viewed as an absolute calamity. Its punishments were severe. Just as we have left behind the food laws so we have left behind this aspect of Hebrew thinking.

17 Schrage, 1988.

18 Michael Williams, 'Romans 1: Entropy, Sexuality and Politics', *Anvil* vol. 10, no. 2, 1993.

19 Henry Liddell and Robert Scott, *Intermediate Greek–English Lexicon*, Oxford University Press, 1959.

20 *The Analytical Greek Lexicon*, revised by Harold Moulton and David Holly, Bagster, 1977.

21 Schrage, 1988.

22 For example, see Richard Hasbany (ed.), *Homosexuality and Religion*, Haworth Press, 1989.

23 John Boswell, *Same Sex Unions in Premodern Europe*, Villard Books, New York, 1999.

Section Five – Pushing Out the Boundaries

Made and remade in the image of God – Anne Primavesi

1 Augustine, *The Confessions*, (trans. R. S. Pine-Coffin), Penguin Classics, 1961, p. 344.

2 J. R. McNeill, *Something New Under the Sun*, W. W. Norton, 2000.

Human nature and image of God – Social and biological factors – Chris Sunderland

1 For example, Immanuel Kant understood true moral capacity would come about when a person rose entirely above their 'passions' and pursued abstract reason.

2 M. Midgely, *Beast and Man – The Roots of Human Nature*, Routledge, 1979.

3 Ashley Montagu, *Anthropology and Human Nature*, Merlin Press, 1960, p. 15.

4 Midgely, 1979.

5 See discussion in R. A. Hinde, *Individuals, Relationships and Culture – Links Between Ethology and the Social Sciences*, Cambridge University Press, 1987.

6 A. Giddens, *In Defence of Sociology – Essays, Interpretations and Rejoinders*, Polity Press, 1996, chapter 4.

7 M. Ridley, *The Origins of Virtue*, Viking, 1996.

8 Hinde, 1987, p. 63.

9 F. de Waal, *Good Natured – The Origins of Right and Wrong in Humans and Other Animals*, Harvard University Press, 1996, p. 102.

10 R. Mason, *Propaganda and Subversion in the Old Testament*, SPCK, 1997.

11 This is illustrated further in C. Sunderland, *In a Glass Darkly – Seeking Vision for Public life*, Paternoster, 2001.

12 See for example N. Klein, *No Logo*, Flamingo, 2001.

13 See for example A. Giddens, *The Transformation of Intimacy*, Polity Press, 1992, pp. 74–5; and A. MacIntyre, *After Virtue: A Study in Moral Theory*, Duckworth, 1981 (2nd edn), p. 217.

14 Jeremiah 31.31ff.

Human individuality and inclusive community: Concepts of self, vocation and *imago Dei* – Donald Macaskill

1　For an excellent discussion on the nature of narcissism, its influence in late modern psychology and theology of the self and identity, see Charles Elliott, *Memory and Salvation*, Darton, Longman and Todd, 1995, pp. 131–56.

2　See Kenneth J. Gergen, *The Saturated Self: Dilemmas of Identity in Contemporary Life*, Basic Books, 1991.

3　See Romney M. Moseley, *Becoming a Self Before God: Critical Transformation*, Abingdon Press, 1991, pp. 38–50.

4　See Anthony C. Thiselton, *Interpreting God and the Postmodern Self: On Meaning, Manipulation and Promise*, Continuum International, London, 1996, p. 121.

5　Thiselton, 1996, pp. 77ff.

6　Thiselton, 1996, p. 158.

7　Alistair I. McFadyen, *The Call to Personhood: A Christian Theory of the Individual in Social Relationships*, Cambridge University Press, 1990.

8　McFadyen, 1990, p. 9.

9　'Persons are a manifestation of their relations, formed through though not simply reducible to them. The Persons of the Trinity, for example, are identified by terms which indicate their most significant relations' (McFadyen, 1990, p. 40).

10　'The three divine persons are not there simply for themselves. They are there in that they are there for one another. They are persons in social relationship . . . Being-a-person (*Personein*) means "being-in-relationship"' (Jürgen Moltmann and Elisabeth Moltmann-Wendel, *Humanity in God*, SCM Press, 1984, p. 97).

11　'Looked at from the angle of personhood man reveals his creaturehood in a way of difference and not division from God. Only through personhood which implies communion as well as the integrity of being, can God and man be clearly distinguished from each other, precisely by affirming their distinct identities in communion' (John D. Zizioulas, 'Human Capacity and Human Incapacity: A Theological Exploration of Personhood', *Scottish Journal of Theology* 28, 1975, pp. 401–448).

12　The description of humanity and humanness advanced by J. Houston in an essay in 1985 is closer to a postmodern concept of the self. He writes, 'Humanity, humanness, involves being vulnerable to emotional hurt and open to emotional pleasure by what others do and think and feel' ('On Being Human', *Scottish Journal of Theology* 38, 1985, pp. 471–9).

13　See Grace Jantzen's essay on the Trinity as offering a cooperative model for the human self and personhood, 'Connection or Competition: Identity and Personhood in Christian Ethics', *Studies in Christian Ethics* 5.1, 1992, pp. 1–21.

14　For a development of this thought see John Macmurray, *Persons in Relation*, Faber, 1995.

15　See Richard J. Neuhaus, *Freedom for Ministry*, Wm B. Eerdmans Publishing Co., 1992, pp. 89, 95.

16 'Becoming a person involves, above all else, acquiring competence in the system of social communication' (McFadyen, 1990, p. 95).

17 'The understanding of oneself as a continuous point of identity ("me") in an extensive range of relations, evidenced in self-referential and self-indexical use of "I", is not the result of some private, inward experience of one's self. It is, rather, the result of others indexing and referring to "you" in this way' (McFadyen, 1990, p. 95).

18 Helen Oppenheimer, *The Hope of Happiness: A Sketch for a Christian Humanism*, SCM Press, 1983, pp. 138–42.

19 '"A person is brought forth by a call." according to Mounier. A person acquires or becomes aware of personal identity when that person is addressed or appealed to by another . . . Someone needs me, or rather, *wills* to need me. Since everyone's life situation is unique, every call to give an answer is also unique . . . We are called from what we are to that which we must become in God's eyes' (Herwig Arts, *With Your Whole Soul: On the Christian Experience of God*, Paulist Press, 1983, pp. 155–6).

20 Iain G. Nichol, 'Vocation and the People of God', *Scottish Journal of Theology* 33, 1980, pp. 361–73.

21 James W. Fowler, *Becoming Adult, Becoming Christian: Adult Development and Christian Faith*, Harper Collins, 1984, p. 95.

22 See Fowler, 1984, pp. 97ff.

23 'There is no personal fulfilment that is not part of a communal fulfilment. We find ourselves by giving ourselves . . . From the standpoint of vocation, fulfilment, self-actualisation, and excellence of being are by-products of covenant faithfulness and action in the service of God and the neighbour' (Fowler, 1984, p. 102).

24 'It is . . . to recognise that nothing which may befall another person is necessarily alien to oneself, and that the question of one's individual identity is intimately and irrevocably bound up with the fact that we are members one of another' (Nichol, 1980, p. 368).

25 Nichol, 1980, p. 369.

26 Fowler, 1984, p. 133.

27 'To be in vocation means to grow in a "grace-full" fitting of our dance to the larger movement of the core plot. To be in vocation means to make creative contributions to the ongoing unfolding of the drama, in accordance with the vision and denouement intended by the playwright' (Fowler, 1984, p. 137).

28 Nichol, 1980, p. 372.

Section Six – The Church 'Between Suffering and Hope'

Created in the image – The suffering, broken Body of Christ, the Church – Mary Grey

1 See M. Grey, *Prophecy and Mysticism: The Heart of the Postmodern Church*, Cassell, 1997, pp. 30ff.

2   Isabel Carter Heyward, *The Redemption of God*, University of America Press, 1982, p. 17.

3   Martin Buber, *I and Thou*, T & T Clark, 1958, (2nd edn), p. 18.

4   See the chapter by Anne Primavesi.

5   Fedorov is cited in Paul Evdokimov, *Le Christ dans la pensée russe*, Editions du Cerf, 1970, p. 115.

6   Leonardo Boff, *Trinity and Society*, Orbis, 1988; Ivone Gebara, *Longing for Running Water*, Fortress, 1999.

7   See Willi Marxsen, *Die Sache Jesu geht weiter*, Gütersloher Verlagshaus G. Mohn, 1976.

8   See Rowan Williams, *On Christian Theology*, Blackwell, 2000.

9   Williams, 2000, p. 124.

10 Jürgen Moltmann, *The Spirit of Life – A Universal Affirmation* (trans. Margaret Kohl), SCM Press, 1992.

11 M. Grey, *The Wisdom of Fools?*, SPCK, 1993 (chapter 9).

12 John V. Taylor, *The Go-Between God*, Collins, 1972 (chapter 1).

13 Nancy Victorin Vangerud, *The Raging Hearth – Spirit in the Household of God*, Chalice Press, 2000.

14 Williams, 2000, p. 231.

15 Simone Weil, *Waiting on God* (trans. Emma Crawford), Collins: Fontana, 1951.

16 T. S. Eliot, 'East Coker' in *Poems 1909–1962*, Faber and Faber, 1963, p. 200.

17 See Mark Wallace, *Fragments of the Spirit*, Continuum, 1996.

18 Wallace, 1996, p. 170.

19 Mark Wallace, 'The Wounded Spirit as the Basis for Hope', in *Christianity and Ecology*, Dieter T. Hessel and Rosemary Radford Ruether (eds), Harvard University Press, 2000, p. 56.

20 Cited in Elizabeth Johnson, *She Who Is*, Crossroad, 1994, pp. 127–8. From *Scivias* 190 and passim.

21 Walter Wink, *Engaging the Powers*, Fortress, 1982.

22 I owe this expression to Professor Timothy Gorringe.

23 Thomas Berry, *The Dream of the Earth*, Sierra Club, 1986.

24 See P. Wilson-Kastner and G. R. Wilson-Kastner (eds), 'The Martyrdom of Perpetua: A Protest Account of Early Christianity' in *A Lost Tradition: Women Writers of the Early Church*, University of America Press, 1981, p. 27.

25 Antjie Krog, *Country of My Skull*, Random House: Vintage, 1999, p. 423.

26 Thomas Merton, 'Hagia Sophia', in *Emblems of Fury*, cited in *The Candles Are Still Burning*, M. Grey, D. Sullivan and A. Heaton (eds), Cassell, 1994, p. 171.

Index of subjects

Note: Where more than one sequence of notes occurs on the same page, references to notes are clarified by the addition of a letter (e.g. 242 n.6b).

Index of references